W9-DJN-551

*The Bible College Story:*

EDUCATION WITH DIMENSION

BY S. A. WITMER

Galilean Fisherman. *Light and Hope Publications, Berne, Indiana. 1940. Sixth edition, 1959.*

*The Bible College Story:*

# EDUCATION
# WITH
# DIMENSION

*S. A. Witmer*

Preface by Dr. Merrill C. Tenney

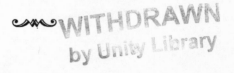

CHANNEL PRESS, INC., MANHASSET, NEW YORK

UNITY SCHOOL LIBRARY
Unity Village
Lee's Summit, Missouri 64063

*The Bible College Story:* EDUCATION WITH DIMENSION

Copyright © 1962 by Channel Press, Inc.

*All rights in this book are reserved. No part of this book may be used or reproduced in any form whatsoever without written permission from the publisher, except in case of brief quotations embodied in critical articles and reviews. For information address Channel Press, Inc., 400 Community Drive, Manhasset, New York.*

Library of Congress Catalog Card Number: 62-13413

PRINTED IN THE UNITED STATES OF AMERICA

BV
4030
W5

DEDICATED

*with gratitude to all of the fine persons who have been my teachers — parents, instructors, pastors, associates; above all, to the grace of God which led me to see that the Bible is the revealed Word of God and that believing in Jesus Christ, His Son, brings life in the dimensions of eternity.*

# CONTENTS

# LIST OF TABLES

# PREFACE

The development of Bible institutes and Bible colleges which began in the United States about three-quarters of a century ago has proved to be a significant movement in the history of American education. Born in revival, it has maintained a constant tradition of Biblical learning with its accompanying high ethical and moral standards. The integration of learning around a common core of interest, its insistence upon the value of practical training, and the moral discipline of dedication were advocated by these schools before these principles became topics of discussion and research among professional educators.

The rapid growth of this movement in the last two or three decades, and its consolidation through The Accrediting Association of Bible Colleges, have brought it into public notice. Its leaders have been pioneers in a new field of education which is now being developed in many countries outside of the United States. The influence of the Bible schools has been enormous, for a large proportion of evangelical Protestant preachers, missionaries, and lay workers are graduates of these institutions. They have contributed to scholarly achievement, for many of their alumni have been stimulated to pursue further study and to enter the fields of research and teaching.

Although Bible schools have been drastically criticized in the past for their supposed narrowness of curriculum, inferior equipment and quality of teaching, and obscurantist viewpoint, they have maintained a defense against rationalism, naturalism, and skepticism that was greatly needed in the

Christian church. They have improved their performance with the passage of time, and with the expansion of their curricula and strengthening of their faculties they are capable of becoming an increasingly powerful factor in the training of Christian leaders, and consequently in the thinking of the Christian public. Together with the Christian liberal arts colleges and seminaries they will undoubtedly be the chief defense of evangelical Christianity against the secularism and apathy of the present century. Their emphatic insistence upon the final authority of God's revelation in the Bible and upon the necessity of a personal experience of salvation in Christ motivates a kind of education that is sadly lacking in secular institutions.

Dr. Witmer is an expert in this field, for he is a graduate of a Bible school and has been the president of one. He possesses a doctoral degree in the field of education and psychology, and is now the Executive Director of The Accrediting Association of Bible Colleges. His history and analysis of the movement is a timely contribution to the annals of education. The facts presented in this book will provide the basis for a better understanding of the origin, history, and character of the Bible institutes and colleges, and for an adequate appraisal of their value.

MERRILL C. TENNEY

*Wheaton College Graduate School,*
*February, 1962*

*The Bible College Story:*

EDUCATION WITH DIMENSION

*Chapter One*

# A STORY THAT
# NEEDS TELLING

At long last the story of Bible institutes and Bible colleges can be told. Here is a movement that has made an immense contribution to evangelicalism. Its impact has been felt in nearly every part of the world; it has given training to over half of all Protestant missionaries from North America. These schools have held the helm of the movement steady to the truths of Revelation and the authority of the Scriptures through three-quarters of a century of theological flux. They have stimulated evangelicalism at home and abroad. They have helped shaped the lives of many distinguished Christian leaders, among whom are Harold Street, Billy Graham, Wilbur M. Smith, Ralph T. Davis, Robert A. Cook, Rachel Saint, Helen Baugh, and Louis T. Talbot. The movement has grown from one school with a score of students in 1882 to 250 with 25,000 day students in 1960. And yet, the full story of this dynamic movement has never been published. There is not a single volume on any library shelf on Bible institute-college education.

Why so little has been written on this movement is difficult to explain. Educators inside and outside of the movement have become aware that here is a lapse in the field of educational literature. In 1947, Mrs. Lenice F. Reed made the following

observation in her thesis entitled, "The Bible Institute Movement in America":

> In spite of the fact that so many Bible institutes dot
> the country from shore to shore, no mention of the
> movement can be found in an encyclopedia. Even the
> founders, such as D. L. Moody, are accorded very
> little space or notice. Though the mission fields are
> manned by hundreds of Bible school graduates, and
> though a great (sizable) proportion of Christian
> work in the homeland is carried on by those who re-
> ceived their training in Bible institutes, yet authentic
> information seems to be very scant. Many libraries
> are unable to furnish even a magazine article on the
> subject.[1]

The most likely explanation is that its educators have been
too preoccupied with their mission of preparing students for
world-wide ministries to give much time to describing themselves or analyzing their practices. However, some gains can
be reported since the assessment by Mrs. Reed in 1947. Bible
school education has become an inviting area of research for
theses and dissertations.[2] Magazines, both evangelical and professional, have begun to publish articles on Bible college education.[3] One of the oldest and most widely read educational
journals, *School and Society,* featured two articles on the
nature and significance of Bible college education.[4] Several
pamphlets and leaflets have been written by Bible college
educators. One short definitive work on the movement has
been published—a chapter in *Christian Education in a Democracy* (Oxford University Press, 1951).[5] Thus, it appears
that the movement is finally "breaking into print" and at least
the Christian public is beginning to become aware of its
significance.

It has taken a friendly observer outside the movement to
speak eloquently on behalf of making known the story of the
Bible institute movement. Said Dr. Frank E. Gaebelein in
*School and Society:*

Here is a story that needs telling, a chapter in the history of education that ought to be widely circulated. For it is not generally recognized that within the last six or seven decades a new and distinct form of education has been quietly and steadily developing in our country. . . . Almost ignored in the histories of education, they have become, in their own right, a distinct educational genre. More than that, they have been exercising in their field a vital and, in some areas, as in the foreign missions enterprise, a crucial significance.[6]

But more compelling reasons than merely adding another book to library shelves call for an exposition of Bible institute education. The movement needs to become articulate for its own benefit. Its front ranks are facing critical questions about the distinctive role of Bible institutes and colleges and the direction in which they are going. Does development beginning with a non-graded Bible training school lead inevitably to a liberal arts college? Is there a significant difference between the Christian liberal arts college and the Bible college? Do Bible schools have to broaden their services to survive? Is the answer to these questions to be found in the principles of the Christian faith and its unique mission, or is direction to be determined by pragmatic considerations?

Moreover, the movement needs to clarify and to make explicit the philosophy of Biblical education to which it professes commitment. It needs to grow in self-understanding in order to discriminate more intelligently between Christian and un-Christian principles. Too frequently alien ideas and methods are introduced so that in a given school a heterogeneous assortment of educational theories is put into practice. There is also the problem of academic integration by the teacher who fails to unify his special field of knowledge with Christian faith. Too often the problem is side stepped by separating the two; Christian theology with its supernatural frame of reference is confined to one compartment and the

specialities in science built upon naturalistic timber are kept
in a completely different compartment.

There is also a need for Bible college educators to look at
the "pit from whence" Bible institutes have been dug; to appreciate the hardships and efforts expended in their founding;
to take a fresh look at the vision of the founders; to understand
the uniqueness and power of Biblical education; to see its relevance to the contemporary crisis and the unprecedented vast-
ness of human need for an abiding faith. When a thousand
voices call for these colleges to conform to the prevailing secular culture, they should realize that there are untapped re-
serves of moral and spiritual power in Biblical faith and that
its implications for education need to be spelled out. It is
hoped that this book on the Bible institute movement will
throw light on its problems, provide historical perspective for
current issues, and provide new inspiration from a story of
Divine Providence and faith's adventures.

## For Public Understanding

This story needs telling, too, for the many groups to which
Bible schools are related. Because the movement has been very
slow in becoming articulate, even its friends are often ill-informed. This includes not only those in the educational world
who have no affinity with evangelicalism, but those who hold
the same Christian beliefs as do Bible schools. Contrary to
what might be expected, secular educators are often more
generous in their readiness to recognize the worth of Bible
college credits than are religionists. However, since Bible
schools serve the church and derive practically all of their
support from Christian sources, it is the church, particularly
the large segment that is committed to Biblical faith, that
needs to appreciate the relation and the worth of these schools
to the Christian mission.

Long considered inferior, sub-standard, or third-rate, Bible
institutes-colleges have suffered from the stigma of being short-
cut training schools rather than educational institutions.

Admittedly, blame must be divided between the schools themselves and the ill-informed who make no distinction between sub-standard and sound institutions, lumping them all into one category. Some schools have been guilty of these educational "sins," but certainly not all. Since The Accrediting Association of Bible Colleges came into being, and its standards have won wide acceptance, some of the stigma has been removed. At least, it has been demonstrated that Bible-centered education is not incompatible with sound educational practices.

## For Relevance

But there is a further, more profound reason for telling the story of Bible institute-college education—its relevance to the crises of contemporary life and education's search for a unifying center for knowledge, for life itself. Dr. Frank E. Gaebelein commented as follows:

> The central feature of the Bible college is well worth looking at, because it carries implications far beyond this one kind of institution. This is a kind of education that solved for itself the perennial problem of educational philosophy, the identification of an integrating principle for the entire curriculum. For it the Bible is, to use Lewis Mumford's brilliant figure, "a magnetic field at the center which will continually polarize each fragment that enters the field."[7]

For at least two centuries or more, American education derived its dynamic, meaning, and purpose from Biblical faith, but for the past century it has been wandering about in "the far country" of naturalism, pragmatism, and secularism in search of ultimate truth that will give it meaning and direction. But like the prodigal, it has exhausted the moral thrust of its heritage and is now left in despair at the very time when American higher education is called upon to give leadership to the Free World in its mortal conflict with communism.

What does it have to offer besides technology and science and a desire for material well-being?

Early American education, based on the Christian concept that man was created in the image of God, had a double function, preparation for earthly vocation and personal fulfillment in the kingdom of God. But when naturalism reduced man to a creature of this world only, educational theory was accommodated to radically reduced dimensions. Social adjustment displaced the traditional emphasis on personal moral development. And since the past with its moral idealism, and the future with its implications for eternity were outmoded, education interacting with the prevailing culture became occupied with temporal values. The good life here and now in terms of material well-being and social success was thought sufficient for man reduced to natural dimensions. And so it was—if the premise was valid.

But the very fact that this generation is asking the deeper questions and is searching for transcendent meaning invalidates the premise. Man is bigger than the role assigned to him by naturalism. He is *anthropos*—the being with the upturned face. It may well be that Pascal's discovery will become the experience of modern man as he rises to assert his true dignity: "It is good to be tired and wearied by the vain search after the true good, that we may stretch out our arms to the Redeemer."[8]

Not only did man's spiritual nature refuse to be penned up in the cage of naturalism, but two horribly cruel and destructive world wars blasted completely the theory of inevitable progress. Disillusionment was accentuated by the fact that these wars were spawned among the "enlightened" nations. Not pagans, but civilized men fought their fellow men with weapons fashioned by science for mass destruction. Justice Robert H. Jackson summarized the paradox of our times by observing that modern society needs to fear only the educated man.

It is now possible to assess educational practices based on

wrong theories. The pragmatic test of the Master, "By their fruits ye shall know them," can now be applied. Secular, naturalistic, socially-oriented education that by-passes the moral and spiritual development of man is weighed in the balances and found wanting. From the theological point of view, it is judged for its idolatry, apostasy, and betrayal. It has worshipped the works of man; it has departed from its Christian heritage; and in many once Christian colleges it has betrayed its trust.

Recent studies on the attitudes of college students indicate that the typical student is not motivated by a faith in ultimate values. No "cause" enlists his loyalties and no moral idealism moves him. He is described as apathetic to moral issues. As an outcome, the crusade has disappeared from the college campus. Without anything big and worthy outside of himself, the student has but one commitment—to himself. According to the findings of Philip E. Jacob of the University of Pennsylvania, "The great majority of students are unabashedly *self-centered*. They aspire for material gratification for themselves and their families. They intend to look out for themselves first and expect others to do likewise. . . ."[9]

The present situation presents an excellent opportunity for American colleges to recover one of their earliest functions, that of stimulating vision and moral idealism and thus developing convictions and motivations for dedicated service. The questions raised by our generation come from the heart as well as the mind, and Christian education is challenged to satisfy both.

It is heartening to note that recent events, beginning with Sputnik I, have had a sobering effect on American education. It appears that the peak of superficialism is past and that an earnest search has begun to recover fundamental principles and values. If not searching, there is at least in most quarters a willingness to listen to truth from sources other than empirical science. Reaction to Dewey's pragmatism and to the excesses of progressive education is widespread. Philosophy is returning to the college curriculum as a respectable discipline. The pros of general education continue to be a leading topic of discussion in educational conferences. The current emphasis on objectives is extended to philosophic dimensions. Religion is returning to many campuses in varied forms: courses and departments of religion, religious programs and events, the appointment of chaplains, and the establishment of denominational foundations. Exponents of neo-orthodoxy draw crowds to college chapels. Among the Roman Catholics, Neo-Scholasticism and Neo-Thomism are in vogue. Inter-Varsity Christian Fellowship is able to attract several thousand students to a conference at a state university campus to sense the impact of Christian witness and the challenge of world missions. Harold J. Ockenga, Billy Graham and other evangelicals are heard by respectful audiences in leading universities.

Of equal significance are the many serious discussions that have begun in America and Europe on a Christian philosophy of education. At least the questions have been raised. Does Christianity provide a tenable world view? Is it possible to formulate a Christian philosophy of education? Is a synthesis possible between reason and faith? Does the revelation of Scriptures yield structures of thought for history, for psychology, for anthropology, for the natural sciences?

Bible institute-college educators hold that there are affirmative answers to these questions. They hold that Jesus Christ is the center, the circumference, and the sum of all knowledge and truth. They believe that the written Word which discloses the Incarnate Word provides a frame of reference in enduring reality from which a valid philosophy of education can be derived. A philosophy of education that answers the deeper questions must begin with the simple question, What is man? And that takes us to God, to Creation, and to His eternal purpose in Creation and Redemption. If "man's chief end is to glorify God and to enjoy Him forever," Christian education must regard this purpose as a fundamental guide in education.

## DIMENSIONS

As the story of Bible college education unfolds, it will become evident that it consists of immeasurably more than a collection of 30 or more credits of Bible study. The whole Bible institute movement has its roots in the Bible as the Word of God. It is the source of vision and dynamic as well as essential subject matter.

From the Bible's wisdom comes the stress on spiritual values. From its redemptive thrust is derived the world missionary outreach of Bible colleges. From gospel imperatives are developed the various training programs in communicative skills. From its living truths come unique and vital principles of education.

Instead of the Bible restricting the dimensions of education, it greatly extends them. The teaching-learning process becomes three dimensional, for to pupil and teacher is added the interacting presence of the Holy Spirit. The concept of redeemed personality takes on the dimensions of Christlikeness. The ends of education extend beyond time to eternity. Provincialism is erased by the one-world concept of John 3:16—"God so loved the world . . ." and the world imperative of Mark 16:15—"Go ye into all the world . . ."

## CLASSIFICATION

Since Bible schools have only recently been accorded a place in the pattern of American higher education and recognition by all educators is still to be achieved, it is necessary to define their uniqueness and their functions. What place do they fill not occupied by other colleges? What services do they render not offered by other theological schools? What needs are met by the services of Bible colleges?

*Primary Function*

There is no question that the purpose of the first Bible schools—Nyack Missionary College established in 1882 and

Moody Bible Institute established four years later—was to train men and women for church vocation or Christian ministries. In both cases they were founded in response to concern for human need. A. B. Simpson had a deep concern for the peoples and nations that had never been touched by gospel light. Dwight L. Moody's compassion stirred him to do something about the neglected, unevangelized masses in the urban centers of America and Britain. For both areas of need, there was a critical lack of trained personnel; seminaries came far short of preparing a sufficient number of men while doing practically nothing to train women for specialized ministries other than the pastorate.

Both Simpson and Moody envisioned the answer in men and women of spiritual maturity with knowledge of the Word of Life, and with communicative skills to serve effectively. That vision called for a suitable course of training, and in turn the program called for an institution to provide it. These were the components of vision that brought the first Bible schools into being. *Their first function was to prepare students for Christian ministries through a program of Biblical and practical training.* Nyack's first curriculum had a third ingredient —general education, for it included English, public speaking, philosophy, and natural science.

From this central purpose follows the place given to Biblical education in Bible colleges. Because the Word of God is the chief instrument ordained of God to mould His servants (cf. II Timothy 3:16-17) and is the message to be communicated, it is given a central place in Bible college curricula. At the same time, it also integrates all knowledge from special fields into a Christ-centered unity.

Other distinguishing features of Bible institute-college education also follow from its central function. Because of the essentiality of Christian life to effective Christian service, Bible schools stress cultivation of the spiritual life—faith, prayer, the Spirit's enduement, self-denial, and dedication. As their graduates enter varied ministries at home and abroad calling for experience in communicative skills, practical training has a vital part in the educational program. Christian service is not an activity chosen voluntarily as in Christian liberal arts colleges; in a Bible institute and Bible college it is an essential part of preparation for "church vocation."

There are many similiarities between the Bible college and the Christian liberal arts college. Both are committed to a Biblical philosophy of education. In both, Christ is the integrating center. Both are concerned with the personal development of students. Both seek to broaden and deepen the education foundation of incoming students by general education.

But from this point the Bible college and the Christian liberal arts college follow divergent objectives. The liberal arts college goes on from a foundation of general education in the humanities and sciences to prepare students for the many professions and vocations. Emphasis is on a liberal arts education. Bible colleges, on the other hand, are specialized. Their primary aim is to prepare students for Christian ministries and church vocations. This they do through a program of Biblical, general, and professional education. Majoring in Biblical studies, therefore, is at the heart of the Bible college curriculum.

The Bible institute and the Bible college differ also from the seminary. Generally, Bible schools operate as post-high school institutions while seminaries operate on the post-college level. This difference is recognized by The Accrediting Association of Bible Colleges, which serves the undergraduate area of theological education, and the American Association of Theological Schools, which serves the post-college or graduate level. A further distinction obtains also in objectives: seminaries specialize in preparation for the pastoral ministry, while Bible institute-colleges offer programs for numerous Christian ministries, both preparatory and terminal.

*Definition*

In defining Bible institute-colleges, a problem arises in finding a single concept that embraces all of the institutions which are variously known as "Bible institute," "Bible college," "Bible school," "training institute." There is no fundamental difference between the Bible college and the day Bible institute.[10] Both offer Bible-centered programs for which the chief purpose is to prepare students for Christian ministries. Both are conservative in theology; both stress the devotional life, Christian service, and the world mission of the church. The one principal difference is that the Bible college includes one additional year of general education. Bible institutes limit general education to only 16 to 32 semester hours, while Bible colleges require from 32 to 64 hours in their four-year programs.

It follows that *a Bible institute-college is an educational institution whose principal purpose is to prepare students for church vocation or Christian ministries through a program of Biblical and practical education.*

The Accrediting Association of Bible Colleges dropped the term "Bible Institutes" from its name several years ago for the sake of brevity, but it includes in the concept of Bible college all Bible schools of college grade whether they have three-, four-, or five-year programs, and whether they are called institutes, colleges, or schools.

To them, Bible college education is education at the college level whose distinctive function is to prepare students for Christian ministries or church vocations through a program of Biblical, general, and professional studies.[11]

*Chapter Two*

# HISTORICAL
# DEVELOPMENT

## SOCIAL BACKGROUND

The growth of the Bible institute-college movement in the latter part of the nineteenth century and the first six decades of the twentieth was conditioned by profound social, theological, and educational developments in America. To this background we must first turn our attention.

For more than two centuries, Protestant, evangelical Christianity gave leadership to American higher education and stamped it with its faith and spirit. Each of the nine colleges founded during the colonial period was prompted by Christian motivations. According to Cubberley, the "prime purpose of each was to train up a learned and godly body of ministers. . . ."[1] The first, Harvard, was essentially a Bible college in its early years. In a pamphlet published in 1754, President Clap of Yale declared that "Colleges are *Societies* of *Ministers,* for training up Persons for the Work of the *Ministry,*" and that "The great design of founding this School (Yale), was to Educate Ministers in our *own* Way." In the advertisement published in New York papers announcing the opening of King's College (later Columbia University) in 1754, it was declared:

> IV. The chief Thing that is aimed at in this College, is, to teach and engage Children *to know God in Jesus Christ,* and to love and serve him in all *Sobriety,*

*Godliness,* and *Richness* of Life, with a perfect Heart and a Willing Mind: and to train them up in all Virtuous Habits, and all such useful Knowledge as may render them creditable to their Families and Friends, Ornaments to their Country, and useful to the Public Weal in their generation.[2]

While the first Canadian institutions were not established until the latter part of the 18th century and the first part of the 19th, religious motivations were dominant. King's College was founded by the Anglicans in 1790, Acadia University by the Baptists in 1839, and Bishop's College by the Anglicans in 1845.[3]

The nineteenth century saw the great surge in the development of Protestant colleges in the United States. In 1800 there were only two dozen colleges; it is estimated that at most there were 100 teachers and from one to two thousand students. Then, from 1820 to 1870 came the major period of denominational effort. By 1870 there were 300 colleges. Actually, almost twice that number were organized as America pushed westward, but scarcely more than half survived. The great majority were Protestant and evangelical. Even the few state institutions established were often under Christian leadership and oriented toward the Christian faith. Many of their first presidents were ministers and many graduates became ministers. Of the first 94 graduates of Illinois, 45 entered the ministry. Thus for 230 years of American higher education, Protestant leadership and motivation prevailed.

## Altered Pattern of American Education

But in the past century three powerful developments have radically altered the pattern of higher education in both the United States and Canada, reducing Protestant higher education to a subordinate role. The first was the development of tax-supported education which must be separate from the church. In the United States, the state universities have developed in size and influence until they eclipse private colleges in many states. In most Canadian provinces, the provincial universities have long since dominated higher education.

In the United States, 60 per cent of all students in colleges and universities are enrolled in tax-supported institutions. With college registrations expected to double in the next 10 years, it is estimated that 80 per cent of all students will be in tax-supported institutions by 1970.

In Canada, the church colleges generally adopted the British pattern by establishing an examining and degree-granting university. In consequence the university became an instructional institution, and then it took over all educational services except theological education. A number of the provincial universities have the sole right to grant degrees (except theological) within their respective provinces. Of the 34 Canadian institutions listed by The National Conference of Canadian Universities that possess and exercise the right to confer degrees, only four are Protestant; six are independent; ten are provincial; while fourteen are Roman Catholic.

This last fact points up the second major development: the great expansion of Catholic higher education, which reflects population growth and the dynamism of Roman Catholicism. In the United States only one Catholic college was founded before 1800, 38 had been founded by 1870, while 222 have been founded since—the majority in the twentieth century. The *Official Catholic Directory, 1958,* placed the total enrollment for these Catholic colleges at 271,493. This figure is enrollment for Catholic higher education and represents only the peak of the pyramid of students enrolled in Catholic schools.

The third major development has been the increasing secularization of higher education in both the United States and Canada. Provincial and state universities are not expected to be committed to religious faith. By their status and function, they are secular. For every Christian professor who bears witness to his faith, there are likely several vocal agnostics. But secularization has gone beyond public institutions. Unfortunately, many church-related colleges have become almost as secular as state universities. The early Biblical content has been drained from the curriculum, and in the classroom the theistic frame of reference has been displaced by pragmatism and naturalism.

The drift from evangelicalism to rationalism to secularism that has characterized Protestant higher education began almost from its inception. When Harvard was suspected of Unitarian and rationalistic views, Yale was founded "to be a truer school of the prophets." When the Great Awakening shaped new churches desiring an evangelically trained ministry, both Harvard and Yale became suspect, and so Princeton was founded.

### Rise of Bible Institute Movement

It was during the past three-quarters of a century of profound changes in American education that Bible institutes and Bible colleges had their origin and their development. They represent a pietistic reaction to secularism, a theistic reaction to humanism and agnosticism, a resurgence of spiritual dynamic in Protestantism, a restoration of Biblical authority and direction in education, and a return to the central concern of Christian education—the implementation of Christ's Great Commission: "Go ye into all the world. . ."[4]

In some states and provinces, the rise of Bible colleges has been the only significant development in Protestant higher education to offset the tragic decline of its early strength. An example is Rhode Island. Rhode Island College (later Brown University) , was founded by Baptists for the "primary task of training clergymen." The charter stipulated that 22 of its 29 trustees must be Baptists and its president "forever" a member of the Baptist church. But by 1942, all such controls had been removed by legislative acts and complete severance from church control had been effected. Today 41 per cent of Rhode Island's students in institutions of higher learning are in independent schools, 38 per cent in public schools and 18 per cent

(2,821) in the three Roman Catholic institutions founded since 1900. Today, the only Protestant institution listed in the *Education Directory* of the U. S. Office of Education is a Bible college, Barrington College, whose more than 400 students represent but three per cent of the total college population in Rhode Island.

The state of Michigan strikingly attests to the development of Bible colleges against the changing pattern of American higher education. According to the United States Office of Education's *Education Directory* for 1960-61, 56 institutions of higher learning in Michigan have sufficient academic standing to merit listing. An analysis indicates that 78 per cent of the 150,000 students are now in the 25 public, tax-supported institutions. Some 8,640, or 5.8 per cent, are in private schools, mostly professional. Only 9,909, or 6.6 per cent, are in the 16 Protestant schools, while 15,163, or 10 per cent, are in the 12 Catholic institutions, ten of which were founded since 1900.

But this pattern differs noticeably from that which prevailed in 1876. Protestants then had established two seminaries, one junior college, and eight liberal arts colleges. No Roman Catholic college had yet been established. There were four state institutions. Protestant churches established two more colleges in the nineteenth century, but their major thrust in higher education was spent, for no Protestant liberal arts college or university has been established in Michigan in the twentieth century. The only Protestant schools founded in this century with sufficient academic standing to be listed in the current *Directory* are three Bible colleges, established by evangelical groups.

Facts are especially sobering for Protestant higher education in the metropolitan area of Detroit, with a two million population. The automobile center of the world has renowned private, professional and technical schools, public schools, and Roman Catholic institutions, but the only Protestant school of any classification—seminary, college, university, or Bible college—is Detroit Bible College, founded in 1945. Six Catho-

lic schools have over 11,600, or 28 per cent of the population's
students.

Other social and religious conditions also contributed to the
rise of the Bible institute-college movement:

> In a sense it is part of the amazing educational de-
> velopment of this period, a development that saw the
> tremendous growth of secondary and college educa-
> tion, the multiplication of vocational schools, the
> growth of adult education, and the new opportunities
> in education for women.
>
> The evangelical revivals in the nineteenth century
> created both a thirst for knowledge and a demand for
> trained laymen. The awakening of the Church to the
> world-wide mission called for many more missionary
> recruits than seminaries were producing. American
> freedom from tradition and the absence of rigid state
> controls opened the way to nonconventional schools
> and provided the conditions for their development.
> Furthermore, the reaction to rationalism in denom-
> inational colleges and seminaries called for schools
> that were unquestionably evangelical. It is not a coin-
> cidence that the Bible-institute movement grew up
> during the very period when the philosophy of nat-
> uralism became prevalent in American education.
> Even in evangelical seminaries first place was usually
> given to language and critical studies at the expense
> of direct study of the Word as an experience of divine
> reality.[6]

## FOUNDING OF BIBLE INSTITUTES
## AND BIBLE COLLEGES

### European Antecedents

Largely through the influence of pietism, the nineteenth century saw the rise and development of numerous groups on the
Continent, principally in Germany, who organized missions for
the propagation of the gospel in Europe and in foreign lands.[7]

Prior to that time "the Moravian Brethren, for a whole century had been the sole representatives of the missionary idea in German civilization." [8] Most of these groups worked outside the established churches and were voluntarily supported. Their methods were often unorthodox. In the training schools which they conducted, admission standards and course requirements were often less than conventional.

One of the best known was the Gossner Mission founded by Johannes Gossner (1773-1855) in 1842. Gossner experienced a spiritual transformation while serving as a Roman Catholic priest. His evangelical zeal led to his imprisonment and to his openly joining the Evangelical Church in 1826. He received his inspiration to carry "the gospel to the heathen" from Spittlar, one of the founders of the Basle Mission Society and a representative of Pietist circles.[9] Gossner began training small groups of missionary candidates, and during the remainder of his life, 141 missionaries were trained for missionary work.

Another significant antecedent was The East London Institute for Home and Foreign Missions founded in 1872 by H. Grattan Guinness. It was established to serve several related purposes: to increase the number of missionaries; to provide education and training for zealous young people who desired to engage in missionary work but were thwarted by lack of education and means; to direct trained recruits into fields for which they were suited and to assist them if necessary; and "to deepen in the heart of Christians at home practical compassion for the heathen." In its first 16 years, 3,000 young men applied for admission, 800 were accepted, and 500 completed their training to become workers at home and abroad.[10] It was this institution along with several others that inspired Dr. A. B. Simpson to urge the establishment of similar schools in America. In fact, it was when Simpson as a teen-age youth in Chatham, Ontario heard the visiting preacher, Rev. H. G. Guinness, that he first became impressed with Guinness and his work.

*First North American Schools*

The two pioneer schools, Nyack Missionary College and
The Moody Bible Institute, not only initiated the movement
in America but they inspired the establishment of many other
similar schools.

Nyack Missionary College came into being through the
gifted leadership of Dr. A. B. Simpson in order to carry out
his vision of disseminating the gospel among the peoples of
the world both at home and abroad. In 1880, he agitated for a
missionary college in an editorial in *The Gospel in All Lands*.
Commenting on a proposed Inter-Seminary Missionary Convention, he wrote:

> We hope this convention will, among its many
> questions, thoroughly discuss the establishment of a
> specific missionary training college, to prepare per-
> sons who may not be able to take a full scholastic
> course for missionary service. . . . We want our best
> scholarship and talent in the mission field, but we
> want all who can go; and with a destitution so im-
> perative, the Church of God should be willing to wel-
> come the humblest "prentice hand," and dispense
> with full technical preparation, wherever she finds
> other qualifications for humble usefulness.[11]

Simpson felt that missionaries with courage, faith, love,
patience, and tact might be more useful than those having
more professional qualifications.[12] He defended his trainees as
"irregulars" by citing the commissioning of such men as
Stephen, Philip, and Barnabas for the great work of first-
century evangelism.

The vision and objective that led to the founding of Nyack
Missionary College were in tune with God's redemptive purpose, but its earthly trappings were very humble. Begun in
1882, it occupied the rear platform of the old Twenty-third
Street Theater in New York City. Classroom facilities consisted
of wooden benches and crude tables. The twelve students were

taught by two teachers. But the high caliber of the faculty and the rich content of the curriculum contrasted sharply with the improvised quarters during those early years. Able men of spirituality and scholarship were attracted to the venture.

The three departments of the curriculum provided theological, general, and practical courses:

1. *Literary*—English, logic, philosophy, natural sciences, ancient and modern history, geography
2. *Theological*—Christian evidences, Bible, New Testament Greek, systematic theology, church history, pastoral theology
3. *Practical*—homiletics, evangelism, Sunday school work, and vocal music

Organized as the Missionary Training College for Home and Foreign Missionaries and Evangelists in 1883, its name was changed several times to The Training College (1890), the New York Training Institute (1894), and The Missionary Training Institute when the school was moved to its present location in Nyack, New York, in 1897. More recently it was renamed Nyack Missionary College.

Dr. Simpson's plea for a special type of training forecast the distinguishing marks of the Bible institute-college movement: "Distinct Bible training . . . practical training in definite lines of Christian work . . . Holy Ghost missionaries . . . simplicity and economy . . . actual results."[13]

Nyack has consistently followed, during its eighty-year history, the pattern of education established by its founder, and has become one of the foremost missionary colleges in the Protestant world. In curriculum, orientation to world evangelism, academic standards, and spiritual emphasis it has given exemplary leadership.

The institution which was destined to become the largest, the most renowned, and the mother of many other similar institutes is Moody Bible Institute of Chicago, founded by Dwight L. Moody and his associates. The Institute claims 1886

as its year of birth, but its actual history can be traced to
earlier beginnings. It goes back to 1872 to Miss Emma E.
Dryer, distinguished teacher, organizer, humanitarian and
servant of Christ. While dean of women at Illinois State Normal School, she happened to be visiting friends in Chicago at
the time of the Great Fire and remained to engage in relief
work. Becoming acquainted with Mr. Moody, she was led to
teach Bible classes for women in his North Side Tabernacle.
With Mr. Moody's encouragement, she gave up her work in
the Normal School to train women as city missionaries. It
was during this period that a regular training school was
contemplated.[14]

Mr. Moody, however, was too engrossed in evangelistic
tours to give time to establishing a regular training school even
though interest mounted. In 1885, while passing through
Chicago, Moody attended a meeting of persons interested in
plans for a school. He consented to give leadership to it if
$250,000 could be raised. The money was soon forthcoming,
and in 1886, following Moody's historic address on "City
Evangelization," The Chicago Evangelization Society was
born. In that address he uttered the famous summons, "I believe we have got to have 'gap men,' men who are trained to
fill the gap between the common people and the ministers."[15]

It took several years of planning and organization to establish the school. The objectives were formulated in 1887 as
follows: ". . . to educate and direct and maintain Christian
workers as Bible readers, teachers and evangelists, who shall
teach the gospel in Chicago and its suburbs, especially in
neglected fields." With the coming of a brilliant Yale graduate,
Reuben Archer Torrey, who had taken postgraduate studies
in Leipzig and Erlangen, as superintendent in 1889, and with
the construction of the first building in the same year, "a full-
fledged training school emerged, dedicated to teaching men
and women the fundamentals of the English Bible and practical Christian work."

From the beginning, the institution had an extraordinary

growth. Eighty students enrolled in the first year, and within ten years nearly 3,000 had received training. In 1905, the legal objectives were broadened and made more specific: "Its object is to educate, maintain and send forth Christian workers, Bible teachers, gospel singers, teachers and evangelists, to preach and teach the gospel of Jesus Christ."

The Institute has become a "mosaic" of Christian institutions. It not only enrolls 1,000 day students and 900 evening students, but it has developed a cluster of service agencies. These include the Correspondence School with 32,429 enrollees; Moody Press; Moody Institute of Science; Extension Department; Moody Literature Mission; and the Radio Division, which broadcasts the Christian message over WMBI and WMBI-FM (Chicago), WCRF-FM (Cleveland), and WDLM (East Moline). Its ministry of producing and distributing gospel-science films is wholly unique; these open doors to the armed services, and to public and parochial schools.

The outstanding success of The Moody Bible Institute has influenced greatly the Bible institute-college movement. Certain features of its program, such as practical Christian training, have been copied by numbers of other institutions. With 2,700 of its alumni in active foreign missionary service, it is the largest evangelical training center in the world.

It is significant that the first two schools, Nyack and Moody, represent quite typically the two chief types of Bible schools. Moody has throughout its history represented the more specialized "Bible institute" with its three-year diploma courses. Nyack is an example of the degree-conferring Bible college whose curriculum includes more liberal arts or general education courses. That both are accredited indicates that the Bible institute as well as the Bible college can conform to sound academic standards.

## Other Nineteenth Century Schools

A modest number of Bible institutes and Bible colleges, besides Nyack and Moody, were established in scattered sections of North America before 1900. Western Baptist Bible College (formerly Western Baptist Seminary) of Kansas City, Missouri, was established in 1890 by the Negro Baptists of Missouri to train men for the ministry in their churches. In 1893, Johnson Bible College, a Christian (Disciples) college was established in Kimberlin Heights, Tennessee, and it has prepared many students for Christian ministries by means of a typical Bible college program consisting of Biblical, general, and professional studies. Two years later, a sister institution with a similar program was established in the West—Northwest Christian College of Eugene, Oregon. It, too, has a notable record of preparing students for positions of Christian leadership.

In 1897, the Advent Christian denomination established Boston Bible School in Boston. From 1917 to 1959, it was known as The New England School of Theology. In 1958, it was moved from the Boston area to Lenox, Massachusetts, and a year later, renamed Berkshire Christian College. In 1899, the Training School for Christian Workers, which later became Azusa College, was founded in California. After holding classes in various locations, it was established in Huntington Park in 1907, and in 1946 it was moved to a new site at Azusa. From 1939 to 1957, it was known as Pacific Bible College; since then it has been known as Azusa College. In its early years it was identified with the Friends; it now is an independent school but has fraternal and participating relationships with several evangelical denominations.

The one Bible college established in Canada in the nineteenth century is historic Toronto Bible College, founded in Toronto in 1894 on an interdenominational basis by a group of ministers and Christian workers. It first met in Walmer Road Baptist Church, but in 1898 it moved to its present site on College Street, where a fine set of buildings now serves its purpose of training "consecrated men and women for Christian service, in the knowledge and practical use of the Bible."

## Twentieth Century Development

The Bible institute-college movement had a steady but not phenomenal growth during the first three decades of the twentieth century. The greater development took place in the following thirty years.

Eleven existing institutions had their beginnings from 1900 to 1910—Barrington College, Barrington, R. I. (1900) ; God's Bible School, Cincinnati, O. (1900) ; Practical Bible Training School, Bible School Park, N. Y. (1900) ; Lutheran Brethren Schools, Fergus Falls, Minn. (1903) ; Fort Wayne Bible College, Fort Wayne, Ind. (1904) ; Bethany Bible Training School, Chicago, Ill. (1905) ; Central Wesleyan College, Central, S. C. (1906) ; Toccoa Falls Institute, Toccoa Falls, Ga. (1907) ; The Bible Institute of Los Angeles, LaMirada, Calif. (1908) ; Owosso College, Owosso, Mich. (1909) ; Central Pilgrim College, Bartlesville, Okla. (1910) .

Of 234 schools that reported their founding dates, 15 had their beginnings from 1911 to 1920, and 26 were established from 1921 to 1930. Thus, 61 of the Bible institutes and Bible colleges that exist today were founded during the first fifty years of the movement. The number of schools established but later discontinued is not known, but it may well be a score or more.

Table I presents the founding of Bible institutes and Bible colleges by decades. It shows that the major development in number of schools took place from 1931 to 1960. In this thirty-year period, 73 per cent of the existing Bible colleges and institutes were established. The peak decade, 1941-50—the World War II period—was the period also when all types of higher educational institutions expanded in number and services. In the eighty-year history of the movement, 35 per cent of the existing Bible colleges were founded in this one decade.

An unexpected contrast is observed in the growth of the movement in the United States and Canada. In Canada, the

majority of schools—69 per cent—came into being in the two
decades from 1931 to 1950, but only 8 per cent were founded
during the decade which followed. It is very likely that in
recent years, more Canadian schools were discontinued or
merged with others than were started. Quite likely the declin-
ing rate of increase reflects not so much on the vitality of the
movement as it does on the normal reduction of surplus institutions. It is generally admitted by Christian leaders that at
one time there was a needless proliferation of small schools
in western parts of the Dominion. The leveling off in number
of schools probably indicates a stabilization and consolidation
of the movement in Canada with more attention given to
improving services.

TABLE I

FOUNDING OF BIBLE INSTITUTES AND BIBLE COLLEGES
BY DECADES

| Decade | United States | | Canadian | | Total | |
|---|---|---|---|---|---|---|
| | Number | Percentage | Number | Percentage | Number | Percentage |
| 1881-90 | 3 | 1.3 | 0 | 0 | 3 | 1.3 |
| 1891-1900 | 7 | 3 | 1 | .4 | 8 | 3.4 |
| 1901-10 | 9 | 3.8 | 0 | 0 | 9 | 3.8 |
| 1911-20 | 13 | 5.6 | 2 | .9 | 15 | 6.5 |
| 1921-30 | 17 | 7.3 | 9 | 3.8 | 26 | 11.1 |
| 1931-40 | 26 | 11 | 19 | 8.2 | 45 | 19.2 |
| 1941-50 | 66 | 28.2 | 16 | 6.8 | 82 | 35 |
| 1951-60 | 40 | 17.1 | 4 | 1.7 | 44 | 18.8 |
| 1961 | 2 | .9 | 0 | 0 | 2 | .9 |
| Total | 183 | 78.2 | 51 | 21.8 | 234 | 100 |

In the United States, by contrast, the greatest increase in the
number of new schools took place between 1941 and 1960—a
decade later. While development reached a peak during the
World War II period, yet it has continued to the present, for
40 schools were founded in the 1951-60 decade.

# EDUCATIONAL DEVELOPMENTS

*Second Generation Leadership*

No doubt the most decisive factor in the growing maturity of the movement is in the quality of second- and third-generation leadership. The history of the movement points up the fact that many schools were established through the strong, dynamic leadership of outstanding men of God. They were men of great faith, spiritual stature and world reputation. They stamped the institutions they founded and the students they trained with their ideals and motivations. If they were not educators themselves, they had the gift of attracting able educators to their ventures. If, in addition, they saw the need of developing leadership in younger men, of broadening the base of responsible participation and control, of delegating responsibility to their associates, their institutions survived their passing to go on to greater achievements. If not, their schools faltered or failed with the passing of their autocratic control.

Boards faced the supreme test of themselves and their institutions when called upon to select successors to the founders. Would the successors share the founders' lofty ideals, selflessness, and understanding of Biblical education? Would they also be gifted in administrative skill and educational know-how to build the second story of the educational structure? The quality of their leadership was put to the test. Would they turn out to be only pale imitators of their illustrious predecessors? Would they become mere "organization men" absorbed in operating a machine acceptably? Would they turn out to be selfish men who used their great opportunities for personal ends? Would they put more reliance on Ph.D.'s than on the blessing of God? Or would they measure up to the high demands of their office?

The all-important quality for success in the second generation of a Bible school is the *persistence of the ideal that brought it into being*—to answer the desperate human need through the gospel of Jesus Christ effectively communicated by men and women who themselves radiate His presence and demonstrate the power of the gospel. And this ideal must be a conviction, a goal, a passion in the hearts of the second-generation leadership. Providentially, many institutions were blessed with the leadership of such men. As a result, the schools not merely survived but advanced to new heights.

However, for the sake of the record, it must be said that this quality of leadership was not always present. In a few cases, men were appointed to positions of influential leadership who neither understood nor appreciated the distinctive principles of a Bible-centered program of education. They only succeeded in redirecting the institutions toward a different set of objectives, thereby changing their character and severing them from the movement.

But Bible colleges by their other-worldly goals and ideals are always confronted with pressures that would obscure or subordinate the ideal for which they were founded. This ideal is easily lost in an effort to build a great institution. It can be subordinated to the ideals of scholarship and academic prestige. It can be reduced to lip profession by men who place pragmatic considerations above their faith. This inversion of values is deadly, for the life of a Bible college is dependent upon keeping *the ideal dominant and alive.*

## Academic Upgrading

Throughout its history, the Bible institute-college movement has experienced a steady upgrading academically. Responsible for this trend are the general rise in the level of education and the desire to improve the quality of preparation for Christian ministries. During the very period of the rise and development of the Bible institute-college movement, a revolution has been going on in American education. Enrollments in public high schools have increased thirty-fold. According to the President's Committee on Education Beyond the High

School, "without realizing it we have become a 'society of students.' " More than 40 million—one-quarter of the nation —are enrolled in formal educational programs. In addition, over one million military personnel are pursuing educational goals, another three million are in business-sponsored training, and one out of three adults, an estimated 50 million, participate in adult educational classes.[16] Sharing modestly in this trend, are the varied types of schools which have been developed in recent years to prepare men and women for lay and professional work in the service of the church.

When Bible institutes were first established, there were few high school graduates among enrollees. Now there are few who have not completed high school. Seven members of The Accrediting Association of Bible Colleges reported not a single non-high school graduate in their 1959-60 enrollments. Even though the Association permits schools to admit up to five per cent non-high school graduates as special students, the number enrolled has steadily declined from 4.1 to 1.2 per cent during the past ten years. Now it is common to select applicants from among high school graduates. Furthermore, a considerable number of students with from one to four years of college enroll in Bible colleges for specialized preparation.

On the other hand, Bible schools have improved their programs with better qualified faculties, greatly enriched libraries, improved instructional procedures, self-evaluating studies and instructional seminars.

*Amplified Curricula*

The first schools stressed training and culture of the spiritual life. Without question they rendered an important service in shaping lives, but their educational diet was quite scanty apart from religious and practical subjects. Some even boasted that students were taught nothing they did not need to know and that they put into actual use all that they knew. Generally, Bible courses were not graded and students were given two years of training. Quite appropriately, many of the older institutions in their early years were called *Bible training schools.*

A trend toward a lengthened curriculum got under way in the twenties and thirties. The two-year course was extended to three years. At the same time specialized programs for the pastorate, missions, Christian education and music came into prominence. Now the more appropriate name became *Bible institute.*

By the time the majority of enrollees were post-high school graduates, new conditions called for further amplification of the curriculum. It became apparent that high school graduates in America, at least in recent times, do not acquire a good secondary education. With few exceptions, they need more English, for many have neither a grasp of the structure of the language nor a command of its use. Many are without an adequate background in history for Biblical and theological studies. Their educational base needs to be both broadened and deepened. This prompted many, but not all, institutes to add a substantial element of general education to their programs.

Concurrently, students became credit and degree-conscious. They became concerned about the length of time required to get a college degree especially if it meant three or four years of college after completing a Bible institute program. Again, the answer was found for some schools in an integrated program of general, Biblical, and professional studies leading to a baccalaureate degree. With this amplification, many schools changed their names from Bible institute to *Bible college.*[17]

According to the 1959-60 survey of Bible institutes and colleges in the United States and Canada, slightly over half—52 per cent—classify themselves as Bible colleges while the remainder regard themselves as Bible institutes. Among the members of The Accrediting Association of Bible Colleges, the proportion is higher. Forty of the 49 members, or 82 per cent, are essentially degree-conferring colleges. Accordingly, "Bible College" occurs more frequently in their names.

Further developments in curriculum came about as schools undertook to prepare students for the increasing number of specialized ministries that have come into being in recent times. In any one or more of the Bible schools there are programs in missionary medicine, missionary nursing service, Christian social service, journalism, missionary aviation, missionary radio communications, linguistics, missionary technical training, elementary education, and various specializations in the field of music.

## Accreditation

One of the most significant developments that has taken place in the Bible institute-college movement is the organization of The Accrediting Association of Bible Colleges in 1947. Long before that, consideration had been given to the formation of an accrediting agency for Bible schools. In 1918, Dr. James M. Gray of Moody Bible Institute called a group of Bible institute men together to consider the problem. An investigating committee which the group appointed came to the conclusion that there were such great differences in curriculum, methods, and doctrine that it was found "impossible to draw up any method of unifying the whole Bible school system, or of establishing a system of interchangeable credits."[18] The effort was abandoned, but the idea lived on while the times increasingly demanded that the issue be resolved.

At the time of the Minneapolis meeting of the National Association of Evangelicals in 1946, Dr. Howard W. Ferrin stated the issue as follows: The distinctive elements of Bible institute education are indispensable and must therefore be preserved. No existing agency assists Bible institutes to upgrade their programs by the process of accreditation. Accreditation by the regional associations is possible only (at that time) by converting institutes to liberal arts colleges, which obliterates their distinctives. The only solution, therefore, is to establish an accrediting agency according to sound collegiate standards but which will be predicated on principles of Bible college education. Thereupon plans were initiated to organize such an agency.

In response to invitations sent to Bible schools of the United States and Canada, a number of representatives met at Winona Lake, Indiana, in October, 1947. At that meeting The Accrediting Association of Bible Institutes and Bible Colleges was formed with Dr. Samuel Sutherland serving as the first president.[19] With the valued counsel of several leading educators, particularly Dr. John Dale Russell, then Assistant Commissioner of the United States Office of Education, the Association made sound progress. The first 12 schools were accredited in 1948 and the Association soon after became recognized by the United States Office of Education as the one accrediting agency in the field of undergraduate theological education.[20]

Through recognition by the United States Office of Education, its accredited members are listed in the annual reports of the Office of Education. They are approved for veterans' training by the Veterans Administration and for the education of foreign students by the Department of Justice. The Association is a constituent member of the American Council on Education.

The Association has two classes of membership: accredited and associate. Accredited membership means that a school has satisfactorily met the standards of the Association and has thereby been granted accreditation. Associate members are identified with the Association in a non-accredited relationship, but such membership is evidence of academic and financial integrity, valid educational service, and conformity to the spirit and objectives of the Association.

The Association has grown steadily so that in 1960 it reported a membership of 36 accredited and 13 associate schools. While this number represents 20 per cent of the Bible institutes and Bible colleges in the United States and Canada, it includes 44 per cent of the total day school enrollment.

The standards and policies of the Association are published in a manual. By insisting on certain qualities and levels of excellence, these criteria are designed to stimulate schools to continued growth and improvement of services. Besides formal accreditation, the Association maintains a number of related services through the executive director's office. A *Newsletter* is published quarterly, consultative visits are made to schools, surveys are conducted on various aspects of Bible college education, and significant information is disseminated. As a service agency, the Association seeks to be helpful to all Bible institutes and Bible colleges.

At its tenth annual meeting, Dr. Enock C. Dyrness, Vice-President and Registrar of Wheaton College, commended the Association on its progress:

> I offer my congratulations for the tremendous progress which has been made during the past ten years. Not only is this true of the schools that are members of the Accrediting Association, but also of those who have not yet taken that step. With the establishment of the Accrediting Association of Bible Colleges, the Bible school movement has really come of age and achieved its rightful place in American higher education.[21]

*Chapter Three*

# DIMENSIONS OF THE BIBLE INSTITUTE-COLLEGE MOVEMENT

How many Bible institutes and Bible colleges are there? Where are they located? Who operates them? How many students do they enroll? These and similar questions are frequently asked about a movement about which little authentic information has been published.

## SURVEY

Many of these questions were answered in a survey conducted in 1959-60 by The Accrediting Association of Bible Colleges on the day-time Bible institutes and Bible colleges of the United States and Canada. No attempt was made to identify the several hundred purely evening Bible institutes conducted principally in church centers for the training of lay leaders. However, data were secured on evening divisions that are conducted in connection with day institutions.

Two problems were encountered in the investigation. The first was to compile an up-to-date, authentic list of day Bible institutes and Bible colleges. It was found that the several available lists contained numerous discrepancies. Names of institutions were misleading in terms of classification. For example, a school might be named a seminary when in fact it is a Bible college operating on the undergraduate level. Some schools listed were no longer in existence. Some had merged with others. Others had changed name or location. A number of recently established institutions did not appear on any list. By a process of elimination and addition, the original composite list was reduced by approximately 50 schools. All of this points up the ever-changing character of the Bible institute-college movement.

The second problem had to do with securing basic data from the schools themselves. Statistical information on the members of The Accrediting Association of Bible Colleges was available from the records of the Association. A brief questionnaire was sent to non-member schools, and while many responded promptly, some failed to reply even after a third request.

## NUMBER AND DISTRIBUTION

There are 248 known Bible institutes and Bible colleges in the United States and Canada. Of this number 54 are located in Canada and 194 in the United States. They are found in 41 States and the District of Columbia and in 9 Canadian Provinces.

Bible institutes-colleges are found in all parts of the United States. There is no distinct pattern in their distribution; generally, they are found in the more populous areas. Several sections of the country have relatively few. There are only five in the New England States, and eleven in the deep South. Likewise, the Rocky Mountain area has relatively few schools of this type. The sections with the highest proportion are the North Central States with 20 per cent, the Pacific Coast States with 15 per cent, and the States of the upper South with 13 per cent.

The first Bible institutes were characteristically established in large urban centers where there were many opportunities for students to minister in homes, missions, churches, Sunday

**TABLE II**

DISTRIBUTION OF BIBLE INSTITUTES-COLLEGES
BY STATES (U. S.)

| State | Number | State | Number |
|-------|--------|-------|--------|
| California | 17 | Iowa | 3 |
| Texas | 11 | Kansas | 3 |
| Illinois | 10 | Virginia | 3 |
| Kentucky | 10 | Arkansas | 2 |
| Minnesota | 10 | Maryland | 2 |
| New York | 9 | New Jersey | 2 |
| North Carolina | 9 | Rhode Island | 2 |
| Michigan | 8 | South Carolina | 2 |
| Missouri | 8 | West Virginia | 2 |
| Ohio | 7 | Wisconsin | 2 |
| Pennsylvania | 7 | Alabama | 1 |
| Tennessee | 7 | District of Columbia | 1 |
| Arizona | 6 | Idaho | 1 |
| Colorado | 6 | Maine | 1 |
| Georgia | 6 | Massachusetts | 1 |
| Oregon | 6 | Mississippi | 1 |
| Washington | 6 | Montana | 1 |
| Florida | 5 | North Dakota | 1 |
| Nebraska | 4 | South Dakota | 1 |
| Oklahoma | 4 | Vermont | 1 |
| Indiana | 3 | | |
| | | Total | 194 |

schools and other Christian agencies. Today most of the
larger metropolitan areas have one or more Bible colleges even
though there has been a modest trend for schools to move from
congested downtown areas to more spacious campuses in suburbs and rural areas. Approximately 60 per cent of the Bible
institutes and Bible colleges of the United States and Canada
are found in sizeable cities. Opportunities for Christian service
in cities tend to make urban locations more desirable for these
institutions. When established schools in downtown locations
grow and expand and are compelled to secure more space for
building and parking, they find it convenient to move to a

suburb where they can be close to some of the opportunities available in urban centers.

There are, however, important exceptions to this trend. A number of schools have especially selected campus sites in rural areas in order to be removed from the distractions of urban life and to provide better conditions for concentrated study. Outstanding examples are Prairie Bible Institute and Briercrest Institute, both situated in rural sections of Western Canada, but to which hundreds of students come from both rural and urban communities of North America.

In Canada there is a more pronounced pattern in the distribution of Bible colleges, for 32 of the 54 are located in the three prairie Provinces of Manitoba, Saskatchewan and Alberta (this is 60 per cent of the total Canadian institutions). As Quebec is predominantly Roman Catholic, there are but a few Protestant Bible schools. In the less populous Maritime Provinces there are six schools.

TABLE III

DISTRIBUTION OF BIBLE INSTITUTES-COLLEGES
BY PROVINCES (CANADA)

| Province | Number |
|---|---|
| Alberta | 12 |
| Saskatchewan | 12 |
| Ontario | 8 |
| Manitoba | 8 |
| British Columbia | 5 |
| Quebec | 3 |
| New Brunswick | 3 |
| Nova Scotia | 2 |
| Prince Edward Island | 1 |
| Total | 54 |

The chief contrast is between Ontario and the three prairie Provinces. Even though Ontario has twice the combined populations of these Provinces, it has only a fourth as many Bible schools. The explanation is no doubt found in the different

social and religious backgrounds of these areas. While Ontario
has always been a center of Protestant strength, it has been
much more conservative than the Canadian West. Evangelicalism outside of the older denominations has not had the varied
and dynamic development found in the Western Provinces.
Furthermore, the large influx of Bible-believing immigrants
who settled in colonies on the prairies following the World
Wars led to the establishment of quite a number of Bible
institutes, particularly among Mennonites coming from Russia
and Germany. At first, nearly all of these institutes were short-
term schools conducted for lay training during the winter
months when the farms made few demands on young people.
Some of these Bible schools have developed stronger three-year
programs, but they continue to serve homogenous communities. For example, in a sizeable Mennonite community in
British Columbia there are two Bible institutes, each having approximately 80 students; neither school provides dormitories because practically all students live within driving
distance!

In any event, the less conservative conditions of the Canadian
West were conducive to the remarkable development of several
outstanding institutions that draw students from all parts of
Canada. Foremost among these are Prairie Bible Institute at
Three Hills, Alberta, and Briercrest Bible Institute at Caron-
port, Saskatchewan.

## DENOMINATIONAL STATUS

In classifying schools as "denominational" or "independent,"
the distinction is clear in most cases. Some institutions are un-
questionably under the control of their own denominations in
organization and accountability. Others are clearly independent of denominational control. Their boards are self-perpetu-
ating, and members are chosen irrespective of denominational
affiliation. These schools are sometimes identified as "interdenominational," although they are not interdenominational in

the strict meaning of that term. The borderline institutions are those which are organized independently of denominational control, but in communion and operation they are identified with a single denomination. Among the Baptist and Christian groups (Church of Christ) there are many such schools. In this survey they are classified as "denominational."

Under this classification approximately two-thirds of all Bible institutes and Bible colleges in the United States and Canada are denominational. Of the 248 schools, 160 institutions, or 64.2 per cent of the total, are denominational. They enroll 63 per cent of the students. In Canada, however, the denominational schools are generally smaller than the independent institutions. There is a valid explanation for this differential. Many denominations feel obligated to maintain their own schools to prepare their candidates for ministry in their churches and missions regardless of the number of ministerial recruits. While these schools do not exclude students from other denominations, they function primarily to serve the single parent denomination. On the other hand, the largest Bible institutes and Bible colleges in both the United States and Canada are non-denominational; several, such as Moody Bible Institute, Prairie Bible Institute, and Biola are among the largest Protestant training centers in the world.

Table IV presents the classification of Bible institutes-colleges by denominational affiliation. It is observed that the Church of Christ and the Baptists sponsor the largest number of Bible colleges. Most of the schools in the Church of Christ group are identified with the conservative movement of that society and have contributed much to the revitalization of Biblical faith in that movement. Half of the Baptist institutions identified themselves in the survey as simply "Baptist"; the other half specified a particular fellowship including Conservative, Free Will, Reformed Baptist Alliance, Fellowship, General Association of Regular Baptists, National Convention, Missionary, North American General Conference, World Baptist Fellowship, and Southern. The Pentecostal groups are third in the number of schools with 25. The largest of the seven Pentecostal denominations is the Assemblies of God, which has eight Bible institutes and Bible colleges in the United States. Its related denomination in Canada conducts four schools. In addition to the church groups given in Table IV, a dozen denominations sponsor a single school each.

TABLE IV

DENOMINATIONAL AFFILIATIONS OF BIBLE
INSTITUTES-COLLEGES IN UNITED STATES AND CANADA

| Denomination | Number of Schools in U.S. | Number of Schools in Canada | Total |
|---|---|---|---|
| Christian (Church of Christ) | 34 | 3 | 37 |
| Baptist Groups | 32 | 4 | 36 |
| Pentecostal Groups | 19 | 6 | 25 |
| Wesleyan Groups | 16 | 5 | 21 |
| Mennonite Groups | 2 | 11 | 13 |
| Lutheran Groups | 6 | 2 | 8 |
| Christian & Missionary Alliance | 4 | 1 | 5 |

While some Bible colleges function within the framework of the larger denominations, the great majority are either sponsored by smaller evangelical churches, or they serve major bodies that stress congregational versus denominational authority. Outstanding among the latter are the Church of Christ and the Baptist Bible colleges. In any event, it appears that both independent and denominational schools grow and function most effectively under conditions of political, religious, and social freedom.

ENROLLMENT

The number of day students enrolled in the Bible institute-colleges of the United States and Canada approximates 25,000. The 217 schools that reported their registrations for the first semester of the 1959-60 school year had a combined enrollment of 23,584 students. Of these, 2,868, or 11 per cent, were part-time students. In the 170 U. S. schools, there are 20,167 students or 85.5 per cent. In the 47 Canadian schools reporting, there were 3,417 day students or 14.5 per cent.

There are more men students than women students, although in some schools women outnumbered men. Total men classified as day students number 13,027 as compared with 10,557 women, or 55 and 45 per cent respectively.

In addition to day school enrollments, 92 schools reported having evening divisions with a total enrollment of 9,058. The combined enrollment for day school registrations and evening division enrollments comes to 32,642 students. If estimates are included for non-reporting schools, the total would approximate 35,000 persons who are receiving education on Bible college campuses.

The average day school enrollment for the 217 reporting schools is 108.7. United States schools average somewhat higher with an average enrollment of 118.6, compared to 72.7 students for Canadian schools. However, there is a wide disparity in size. For example, three independent schools in Canada—Prairie Bible Institute, Briercrest Bible Institute, and Toronto Bible College—have a combined enrollment of 1,086 students, thus accounting for 31.2 per cent of all students in Canadian Bible institute-colleges.

In spite of some weak and struggling schools in the Bible institute-college movement, the majority are well-established institutions. The distribution of 250 schools with 25,000 students throughout the United States and Canada constitutes a significant force for evangelicalism. Their influence is incalculable. Other Christian movements such as Child Evangelism Fellowship and evangelistic crusades find in the student bodies trained and dedicated talent for teaching and counseling. The thousands of laymen who are given Biblical and practical training in adult education classes add to the strength of lay service and witness.

Communities with Bible colleges and institutes have a moral and spiritual tone that is at times noticeably lacking in communities without them. The presence of a Bible institute adds moral and spiritual strength to the church and the community.

*Chapter Four*

# BIBLE COLLEGES
# IN THE PATTERN OF
# AMERICAN CHRISTIANITY

The Bible institutes and Bible colleges in the United States and Canada have as many facets as the mosaic pattern of American Protestantism. The 160 denominational schools are identified with 52 denominations. The remaining 88 schools are classified as independent.

But in spite of their being intertwined with the complexities of Protestantism, even with its family quarrels and divisions, they belong to one general theological family. All Bible institutes and Bible colleges are conservative in theology with little deviation from the orthodox position of Trinitarianism and its related doctrines of the sinfulness of man, the necessity of regeneration, the inspiration of the Scriptures, the Saviourhood of Jesus Christ. Bible schools take the Scriptures seriously— its presuppositions, its doctrines, its moral imperatives, and its implications for eternity. They are not given to displacing faith with rationalism, supernaturalism with naturalism, nor theology with philosophy.

It would be expected, therefore, that Bible institutes and Bible colleges in their service and church relationships are identified with the Protestant groups that are evangelical and avowedly conservative. They find their affinity with those agencies, missions, and church groups that are committed without apology "to the faith which was once delivered to the saints" and its proclamation to all the world.

Although it is impossible to make an accurate assessment of the contribution of Bible institutes-colleges to evangelicalism, yet it can be said that they stood uncompromisingly for orthodoxy during the halcyon decades of liberalism when, during the 20's and the 30's, the church was tolerant of rationalism, and when the "new theology" and the "social gospel" all but carried the day. The Rev. Oscar E. Feucht, Secretary of Adult Education of the Lutheran Church, Missouri Synod, paid this tribute to them: "The Bible Institutes have been one of the citadels of strength for the preservation of Biblical theology when modern religious liberalism made serious inroads on many Protestant churches." [1]

By defending the faith not so much by apologetics as by propagation, Bible schools have made a vital contribution to the life of the church. By their stress on Christian experience, dedication, personal evangelism and missions, they have been instruments of God to keep the faith dynamic as well as intact. Mr. Feucht stated further that the most significant contribution of the Bible institute movement "has been the new vitality it gave to the drooping life of the church."

## SERVICES IN MAJOR DENOMINATIONS

While Bible institutes-colleges are found principally among the smaller and newer evangelical bodies, yet a growing place is found for specialized Bible training schools among some of the well-established, larger denominations.

In several denominations that follow the regular college and seminary pattern for ministerial preparation, the Bible institute has been "discovered" as a type of school that provides educational services not available in conventional institutions.

For example, the several intersynodical Lutheran Bible institutes have met a definite need in Lutheranism by offering preparation for church vocation not provided by Lutheran teachers' colleges, seminaries, and liberal arts colleges. One institute is training 50 parish workers each year, but it could place 150. In 1961, the Lutheran Church, Missouri Synod, established a school in Milwaukee to train parish workers. Hundreds of Lutheran missionaries have received specialized missionary preparation in the several Lutheran Bible institutes.

Pastoral training in Bible institutes has a place even in one of America's largest denominations, one noted for the size and prestige of its seminaries—the Southern Baptist Convention. In order to provide educational opportunity for pastors and other church workers who cannot or do not choose to meet seminary admission requirements, several state associations are sponsoring Bible institutes. An example is Baptist Bible Institute of Graceville, Florida, owned and operated by the Florida Baptist Convention. It offers a Bible-centered program that is patterned in content after the regular seminary curriculum. Its policy is to have on the faculty only men with earned doctorates. The need for institutes arises from the fact that the seminary, which is limited to admitting college graduates, is not the complete answer for ministerial preparation among the Southern Baptists.

In President James E. Southerland's inaugural address in 1958 on "The Role of Bible Schools in the Southern Baptist Convention," he noted the great progress that has been made in establishing seminaries and observed, "Today theological seminary education is thoroughly entrenched in our denominational life. . . . This, of course, is as it should be." But he also presented compelling arguments in favor of additional types of theological schools:

> First: Baptists must always remember who they are. We are people of every class and our ministers are God-called men who have been called from the people and who have identified themselves with the people.

Second: We believe in education, but we must not place undue stress upon a man's having a certain type of formal education before he can be considered to be qualified to serve a church as pastor. He may choose a route other than by one of our seminaries.

Third: We must recognize that God still calls men to the ministry who are not high school or college graduates and that by far the majority of our preachers today are noncollege and nonseminary trained men. "The theological survey of the Southern Baptists in 1949 reveals that less than one-third of our ministers had both college and seminary training at that time." (*Encyclopedia of Southern Baptists,* page 1410.) We are only ten years removed from the date of that survey. It is generally recognized that today at least one-half of our pastors do not have a college degree, and have never attended one of our seminaries.[2]

In the largest Negro denomination, the National Baptist Convention with 5,000,000 members, the undergraduate Bible college is serving as the principal type of theological school. A unique Bible institution is the American Baptist Theological Seminary of Nashville, Tennessee, operated under the joint auspices of the National Baptist Convention and the Southern Baptist Convention for the training of Negro ministers and church workers. Another Negro school is Western Baptist Bible College of Kansas City, Missouri, sponsored by the Missouri Baptist Convention of the National Baptists.

In Canada, the major denominations—Anglican, United and Presbyterian—do not operate Bible institutes or Bible colleges. However, a number of the smaller denominations whose United States components conduct liberal arts colleges and seminaries, rely on Bible colleges to prepare their young people for church vocations, including the pastorate. There are at least two contributing causes for this situation. In Canada, these denominations or sects are often too small in membership and resources to support an extensive system of higher education. Then too, Canada's educational policies are not conducive to the building and maintaining of liberal arts colleges by religious denominations.

Accordingly, a number of groups such as the Evangelical United Brethren (Hillcrest Bible Institute), Nazarene (Canadian Nazarene College), Free Methodist (Moose Jaw Bible College), North American Baptist General Conference (Christian Training Institute), General Conference Mennonites (Canadian Mennonite Bible College), Mennonite Brethren (Mennonite Brethren Bible College), and United Missionary Church (Mountain View Bible College, Emmanual Bible College) maintain theological-Bible colleges to train their candidates for the ministry. Several of these schools offer three-year pastoral training programs comparable to seminary curricula, but only require two years of university work for matriculation instead of the three or four required by the standard seminary.

## BIBLE INSTITUTES-COLLEGES AND THE "THIRD FORCE"

Ever since Dr. Henry P. Van Dusen coined the term "Third Force of Christendom" for a host of sects, cults, and small church movements, the *force* of these varied Protestant groups outside the traditional, historic churches has been more definitely recognized. Few would take issue with Dr. Van Dusen that there is a dynamic force of evangelicals outside of the old line churches. They are evangelistic as well as evangelical. They look upon Christianity as a new life begun by regeneration. With few exceptions they hold to faith rather than to infant baptism. Most distinguish between mystical membership in Christ's body and formal membership in a visible church.

The significance of the "Third Force" is its dynamism and growth. Dr. Van Dusen enumerated six factors that contributed to its vitality:

(1) They have great spiritual ardor, (2) they commonly promise an immediate, life-transforming experience of the living God-in-Christ, (3) they directly

approach people, (4) they shepherd their converts in an intimate sustaining group-fellowship, (5) they place strong emphasis upon the Holy Spirit, and (6) they expect their followers to practice an active, untiring, seven-day-a-week Christianity.[3]

Two additional characteristics should be added: They regard the Bible as the revealed Word of God, and they preach a positive message of salvation through Christ.

Now the majority of Bible institutes-colleges in the United States and Canada are identified with this "Third Force" which represents a combination of orthodoxy and spiritual dynamic. The Bible institutes-colleges serve these sects and in turn are supported by them. Many of their leaders and most of their missionaries are products of these schools. In this way, these minor sects have been able to transmit the faith, the evangelistic impulses and the spiritual ideals of the parent groups to their youth. By seeking to incorporate the eight factors above into the educative process, they prepare their students for a Pauline type of ministry distinguished by the word of the Apostle in his first Corinthian letter: "For I determined not to know any thing among you, save Jesus Christ, and him crucified. . . . And my speech and my preaching was not with enticing words of man's wisdom, but in demonstration of the Spirit and of power." [4]

Not all groups of the "Third Force" operate Bible colleges; several look to liberal arts colleges and seminaries to prepare students for Christian leadership, but the majority have relied on Bible institute-colleges for ministerial preparation. While groups of the "Third Force" hold to a common core of evangelical doctrine, yet they span a broad spectrum of variation in faith and practice. Admittedly, there are some schools at the fringe of the movement that seem to get students and support by their negative attitudes. "Occasionally strong individualistic leaders have stamped their personal prejudices and peculiar interpretations of Scripture upon institutions," making them reactionary and highly sectarian.[5]

However, there is less of the petty divisiveness that marked "Third Force" groups 30 or 40 years ago. By more association through such organizations as the National Association of Evangelicals and The Accrediting Association of Bible Colleges, they have discovered that the areas of agreement are greater and more important than their differences. In addition, they have become very much aware that their common enemies are the anti-Christian ideologies of communism, pragmatism, relativism, evolutionism, and materialism.

## Baptists

Baptist-affiliated Bible institutes-colleges are the second highest in number according to our 1959-60 survey, with a total of 36 in the United States and Canada. It is impossible to classify all of them according to particular Baptist connections, for half of the schools simply reported their denominational affiliation as "Baptist." However, it can be said that the groups that represent various degrees and shades of digression from the older denominations generally sponsor Bible institutes and colleges.

Among these groups is the General Association of Regular Baptists. While it operates a liberal arts college and a graduate seminary, it sponsors four Bible colleges: Western Baptist Bible College, El Cerrito, Calif.; Omaha Baptist Bible Institute, Omaha, Nebr.; Grand Rapids Bible Institute and School of Theology, Grand Rapids, Mich.; and Baptist Bible Seminary, Johnson City, N. Y.

The Baptist Bible Fellowship has a rapidly growing institute —the Baptist Bible Institute at Springfield, Mo. Just seven years after it was founded in 1950, it had an enrollment of 485 students, 391 alumni, and close to 100 graduates in foreign missionary service.

While the Conservative Baptist Association looks to its several seminaries to train its pastors, it has several Bible colleges for ministerial preparation and training of church workers. Pillsbury Conservative Baptist Bible College is operated

by the Minnesota Baptist Convention which is in the hands
of the Conservatives. Baptist Bible College of Denver, Colorado, and South Western Baptist Schools of Phoenix, Arizona, are other schools identified with this group.

The establishment of one Bible college—Free Will Baptist
Bible College—is involved in the remarkable restoration of the
Free Will Baptists as an organized denomination. When the
Free Will Baptist denomination united with the Northern
Baptist Convention in 1911, many scattered congregations in
the South remained outside the merger. Even though they
number 184,287 adherents,[6] they continued for 30 years with
little denominational consciousness or cohesiveness. Their colleges in the North and their denominational agencies had all
been absorbed in the merger. It was not until about 1940 that
a number of projects were initiated that called for concerted
effort, giving the scattered churches a common purpose. One
was a missionary enterprise, and the other, a theological college to train pastors, missionaries, and other workers for the
churches.

The plans for a Bible college were realized in 1942, when
Free Will Baptist Bible College, Nashville, Tennessee, opened
its doors. Under the leadership of President L. C. Johnson, the
college has grown rapidly, strengthening its curriculum, faculty, and services. The college already has two noteworthy
achievements to its credit. In 1951, when the first A.B. degrees
were conferred, it marked the first time in almost 40 years that
a degree was granted by a Free Will Baptist institution. A
second goal was achieved in 1958 when the college was accredited by The Accrediting Association of Bible Colleges. The
college is not only preparing students for Christian leadership,
but it is unifying the churches of the denomination doctrinally
and stimulating them to evangelistic and missionary en-
deavor.

Two Baptist schools in Canada are sponsored by Baptist
denominations that have European antecedents. Vancouver
Bible Institute, Vancouver, British Columbia is operated by

the Baptist General Conference (Swedish), and the Christian Training Institute of Edmonton, Alberta is backed by the North American Baptist General Conference (German). In order to serve recent immigrants from Germany, the latter school continues to be bi-lingual.

## Christian Churches

The branch of the Christian Church (Disciples) known as the independent Churches of Christ and representing a resurgence of the movement to restore New Testament Christianity, is one of the most significant bodies of the "Third Force." [7] Begun as a reaction to liberalism which came to be associated with hierarchical tendencies, the movement is growing rapidly in number of churches and adherents. It is estimated that the total number now exceeds one million, and newly established churches are steadily adding to its strength. Its national convention in Columbus, Ohio, in 1960 brought together more than 4,400 delegates from all sections of the United States and Canada.

Thirty-seven Bible colleges with an approximate enrollment of 3,000 contribute trained pastors, missionaries and other church workers to the movement. While their relationships to the parent "brotherhood" vary from identification to disassociation, they are all in the tradition of Alexander Campbell's conservative theology and his emphasis on Bible study. Those with the largest enrollments are Cincinnati Bible Seminary, Johnson Bible College, Kentucky Christian College, Lincoln Bible Institute, Minnesota Bible College, Northwest Christian College, and Ozark Bible College.

A number of schools spearhead the advance of church propagation at home. By this method a school is established in an area where there are few Christian churches for the purpose of training lay and full-time workers to open up and man new churches. In Canada, where there are few Churches of Christ, only one Bible college, Alberta Bible College at Calgary, Alberta—a small school with a strong program—has been in operation. In 1958, Toronto Christian Seminary was begun and is conducting an evening program to provide training for both lay and full-time workers. In the fall of 1960, a third school was opened in Charlottetown, Prince Edward Island.

A proliferation of Bible colleges in some parts of the country has resulted in schools with small enrollments, limited facilities, and doubtful academic quality. Administrators justify many schools versus a few large ones on the ground that the larger the number of geographical areas served by schools the greater the opportunities of field work in which student pastors can engage in church extension. Accordingly, the future of some schools is yet to be assured, depending on the success of the church extension enterprise. In any event, a Bible-centered program of ministerial preparation has demonstrated its effectiveness in the growth and vitality of this dynamic movement. Dr. Murch summarized the significance of these schools as follows:

> These new schools are yet in their infancy. The Lord willing, most of them will grow in stature and quality to form the greatest contribution that the Restoration Movement has made to higher education. This generation is too close to this phenomenal development to fully appreciate its significance.[8]

## Missionary

Several schools besides Nyack Missionary College owe much of their origin and development to the spiritual emphasis and missionary vision of Dr. A. B. Simpson. Until 1916, Nyack was the only Bible college operated by The Christian and Missionary Alliance. In that year, St. Paul Bible College was founded by the Rev. J. D. Williams to serve the Midwest. Five years later, Simpson Bible College was founded in Seattle to serve the Pacific West where it remained until 1925 when it moved to San Francisco. In 1941, Canadian Bible College was established in Regina, Saskatchewan, to serve the Canadian

Districts of the society. This youngest of Alliance schools has already trained more than 100 missionaries and is a leader among the Bible schools of Saskatchewan in terms of academic progress.

All four Alliance schools have developed sound academic programs and maintain a strong orientation toward world missions. All are members of The Accrediting Association of Bible Colleges. All are open to Christian young people from non-Alliance churches.

Toccoa Falls Institute, Toccoa Falls, Georgia, while not officially sponsored by The Christian and Missionary Alliance, has been maintained in the Alliance tradition since its founding in 1907 by Dr. R. A. Forrest. The first gift of $1,000 for a campus site came from Dr. A. B. Simpson. It was established to provide Bible teaching and training for Christian workers for the educationally underprivileged, and today provides many work opportunities for students of limited means. It consists of a high school and a Bible college, both accredited. The latter has an enrollment of 170.

Fort Wayne Bible College, controlled by The Missionary Church Association but operated interdenominationally, has been fraternally related to The Christian and Missionary Alliance since it was founded in 1904. It has Alliance representatives on its governing board, its faculty, and the student body.

The six schools in this group have a combined enrollment of more than 1600.

## Pentecostal

Among the most rapidly growing denominations in the "Third Force" are some of the Pentecostal bodies. The largest, Assemblies of God, has passed the half million mark in membership. It has depended on its Bible colleges and Bible institutes to prepare its young people for Christian ministries at home and abroad. Besides Central Bible Institute at Springfield, Mo., there are six regional Bible schools: Eastern Bible Institute, Green Lane, Pa.; South-Eastern Bible College, Lake-

land, Fla.; North Central Bible College, Minneapolis, Minn.;
Southwestern Bible Institute, Waxahachie, Texas; Bethany
Bible College, Santa Cruz, Calif.; and Northwest Bible College,
Kirkland, Wash.

An additional institute was founded by the Italian branch of
the Assemblies in 1958 at Salisbury Center, N.Y., known as the
Pine Crest Bible Institute. The eight schools had a total day
school enrollment of 2,200 in 1959-60. While not much academic strength could be credited to the Assembly schools fifteen years ago, there has been a substantial upgrading in
quality so that now all but the recently established Pine Crest
Bible Institute are members of The Accrediting Association of
Bible Colleges. Five have accredited status, while two are associate members.

Besides the Assemblies of God (United States), nine other
Pentecostal denominations operate 16 Bible colleges, according
to our 1959-60 survey. The total membership of the Pentecostal
bodies served by Bible colleges is well over one million, according to membership statistics given by the 1960 Yearbook of
American Churches.[9]

TABLE V

BIBLE COLLEGES IN PENTECOSTAL DENOMINATIONS

| Denomination | Membership | Number of Bible Institute-Colleges |
|---|---|---|
| Apostolic Church of Pentecost | | 1 |
| Assemblies of God | 505,703 | 8 |
| Church of God (Cleveland) | 162,794 | 3 |
| International Church of the Foursquare Gospel | 79,012 | 2 |
| Open Bible Standard Church | 25,000 | 3 |
| Pentecostal Assemblies of the World | 50,000 | 1 |
| United Pentecostal Church | 160,000 | 1 |
| International Pentecostal Assemblies | 5,000 | 1 |
| Pentecostal Assemblies of Canada | | 4 |
| Pentecostal Church of God | 103,500 | 1 |
| Total | 1,091,009 | 25 |

*Wesleyan*

Bible colleges are found also among the institutions with a Wesleyan emphasis or background in theology. The Pilgrim Holiness Church operates five Bible colleges: Eastern Pilgrim College, Allentown, Pennsylvania; Central Pilgrim College, Bartlesville, Oklahoma; Frankfort Pilgrim College, Frankfort, Indiana; Southern Pilgrim College, Kernersville, North Carolina; and Owosso College, Owosso, Michigan. The latter institution is developing a liberal arts division in addition to the Bible college.

Other Wesleyan groups that are served by Bible colleges are the Church of God (Holiness) —Kansas City College and Bible School, Overland Park, Kansas; the Holiness Methodist Church —Holiness Methodist School of Theology, Minneapolis, Minnesota; Churches of Christ in Christian Union—Circleville Bible College, Circleville, Ohio; and Emmanuel Association—Peoples Bible College, Colorado Springs, Colorado. One of the Wesleyan Methodist colleges in the United States, Central Wesleyan College of Central, South Carolina, has a Bible college division. Sharing the Wesleyan tradition are two conservative Friends Bible colleges—Friends Bible College of Haviland, Kansas, and Union Bible Seminary, Westfield, Indiana.

The Church of God (Anderson, Ind.) operates several colleges with a Biblical emphasis: Gulf Coast Bible College, Houston, Texas; Warner Pacific College, Portland, Oregon; and Alberta Bible Institute, Camrose, Alberta.

In Canada, the Free Methodists maintain the Moose Jaw Bible College at Moose Jaw, Saskatchewan and the Lorne Park College in Ontario. The Church of the Nazarene has a Bible college at Winnipeg, Manitoba. Two other Canadian Bible colleges, Mountain View Bible College at Didsbury, Alberta, and Emmanuel Bible College at Kitchener, Ontario, are operate by the United Missionary Church.

There are also a number of interdenominational Bible colleges and institutes, Wesleyan in theology, which serve holiness churches and missionary societies. Among these are Azusa College, Azusa, California; Kentucky Mountain Bible Institute, Lawson, Kentucky; Vennard College, University Park, Iowa; God's Bible School and College, Cincinnati, Ohio; John Wesley College, Greensboro, North Carolina; and Salem Bible Institute, Salem, Ohio.

## Non-Denominational Agencies

Non-denominational churches, evangelistic agencies, schools, home mission enterprises, and foreign mission societies make use of the services of Bible institutes-colleges. Such organizations as Child Evangelism Fellowship, American Sunday School Union, and the mission boards of the Independent Faith Mission Association draw most of their recruits from Bible institutes and Bible colleges. The principal function of several schools is to train personnel for these organizations.

## SUMMARY

The Bible institutes-colleges of the United States and Canada must be seen in the perspective of the persistent cycle of revival-formalism-rationalism-decadence that has marked Christendom from the first century of the Christian era to contemporary Protestantism in America. After one cycle has run its full course and a second begins with a resurgence of spiritual life, a demand arises for new schools to prepare men and women for Christian ministries in the spirit and faith of revitalized Christianity. Thence are born theological institutions that are committed to Biblical faith, spiritual experience, gospel propagation and renunciation of compromising practices. Their function is to serve the dynamic movements that give them birth and to safeguard them from the forces of decline.

*Chapter Five*

# LEADING BIBLE SCHOOLS IN THE UNITED STATES AND CANADA

In a single volume dealing with the Bible institute-college movement, not all the schools can be mentioned individually.[1] Of necessity, we can only include those that are *among* the leading schools, not *the* leading schools, as others are equally deserving of mention. Factors taken into account are historical significance, size, noteworthy features, influence, supplementary services, academic strength, record of service and contributions to the Bible institute-college movement.

To review the histories of even a few of the 250 Bible institutes and Bible colleges is an inspiring experience. Behind each and every school stands a man or group of men possessed of great faith, great vision and great sacrifice whose personal example of Christian dedication set the standard for their institutions and their students.

## BAPTIST BIBLE SEMINARY

### Johnson City, New York

Baptist Bible Seminary, located in the "Triple Cities" area of New York, serves one of the newer Baptist groups that have been established—the General Association of Regular Baptists.[2]

The school came into being in 1932 through the conviction of Dr. Richard J. Murphy, pastor of Johnson City's First Baptist Church and several of his colleagues that a sound theological school was needed. A meeting of interested ministers and laymen led to the establishment of the Baptist Bible Seminary Fellowship. The trustees of the First Baptist Church opened the way for the school to begin in the fall of 1932 by granting permission to use its Sunday school building. Ever since, the college has been closely identified with the First Baptist Church. Some of the church facilities are still used for classrooms and offices, although the school now has nine buildings of its own.

Beginning with 32 day students in 1932, the college has steadily grown until its enrollment now exceeds 450; its alumni roll has grown to 1,000.

Baptist Bible Seminary is chartered and accredited by the New York Board of Regents. It offers three undergraduate programs: a five-year program leading to the Th.B., a four-year curriculum leading to the B.R.E., and a three-year Bible diploma course. Of the regularly enrolled students, 40 per cent are pursuing the Th.B. curriculum, 48 per cent the B.R.E. program, and 12 per cent the Bible curriculum.

After 14 years as president, Dr. Paul R. Jackson resigned, and the office is now temporarily filled by the Rev. G. Arthur Woolsey.

## BARRINGTON COLLEGE
### Barrington, Rhode Island

Barrington College represents an unusual and strategically important institution, for it has developed into a sizeable and influential Christian college in New England, long noted for its rationalism, now predominantly Roman Catholic. A "Bible School in New England" was the vision given to Mr. and Mrs. John Marble at the turn of the century. They shared their vision with the Rev. Essek W. Kenyon, who was receiving young people into his home for Bible study. In May, 1900, the home was dedicated as *Bethel Bible Training School*. The school has occupied several sites since. In 1923 it was moved to Dudley Hill. In 1929, a site was secured on Capitol Hill in Providence, Rhode Island, and the school was then re-incorporated as Providence Bible Institute.

In 1950, the jubilee year, the "Miracle Dollar" campus was obtained at Barrington, nine miles from the Providence site. The school operated on both campuses until 1961, when additional buildings were erected at Barrington to accommodate its entire student body of 400 or more. Changes in name have also marked successive changes in location and academic development: Providence-Barrington Bible College in 1954 and Barrington College in 1959. The college is a charter member of The Accrediting Association of Bible Colleges and is also accredited by The New England Association of Colleges and Secondary Schools. By adding departments in the arts and sciences, Barrington is increasingly becoming a general college.

In the history of Barrington College, two men have been guiding forces in the school's development: Dr. Howard W. Ferrin, who has been President since 1925, and Dr. T. B. Crum, who joined the faculty in 1932 and who has been Dean since 1948.

## THE BIBLE INSTITUTE OF LOS ANGELES
### La Mirada, California

The Bible Institute of Los Angeles, Incorporated, was founded in 1908 by Mr. Lyman Stewart, a devoted Christian layman, and the Rev. T. C. Horton, pastor of the Immanuel Presbyterian Church. Organization was effected with the appointment of Mr. Stewart as President and Mr. Horton as Superintendent. The school developed rapidly with a practical outreach to gospel opportunities in the city. A forward step was taken in calling Dr. Reuben A. Torrey to serve as Dean, who began a twelve-year period of service on January 1, 1912. Before long the school became the leading Bible institute on the West Coast.

The institution has branched out into several distinct divisions with deans heading the divisions and a president in charge of the entire institution. Biola College is the collegiate division in which Bible, Christian service, and liberal arts majors are offered leading to baccalaureate degrees. The School of Missionary Medicine offers one year of intensive medical training for missionary candidates. Talbot Theological Seminary is the graduate division offering regular seminary courses. The Bible Institute is the three-year Bible training division. Related services include radio broadcasts, publication of *The King's Business* and other Christian literature, and Bible conferences.

From 1912 to 1959, Biola occupied quarters in downtown Los Angeles at Sixth and Hope Streets. In 1959 it moved 22 miles southeast to La Mirada, where a magnificent campus has been set up on a 70-acre site. Extraordinarily, the initial stage of development, which cost well over two million dollars, was dedicated free from debt. At the same time the school was able to hold its Los Angeles property for some of its subsidiary operations and for income. All of this is a tribute to God's providence, to prudent management, and to the conservative policy of the Board to avoid debt—a policy born of experience years before, when—in a period of financial stringency—the property was barely recovered at a forced auction!

Biola has an enrollment of more than 800 students. Its President is Dr. Samuel H. Sutherland. The college is accredited by both The Accrediting Association of Bible Colleges and the Western College Association.

## BRIERCREST BIBLE INSTITUTE
### Caronport, Saskatchewan

Briercrest Bible Institute, "The Miracle of the Prairies," is located about 15 miles northwest of Moose Jaw, Saskatchewan, on open wheatland prairie. It was founded in 1935, and in a relatively short time became Canada's second largest Bible institute. It began with 11 students and now has an enrollment of 500. Three hundred students are in the Bible Institute proper; the remainder are in the high school division, which is accredited by the Provincial Department of Education.

Following World War II, the school acquired the Caron Airport. Barracks and hangars formerly occupied by contingents of the Canadian Royal Air Force are now used for dormitory, classroom, office, gymnasium, and auditorium purposes. The school has begun to replace its temporary frame quarters with durable buildings.

The Institute offers a three-year, Bible-centered program with minors in pastoral work, Christian education, and music. It also offers courses in missionary work, and has trained a considerable number of missionaries. Its six-month school year is common in the rural areas of the Canadian West. The school has its own water plant and processing facilities for beef and flour.

Able leadership has been given to the institution by its principal, the Rev. H. Hildebrand.

## CENTRAL BIBLE INSTITUTE
### Springfield, Missouri

The Assemblies of God, one of the fastest growing of the "Third Force" groups, with a current membership in excess of one half million, owes much to its Bible colleges, which have prepared its pastors, missionaries and church leaders. The denomination in the United States has seven regional Bible colleges, and one that is denomination-wide—Central Bible Institute near the denomination's headquarters at Springfield, Missouri.

The Institute was founded in 1922 in response to a need for trained workers in the infant denomination which was organized barely six years earlier. It has since given training to more than half of the denomination's missionaries and many of its leaders.

Several mergers added to the development of the school: Bethel Bible Training Institute of Newark, New Jersey in

1929; South Central Bible College of Hot Springs, Arkansas in 1953; and Great Lakes Bible Institute, Zion, Illinois in 1954.

In 1948, the school extended its curriculum by adding four- and five-year degree programs. In the same year it became a charter member of The Accrediting Association of Bible Colleges. In 1957, a graduate division was added, offering a Master's degree in the several fields of Bible, Missions, and Religious Education.

The Institute has approximately 400 students. Its president since 1958 has been Dr. J. Robert Ashcroft.

## THE CINCINNATI BIBLE SEMINARY
### Cincinnati, Ohio

This institution, founded in 1924, has been an influential force in the independent movement of the Churches of Christ. It has produced many leaders for the movement who are serving as teachers in Bible colleges, authors of Christian literature, pastors, and missionaries to 20 countries. With two related institutions located in Cincinnati, Standard Publishing Company and the Christian Restoration Association, the seminary is at the functional as well as the geographical hub of the movement.

The Cincinnati Bible Seminary came into being through the consolidation of two colleges that were organized a year before—McGarvey Bible College of Louisville, Kentucky, and Cincinnati Bible Institute of Cincinnati. The 27-acre campus is situated on a skyline knoll in the western part of the city. Substantial modern structures, which are replacing the original frame buildings, provide dormitory and classroom facilities for the growing institution.

The Cincinnati Bible Seminary is largely an undergraduate Bible college offering programs leading to the B.S.L., B.A. (Bible), B.Th., and B.S.M. degrees. The *Annual Bulletin* listed 461 undergraduate students for the 1959-60 school year. The Graduate School, which operates on the seminary level, offers a three-year B.D. program and had 31 students in 1959-60. President of the school is Dr. Woodrow W. Perry.

## COLUMBIA BIBLE COLLEGE

### Columbia, South Carolina

Columbia Bible College, a leading Bible college of the South, has achieved a place of high regard among evangelicals for its Christian integrity, its orientation to missions, and the combination of spiritual, academic and practical education that it offers.

The school was founded in 1923 as Columbia Bible School after four years of prayerful preparation. Dr. Robert C. McQuilkin, distinguished Bible conference leader, teacher, and editor, became the first Dean and later President, the office he held until his death in 1952. The school began with four regular and four special students, and graduated the first class of three in 1925. When a four-year Bible college program was inaugurated in 1929, the name was changed to Columbia Bible College. The school is chartered by the State of South Carolina to grant degrees and is accredited by its State Department of Education and The Accrediting Association of Bible Colleges. The Bachelor of Arts in Biblical Education is granted for the four-year course.

Columbia Bible College offers several related services. The Ben Lippen Conference Center at Asheville, North Carolina, provides facilities for summer conferences. The Missionary Training Camp, Ben Lippen Camp, and Ben Lippen School— a Christian high school—are also affiliated with Columbia Bible College. The Graduate School of Missions was established in 1947.

The college was formerly situated near the center of Columbia on properties previously used by a hotel and a seminary. In 1960 it developed a new campus on an attractive 300-acre site several miles north of Columbia along the Broad River.

Columbia Bible College has more than 400 students, 1,500

graduates, and 700 missionaries among its alumni. The present President, Dr. G. Allen Fleece, has given leadership to the institution since 1952.

## FORT WAYNE BIBLE COLLEGE
### Fort Wayne, Indiana

Begun by The Missionary Church Association in Bluffton, Ohio, in 1903, the school was relocated in Fort Wayne, Indiana the following year and renamed The Fort Wayne Bible Training School. Later, when a three-year program displaced a two-year course, the name was changed to The Fort Wayne Bible Institute. After college programs were introduced in 1946, the name was again changed to Fort Wayne Bible College.

While the school is controlled by The Missionary Church Association, it has been operated interdenominationally from the beginning. Several denominations are officially represented on the board, and 25 or more are represented in the student body.

Fort Wayne Bible College occupies a 26-acre campus in a beautiful residential area in Southwest Fort Wayne. It has recently begun the development of a new section of the campus with the construction of a modern library building at a cost in excess of $300,000.

Fort Wayne has several "firsts" to its credit. It was the first Bible college to introduce a missionary nursing program. Through an affiliation with the nearby Lutheran Hospital, the program combines regular nurses training, general education, a Bible major and a missions minor into a five-year program leading to the Bachelor of Science in Missionary Nursing. It is also the first Bible college to become fully accredited by a state department of education for the training of teachers. This program, which combines the professional requirements for teaching in the public schools with a Bible major, was developed in response to an appeal from the sponsoring society for missionaries with professional teaching qualifications. Fort Wayne has also served as a center for Bible college educators in developing a Biblical philosophy of education. For some years it has been host and co-sponsor of a summer seminar on the improvement of instruction and the Biblical implications for education.

Dr. Jared F. Gerig has been President since 1958. The student body numbers 350. It is a charter member of The Accrediting Association of Bible Colleges.

## GRACE BIBLE INSTITUTE
### Omaha, Nebraska

The significance of Grace Bible Institute lies in the fact that it answered a latent but growing desire among American Mennonites for a Bible-centered institution. The traditional attachment of Mennonites to the Word of God fostered a hunger which colleges devoted largely to the liberal arts and sciences did not satisfy. The hopes and prayers of a number of ministers and laymen for an inter-Mennonite school came to fruition in a meeting held in Omaha on June 1, 1943. Steps were immediately taken to establish a Bible institute in that city. The school opened on September 8, 1943, with 23 students. The student body has since grown to more than 300. The majority are Mennonites, although the school is open to all students of evangelical faith.

The Institute owes much to the able leadership of its three presidents: Drs. C. H. Suckau (1943-1950), H. D. Burkholder (1950-55), and J. W. Schmidt (1955-60).

After occupying temporary quarters for several months, the Stuntz Hall property at 1515 South Tenth Street in Omaha was acquired. The school now has substantial facilities in renovated and new buildings.

The Institute offers both three-year diploma courses and four-year degree programs with options of specialized training in the pastorate, missions, Christian education, sacred music, and nurses training in affiliation with Immanuel Hospital.

Since 1948 it has been an accredited member of The Accrediting Association of Bible Colleges.

Acting president is the Rev. Waldo Harder.

## LINCOLN BIBLE INSTITUTE
### Lincoln, Illinois

While several of the two score Bible colleges identified with the independent movement of the "Church of Christ" have a much longer record of service and might well have been included in this series, Lincoln Bible Institute has been selected because of its remarkable growth and representative qualities. Founded only in 1944 with 19 regular enrollees, it grew rapidly so that in its twelfth year it enrolled 431 students.

The school grew out of a concern and a vision of its founder, the Rev. Earl C. Hargrove, who has served the school as its president throughout its history. As pastor of the First Christian Church of Lincoln, Mr. Hargrove became deeply concerned about the number of "dead and dying churches in which there was a tragic decline in Christian evangelism and its fruits." To accentuate this condition, there was a "general dearth of ministers and other Christian workers over the entire state and in the regions beyond." Hargrove saw the answer in young men prepared to preach the gospel with "preaching fervor" wherever there was need. This vision yielded fruit in a remarkably short time. In the seventh year, the school enrolled 129 young men and 99 women. The men as student pastors were reviving 130 churches in the southern half of Illinois!

After occupying the limited quarters of an old business college building for several years, the Institute moved to a new 35-acre campus at the edge of Lincoln. There it has built modern brick buildings for its expanding services. The college offers the following programs: Bachelor of Arts (Ministerial-Missionary), Bachelor of Christian Education, Bachelor of Sacred Music, Bachelor of Secretarial Science, and Bachelor of Theology. The Graduate School offers programs leading to the M.A. and B.D. degrees. The undergraduate division is accredited by The Accrediting Association of Bible Colleges.

## LUTHERAN BIBLE INSTITUTE
### Minneapolis, Minnesota

A fascinating story is found in the origin and growth of Lutheran Bible Institute. It represents a link in a chain of providentially directed influences. As one of the first Bible schools, The East London Institute of Home and Foreign Missions, inspired Dr. A. B. Simpson to establish Nyack Missionary College, so was a young Lutheran girl from Minnesota inspired to establish a Bible institute for Lutherans after she attended Nyack.

But the chain of influence did not end with "LBI." This first Lutheran institute fostered the establishment of three allied institutes, one in Seattle, Washington, another in Los Angeles, and the third in Teaneck, New Jersey. And the chain has forged another link: Largely through its example, the Lutheran Church, Missouri Synod, acquired property in Milwaukee, Wisconsin and in the fall of 1961 began the Lutheran Lay Training Institute.

Lutheran Bible Institute, founded in 1919, has given training to over 400 missionaries serving under Lutheran boards. This is in effect one-fourth of the total Lutheran missionaries from North America. The Institute believes in inductive methods of Bible study with an effective field work program. A curriculum to train parish workers is meeting a definite need for trained church staff workers in Lutheran churches of the area. The school also provides extensive services in teaching and disseminating the Word of God through a correspondence school, a publishing department, radio outlets, summer camps and Bible conferences.

A beautiful new campus for its growing ministries has been

recently built. The Rev. Bernt C. Opsal is president of this family of four inter-synodical institutions.

## MENNONITE BRETHREN BIBLE COLLEGE
### Winnipeg, Manitoba

Mennonite Brethren Bible College was founded by the Canadian section of the Mennonite Brethren denomination in 1944 to meet a definite need for advanced Biblical education. Mennonite Brethren came to Western Canada in two waves of migration of Mennonites from Russia following the World Wars. The first wave took place in the twenties and the second in the years immediately following World War II. Their adherence to Biblical faith and their need of trained Christian workers led these devout Christians to found a number of Bible institutes, beginning with one in Ontario and others extending across the four Western Provinces. These schools stressed Biblical and practical training for students irrespective of academic standing.

A long-felt need for an advanced theological school to provide teachers for the Bible institutes and leadership for the denomination led to plans for a college in 1943 and the purchase of a site in Winnipeg in 1944. The school was officially opened on October 1, 1944, and Rev. J. B. Toews became the school's first president.

Mennonite Brethren Bible College requires two years of university work for admission to its three-year theological program (Th.B.). Students with one year of university take four years, including one year of general education. Diploma courses in Sacred Music and General Bible are available to high school graduates (Junior matriculation). The course in Religious Education requires first year university. The college has an enrollment of well over one hundred and was the first Canadian institution to be accredited by The Accrediting Association of Bible Colleges. Recently its Arts Division became affiliated with Waterloo Lutheran University.

## MOODY BIBLE INSTITUTE
### Chicago, Illinois

Variously designated the mother of Bible institutes, the West Point of Christian training, Moody Bible Institute, whose modest beginning is traced in Chapter II, has become an institution of world-wide fame. It is without doubt the largest Protestant missionary training school in the world. Twenty-seven hundred of its alumni are active missionaries. Its Moody Literature Mission sends the gospel in print to chaplains, workers in hospitals, prisons, rural schools, other home mission fields; Moody literature is printed in 70 languages and distributed in 160 countries. Its unique ministry of producing and distributing gospel science films has opened doors to the armed services, to public and parochial schools. Several thousand prints have been used for orientation by the U. S. military services. Students have come to Moody from numerous foreign countries and from more than 100 denominations. Its famous Moody Chorale has made several tours of Europe.

The heart of this complex institution with its many gospel and educational services, is the day Bible Institute, which enrolls 1,000 students. The facilities limit admissions to this number although there are generally three or four times that number of applicants. The following courses are offered, each having a Bible major: *General Bible; Pastors; Missionary*—in Modern Languages, Christian Education, and Biblical Languages; *Sacred Music*—in Instrumental, Composition, and Church Music; *Christian Education; Christian Education-Music; Jewish Missions; Missionary Technical*—in Aviation Flight and Mechanics, and Radio Communications. The Institute is accredited by The Accrediting Association of Bible Colleges.

Moody Bible Institute is continuing to grow under the leadership of Dr. William Culbertson, President.

## MULTNOMAH SCHOOL OF THE BIBLE
### Portland, Oregon

Multnomah School of the Bible, in its relatively short life span of 25 years, has become the largest interdenominational Bible school of the Northwest. It owes its establishment to the inspiration and vision of the Rev. John G. Mitchell, pastor of the Central Bible Church. On February 14, 1936, Dr. Mitchell called a group of ministers and Christian businessmen to lay the foundation for a Bible school in the Pacific Northwest. At that meeting a board was organized and officers were appointed. The following fall, on October 5, the first session of Multnomah School of the Bible opened in a rented residence with 39 students. Since that time the school has grown to a student body of 400. Altogether, the school has graduated more than 1,200 students.

For sixteen years the school was quartered in scattered buildings in a downtown section of Portland. By 1952 it was able to purchase the 11-acre campus of the former Oregon State School for the Blind in the eastern part of Portland. Additional facilities have been built since.

Three men have given outstanding leadership to Multnomah's development. Dr. Mitchell as founder, teacher and board chairman; Dr. B. B. Sutcliffe, President from 1936 to 1943; and Dr. Willard M. Aldrich, President from 1943 to the present.

Multnomah features a three-year Bible major course. It also offers a five-year program leading to the Th.B. A special feature is a one-year course of intensive Bible study for college graduates. The school is an accredited member of The Accrediting Association of Bible Colleges.

## NYACK MISSIONARY COLLEGE
### Nyack, New York

The early history of Nyack Missionary College has already been sketched in Chapter II on the historical development of the Bible institute-college movement. It was the first Bible college to be established in America, and it has been the leading Bible college operated by The Christian and Missionary Alliance. It has a record of distinguished service as a training school for missionaries and home workers. Its present enrollment is more than 500.

Nyack Missionary College has a beautiful site of 63 acres on the western palisades of the Hudson River only 25 miles north of New York City. It is chartered to grant undergraduate degree programs in Theology (B.Th.), Religious Education (B.R.E.), Missions (B.S.), Sacred Music (B.S.M.), and Pre-Seminary (B.A.) by the New York Board of Regents. It is accredited by both the Board of Regents and The Accrediting Association of Bible Colleges. It recently established the Jaffray School of Missions to offer graduate preparation for missionary service.

From its inception, the president of The Christian and Missionary Alliance also served as president *ex officio* of the college—until 1940, when the late Dr. Thomas Moseley became president. He served in that office from 1940 until his retirement in 1959. Dr. Harold W. Boon, formerly dean of the college, was appointed his successor.

## PHILADELPHIA COLLEGE OF BIBLE
### Philadelphia, Pennsylvania

Philadelphia College of Bible enshrines in its history great evangelical traditions and the names of great Christian leaders. The institution represents a merger in 1951 of two Bible institutes, both with distinguished records and both situated in the same section of Philadelphia.

The Bible Institute of Pennsylvania was founded in 1913 by W. W. Rugh, who is described in the school's catalog as "saintly," "humble," and "mighty in the Scriptures." Philadelphia School of the Bible also had a progenitor who was "mighty in the Scriptures," Dr. C. I. Scofield, editor of the well-known reference Bible that bears his name. The school was founded October 1, 1914; Dr. Scofield became the first president and Dr. William L. Pettingill, the first dean. A number of noted Bible teachers were associated with these two interdenominational institutions, which merged in 1951, and assumed the name of Philadelphia School of the Bible until 1958. In that year the school became a state-accredited Bible college authorized to confer the degree of Bachelor of Science in Bible. Thereupon the name was changed to Philadelphia College of Bible. It is also accredited by The Accrediting Association of Bible Colleges.

The college is located at 1800 Arch Street in downtown Philadelphia. It combines a well-rounded program of general education with strong Biblical content and practical training in four fields of specialization: Theology, Missions, Christian Education, and Music. It has 400 students in the day school and 650 in the evening division. Dr. Charles C. Ryrie has been President since 1958. His predecessor was Dr. William A. Mierop.

## PRAIRIE BIBLE INSTITUTE
### Three Hills, Alberta

This is one of the most remarkable of all North American Bible schools. Out on the broad expanse of Alberta's great wheat country, miles removed from any metropolitan center, is Canada's largest and one of the world's largest Bible institutes. Its fascinating story began with humble origins in 1922, when cottage Bible classes were begun in a farmhouse a little over a mile north of the village of Three Hills, Alberta. Several Christian farm families, hungry for a deeper knowledge of God's Word, invited Mr. L. E. Maxwell of Kansas City, Missouri, to be their pastor. With no thought of founding a school, Mr. Maxwell began teaching the Bible to seven young people. The infant "school" was given an orientation in missions the following year in a missionary conference. In 1923, the first section of a Bible school building was erected on the edge of the town of Three Hills.

From this modest beginning, the institution has grown steadily until today it has an extensive campus, an enrollment of over 600 in the Bible school, 400 in the high school, and 200 in the grade school. From this evangelical center in a rural community emanate evangelical forces that girdle the globe. It has trained over 1,000 missionaries. Its "Prairie Press" publishes Christian literature that goes to many lands. One of Mr. Maxwell's books, *Born Crucified,* has been translated into six languages. *The Prairie Overcomer* goes out to 45,000 addresses each month, and close to $2,000,000 has been contributed for missions.

The human instrumentality whom God has used to guide the school's development has been Mr. Maxwell—its first and only principal. Through educational principles advocated in the early years by the Rev. C. W. Stevens and Miss Ruth Miller, the school continues to stress inductive methods of Bible study. It also emphasizes self-denial and the lordship of Christ in daily Christian living.

## TORONTO BIBLE COLLEGE

### Toronto, Ontario

Toronto Bible College has the distinction of being the first Bible school in Canada. It was established in 1894 by a group of Christian workers who regularly met for prayer and fellowship in the home of Dr. Elmore Harris, pastor of the Walmer Road Baptist Church. Dr. Harris became the first president, and Dr. William Stewart, its first principal. The school was founded to train consecrated men and women for Christian ministries at home and abroad. By holding steadily to this purpose, it has given preparation to many hundreds of pastors, missionaries and teachers.

Toronto Bible College bears the stamp of the life and ministry of the Rev. John McNicol, who as a young Presbyterian pastor joined the faculty in 1902 and gave more than fifty years of service to the institution. Dr. McNicol served as principal from 1906 to 1946. He was succeeded by Dr. J. B. Rhodes, who served until he succumbed to ill health in 1953. Since 1954, the Rev. E. L. Simmonds has been filling the office of principal.

The college is situated near the campus of Toronto University on 16 Spadina Road. It offers diploma and degree courses with specialized training for the pastorate, Christian education, sacred music, and missions. The day school enrollment is approximately 200.

A feature of Toronto's program is the emphasis given to the corporate leadership of the Holy Spirit demanding obedience to the lordship of Christ in the exercise of self-discipline. Reliance is placed upon this principle rather than upon rules to regulate the life of the college.

*Chapter Six*

# BIBLIO-CENTRIC
# EDUCATION

Having sketched the history and the external dimensions of the Bible institute movement, we now turn to the vital principles within that have given life and power to the movement. This takes us at once to the centrality of the Word of God in the educative process.

Bible institutes-colleges have at least one characteristic in common—they give the Bible the central place in their curricula. A Bible major is required in practically all schools of this type. The Accrediting Association of Bible Colleges requires a *minimum* of 40 semester hours of Bible and Biblical theology in curricula aimed at preparing students for Bible teaching and preaching ministries and a minimum of 30 hours in other programs.

But why give this prominence to the Bible? Why are 250 North American institutions willing to be identified as *Bible* schools? What is the rationale of using a 2000-year old book as a text for college students in the twentieth century? The reasons rest on one basic assumption—*the Bible is regarded as being uniquely the Word of God*. The conviction that God by the Holy Spirit spoke through the prophets and apostles, to communicate an authoritative message of life and destiny to mankind, is fundamental to the whole concept of Biblical education.

Bible college educators hold that the Bible had a divine origin: "Men spake from God, being moved by the Holy Spirit." They hold too that it is the oracle by which the living God speaks in the present to the human mind and heart. "For the word of God is living and active, sharper than any two-edged sword, piercing to the division of soul and spirit, of joints and marrow, and discerning the thoughts and intentions of the heart."[1]

If the divine element in the Scriptures is denied, the Bible becomes nothing more than a collection of ancient writings purely human in their origin. If, on the other hand, the Scriptures are regarded as the Christian church has historically accepted them—the inspired, living, authoritative revelation of God—they should be a determinative factor in all education. No valid philosophy of education can be formulated without taking into account the Scriptures. They have profound implications for the educative process.

## THE BIBLE AND GENERAL EDUCATION

1. *The Bible answers the deep questions of life*—answers which are not found by scientific investigation but by divine revelation. According to the Word of God, there is a moral universe as well as a natural universe; a realm of spiritual reality, the kingdom of God, as well as a realm of physical-psychic being. The supreme fact of all is GOD—personal in His being, holy in His nature, and sovereign in His majesty. To man and his cosmic environment, He is Creator, Sustainer, and Redeemer. Man was created in the image of God, a personality capable of moral choice destined to be a finite partner with the infinite Creator.

Through moral failure man is now a sinner, estranged from his Maker. But God through His own self-giving in the person of Jesus Christ sought man's restoration: "God was in Christ, reconciling the world unto Himself." Man individually may now have forgiveness and life eternal. He may share in the eternal blessings of a new creation flowing from atonement and resurrection. In reconciliation he also becomes a member of the corporate body of Christ—the central unity of an ultimate universal unity when "in the dispensation of the fullness of times" God will "gather together in one all things in Christ, both which are in heaven, and which are on earth; even in him."[2] Then history will be consummated in the final triumph of righteousness over evil.

This, in brief, is the Bible's answer to the deep questions of the human mind. At the center of the universe is a heart of infinite compassion. *God cares,* and He is doing something about man's sin and despair. There is an answer to man's yearning for fulfillment, for satisfying reality, for God Himself. God offers all in Jesus Christ—the Way, the Truth, and the Life. In Christ, man has life in the dimensions of eternity. In Him also, he finds One who is worthy of his complete devotion. The Bible discloses that the supreme good—the *summum bonum* of the philosopher's quest—is Christ Himself. To know Him and to love Him is to realize the highest good. He is the measurement of all values, for He is the Supreme Value.

Obviously, education must begin with the first fact of all facts—God. "The fear of the Lord is the beginning of wisdom." But it cannot be said that American education is any longer predicated on Christian theism. Having been drained of its early moral and religious content, it is predominantly secular and its educational theories are derived from principles of naturalism.

But where does this leave youth with the deep questions as to the meaning and end of human existence? It leaves him with a question mark that has been greatly enlarged by the contemporary explosion of knowledge. The disclosures of science have only enlarged the metaphysical question. They have not yielded answers to the great questions about enduring values and destiny.

The tragedy of our age is that it has removed the ground of great faith just when the times call for new altitudes of moral achievement. The physical outreach of the space age demands a comparable outreach of the human spirit. Indeed, this age has been compared to a previous period of exploration when the white race broke the cordons that bound it to the old world and released it to circumnavigate the globe. But not so. That age had its Renaissance and its Reformation *to free the spirit and mind of men.* This age has yet to recover the truth that makes men free—the truth as it is in Jesus Christ. And it has yet to discover that basic security rests on inner peace through faith rather than on external conditions.

2. *The Bible teaches students how to live in their total environment.* Education can be properly conceived as preparation for living in one's environment, but education can be mis-education when its aims are limited to only a part of the environment. Most modern educational theories are based on partial views of man's total context.[3]

One of these views is *naturalism.* It sees man as a physical organism, part of the physical universe which stretches from the tiny atom to distant galaxies of immeasurable space. This earth is his home—at least it was so considered until the advent of Sputnik! His education consists of learning as much as possible about this physical universe through mathematics and science, then of using technology to increase material goods.

The Bible, of course, recognizes the physical nature of man and his physical home. It tells us that God created both, and that He charged man "to have dominion . . . over all the earth." When men alleviate poverty, starvation and disease by the application of science, they are carrying out the Edenic commission. But the Word of God does not limit man's environment to the observable universe, for the Bible reveals a far wider and greater sphere for his being.

Another aspect is *socialization.* Emphasis shifts here from man as a biological being to man as a social being. He belongs to the group, the community, "the democratic social order," etc. This view looks at man not as an individual but as an organism interacting with his social environment. His education is concerned with social adjustment. He is taught to become part of a team, to think and work together with a group. The Bible, of course, recognizes that man is a social being, and by moral renewal it equips him for living in harmony with his fellow men. But ultimately the Word of God is aimed at preparing him for a social order that is spiritual and eternal, the kingdom of God.

Another one-sided view is based on *statism;* the state is the essential sphere and end of education. The citizen exists to further national ends. In contemporary totalitarian countries, education has been prostituted to a brain-washing proposition which destroys human dignity and freedom. While this view is wholly repugnant to Americans, yet perceptive educators detect a creeping trend to shape educational policy in the national interest. The Word of God recognizes the state and the obligations of Christian citizenship, but it severely condemns the idolatry of statism. There is a higher kingdom than Caesar's— the kingdom of God.

Another sphere that concerns education, but which is only partial, is that of *culturalism.* It embodies loosely the intellectual, literary, aesthetic, philosophical and traditional body of values handed down to us through the ages. The essentials of this heritage are embodied in the liberal arts, and the function of education is to imbue students in this culture.

Without question, many elements of truth, beauty and morality in literature, art and the philosophies are found in this cultural heritage. But the liberal arts include, as well, many contradictory philosophies—from theism to atheism. While the liberal arts stimulate thinking, raise sights, broaden knowledge, enrich experience—they do not unify human experience. There must be a hierarchy in the realm of truth and goodness and beauty and a standard by which all values and systems can be appraised. According to the Biblical claim, Jesus Christ as Lord of all is both the standard and the Judge of all cultures and all values.

*American culture* with its ideals of getting ahead, of social acceptance, material success and security is another sphere which has almost pre-empted the older and deeper concerns of education. But the spiritual vacuum produced testifies to the shallowness of this type of educational emphasis.

All of these views of man's development tend to disregard the most important and fundamental of all—the kingdom of God. This is the realm of spiritual reality, which is more real and permanent than the observable universe. God created man a bi-world creature. He was given feet of clay to walk the earth and a spiritual nature to converse with God. Rebirth by faith in Christ confers upon him citizenship in the spiritual world, grants him the privilege of fellowship with God, and makes him alive to spiritual reality.

Education for the Christian, therefore, takes on entirely new dimensions. It embraces not only preparation for useful living in the world here and now, but orientation in and adjustment to the kingdom of God. In other words, to know how to pray, to live by faith, to love what God loves, to "walk in the Spirit" are essentials in Christian education. And for this phase of education, the Bible is indispensable. It is a manual on spiritual orientation. It seeks to shape thinking, aspirations, and affections and conduct according to the claims of God's kingdom.

3. *The Bible provides a unifying center for all knowledge.* According to the Word of God, truth inheres in God. In the great paean of Moses in Deuteronomy 32:1-4, it is asserted that He is "a God of truth." The Psalmist adds that all His ways are truth. Every manifestation of God—the creation of the universe, the revelation of Himself through the prophets and apostles, the Incarnation—has been a manifestation of *truth*. The same God whose handiwork is displayed in the galactic heavens manifested His grace and truth in Jesus Christ. Every single truth, therefore, is consistent with every other truth and with the whole body of truth. It follows also that there is no

essential difference between secular and sacred truth, for all is revelatory of God.

But knowledge, which is the human apprehension of truth, is limited and imperfect. Even the peer of theologians, the Apostle Paul, acknowledged that now "we see through a glass darkly." Even so, the difference between Paul's experiential knowledge of reality and the speculations of Greek philosophy is striking. Because Paul had experienced Truth in the person of Christ, He could affirm with certainty, "I know whom I have believed, and I am persuaded. . . ." Paul found in Christ the Person—not an abstract principle—who unifies all: the temporal and the eternal, the earthly and the heavenly, the physical and the spiritual, even the human and the divine. That encounter with the living Christ on the Damascus Road not only revolutionized and reorganized his religious life, but it completely re-oriented his intellectual life as his knowledge and thinking were all brought into harmony with Him who is *the Truth.*

Bible college educators have also been wrestling with the problem that has engaged the minds of Christian scholars in recent years—the problem of integrating knowledge in the fields of the humanities and sciences with Christian faith. Their practical interest in the problem is in the teaching of general education, for the liberal arts courses taught in Bible colleges are offered not so much for culture *per se* but rather for the breadth of education needed by Christian workers in service at home or abroad. But the Bible college offers a strategic as well as a compelling opportunity for teachers in general education to point out some of the implications of Christian faith for their fields.

Dean S. Maxwell Coder of Moody Bible Institute pointed out the possibilities and benefits of integrating general education with the Word of God:

> It is obviously a simple matter to relate subjects like personal evangelism and historical geography to the

Word of God, since much of the material is drawn
directly from the Bible, but it is not always so easy
with non-Biblical material. Nevertheless, it is possible
to relate every subject to this central factor of our
curriculum. Some years ago students complained that
a class in general education was dry and uninterest-
ing. However, when in a later semester the subject was
assigned to another teacher, who found it possible to
cast more of the light of the Word of God upon it,
students began to speak of the profitableness of the
class to them and even of personal blessing received
when the material was compared with revealed truth.[4]

4. Finally, *the Bible is a perennial source of vision, dynamic,
idealism, moral purpose, faith, and hope.* "There is a spirit in
the Bible, which, if it gets into men, makes them tall of soul,
tender in heart, just, gentle, patient, strong, faithful and
fearless."

But today the typical college student is without the motivation of a great vision, a great faith and a great purpose. In the
study of college influence on student character sponsored by
the American Council on Education, it was found that apathy
is common among students. A faculty member defined it as an
"attitude that registers superficial or studied indifference." One
observed, "Nobody cares any more. Being a leader takes more
time than it's worth." [5] So much does apathy reflect the spirit
of our times that evangelical colleges are not immune from its
inroads.

This, then, is the outcome of education predicated on naturalism. It removed the context of a moral order and reduced
man to an animal. It replaced the transcendent God by the
sovereignty of nature. It reduced the Bible to a collection of
legends, thus insuring the decline of religious and moral controls. It opened the way for the demonic wickedness of man to
break loose and then furnished him with the atomic bomb.
Little wonder that disillusionment and indifference are common among college youth.

An honored coach and a great leader of youth, Amos Alonzo Stagg, offered this counsel to students:

> The days through which we are passing seem to be fateful days. In some ways the future is uncertain. At the same time the future is largely in the hands of the youth of today. . . . The leaders in other days in our western world were steeped in Scripture. In former generations men read and knew their Bibles, and at periods of crisis such men gave leadership and guidance. Cromwell, Wilberforce, Washington, Lincoln are only a few of many that might be named. As leaders of other times received light and leading from the Book, so may modern youth, the leaders of tomorrow. . . . Youth needs inspiration to great daring and noble personal living. Others have found it, and I gladly testify that I have found it, in the pages of the earth's greatest book—the Bible.[6]

## THE BIBLE AND THEOLOGICAL EDUCATION

Bible colleges are concerned not only with the spiritual growth and intellectual maturity of their students, but with the preparation of prophetic voices to speak with conviction "Thus saith the Lord." That there should be a substantial amount of Bible in the theological curriculum rests again upon the basic assumption that the Bible is the Word of the Living God to be communicated to men for their salvation. The charge of Paul is as valid today as when it was first made to Timothy: "Preach the word. . . For the time will come when they will not endure sound doctrine, but after their own lusts shall they heap to themselves teachers, having itching ears. And they shall turn away their ears from the truth, and shall be turned into fables." [7]

In modern times, a Christian educator applied this charge to the current situation in a clarion call for a new strategy for theological education. Dr. Abdel Ross Wentz of Lutheran

Theological Seminary observed that training schools for the Protestant ministry were not fulfilling their roles as "schools of prophets" but were adapting their curricula to the *wants* of the churches rather than to their *needs*. The churches in turn have so domesticated themselves in the national culture that they are in no position to challenge that culture. By conforming, they have lost their power to transform.[8] Dr. Wentz asked, "How can American Protestantism break the shackles of secularism and become the Lord's salt for society?" His answer was that it can be done only as pulpits recover a strong Biblical tone.

> Our preachers need to be suffused with the moral sternness of the prophets. They need to be imbued with the vitalizing message of the apostles. . . . This is not a mere matter of using Bible texts, or Bible passages, or Bible analyses. It is a matter of personalities drenched in the message of the prophets and apostles. It is a matter of communicating that message through pulpit and pastoral relations to all the churches. It will bring God near and send ideals soaring. It will exorcise the demon of secularism and will annihilate the pestiferous nit of prudential morality and probationary ethics which this evil spirit has spread through the whole fabric of American life.[9]

With this conviction Bible college educators are in complete agreement. But for the pulpit to recover not only the tone but the message of the prophets and apostles means that the living Word of God must be the central, vitalizing elements in ministerial preparation. Not only preachers, but theological students need first to be suffused with the moral earnestness of the prophets. *They* need to be imbued with the vitalizing message of the apostles. As students—while *becoming* preachers—their personalities need to be "drenched in the message of the prophets and apostles."

But a critical question follows: When does preparation for the ministry begin? If men of God are "made by God," it is obvious that the process begins long before seminary. The shaping of heart and mind for the sacred calling involves immeasurably more than a collection of credits and degrees. It involves a continuous process that certainly begins no later than "rebirth" and includes dedication, devotion, reverence, compassion, conviction, prayerfulness, an experiential knowledge of God's Word, self-discipline, and a passion for service. The important college years cannot be left out of this continuous process.

In Catholic and certain Lutheran denominations pre-theological and theological education are co-ordinated, but in most Protestant denominations there are no requirements beyond education in the liberal arts or graduation from a regionally accredited college. But this opens the door for programs that have little or no relation to theology. In the 1957 investigation of theological education, it was observed that "no necessary congruence between liberal arts training and theological study can be assumed."[10] In other words, the presuppositions of revelational theology belong to one pole of thought while the humanism and naturalism inherent in the liberal arts belong to the opposite pole.

From the two premises that the Bible is the Word of God and that ministerial preparation is a continuous process that begins early in life, Bible college educators hold that the Bible should have an important place in both the pre-theological and the theological phases of preparation. In college preparation for the seminary, the student should have the general education in Biblical knowledge that all students should secure in a Christian college. In addition, he should secure basic work in the Biblical and theological fields as a foundation for advanced seminary studies. This may well include courses in the Biblical languages, basic courses in Bible content, Biblical history and geography, introductory courses in doctrine and the mission of the church. These courses are in addition to those in philosophy, history, psychology, etc., which a pre-theological college

program offers. It is this kind of a program that a number of
Bible colleges have devised for the pre-seminary phase of
ministerial preparation.

The advantages of early study of God's Word in the preparation of students for the ministry are pointed out by Professor
Edwin V. Hayden:

> There is an important psychological value in teach-
> ing Bible early in the student's career. Being first in
> the order of studies, it is likely to remain first in
> importance. Being central in his studies in the begin-
> ning, it is more easily kept central in his life and
> ministry. For the Bible college student the Book of
> God is not likely to become an appendage to his
> library, introduced for mere professional purposes.[11]

In terminal programs, Bible colleges generally require a
sequence of introductory and advanced theological studies. The
criteria of The Accrediting Association of Bible Colleges at this
point are as follows:

> A study of the Bible should begin with basic
> courses that introduce the student to all of the books
> of the Bible, to Biblical history and geography, and to
> God's unfolding and unifying redemptive purpose.
> Introductory studies should come in the first years or
> semesters of the college program and lay the founda-
> tion for advanced depth in exegetical and expository
> studies. . . .
> Theological studies are meant to supplement Bibli-
> cal studies and to yield a thorough understanding of
> Christian doctrine and its application to practical
> problems and needs. Here, too, the growing maturity
> of students must be recognized. Elementary doctrine
> may be suited to the first-year student, but regular sys-
> tematic theology is ordinarily for the advanced stu-
> dent and normally comes in the upper division after
> students have completed their basic courses in Bible.[12]

## THE BIBLE IN EDUCATION
## FOR LIFE

The implications of Biblio-centric education go far beyond formal courses in the theological curriculum. They extend to the whole range of Bible college education.

The first concern of Bible college education relates to the student himself—his growing into maturity as a person, a Christian, and a responsible citizen. In keeping with the Scriptural order of values, what a servant of Christ *is*, is more important than what he *does*. The Christian worker who is not yielded to the will of God even though he performs "many wonderful works" in Christ's name receives not His approbation but His fearful censure: "I never knew you: depart from me, ye that work iniquity." [13]

The wide and varied set of learning experiences that seek the personal development of students is embraced in the concept of *general* education. It "includes all the those experiences, both curricular and extracurricular, which make for the growing maturity of students in preparing them for effective living. . . . Foremost in the total development of students, is the cultivation of Christian life and experience." [14]

This kind of education includes good sportsmanship on the basketball floor, working cooperatively with a staff on a yearbook, facility in reading, good manners in the dining hall, ability to think logically, appreciation for our cultural heritage, public and private devotions, and many more items, yet the Bible is relevant to all. It is a guide for every facet of life. Its precepts for daily living are timeless. It is the best of all devotional literature. A person can hardly claim to be an educated person who is ignorant of its history, its literature, its spiritual truths, its moral teachings, and the great persons and Person whom it portrays.

Above all, the Bible is indispensable to cultivation of the spiritual life. It furnishes all of the vitamins needed for spiritual health. The written Word reveals the Living Word, the

Lord Jesus Christ, who alone is able to integrate the whole of our personalities for effective living.

Finally, the Bible is central in the practical preparation of men and women for Christian ministries. It is the message of salvation committed to them for faithful transmission. Its pastoral epistles are treatises on pastoral theology. The Corinthian letters give instruction on church life and administration.

Thus, Bible college education is a three-sided pattern of theological, general, and practical education. At the center of the triangle is the Bible. It is the vital ingredient of every phase of education.

Because Bible institutes-colleges give first place to the Word of God, they have made an invaluable contribution to the life and the work of thousands of servants of Christ. Graduates from non-academic Bible institutes have been heard to say after having gone to other institutions for more advanced education: "The Bible that we received in Bible school has meant more to us than all other educational experiences we have had. It gave us a foundation for life." The Christian leaders who are sincerely grateful for the Bible training they received in a modest Bible school are legion.

*Chapter Seven*

# BIBLE SCHOOL
# CURRICULA FOR THE
# WORLD MISSION
# OF THE CHURCH

*Go ye into all the world and preach the gospel to every creature.* This parting command of the risen Lord is the *raison d'être* for Bible institutes and colleges. It is the base of reference for the direction, the purpose, and the subject matter of Bible college education. The founders and their successors were dominated by the conviction that the church is under a compelling obligation to make the gospel of salvation known to all mankind. This mission begins with the man next door and extends to the "uttermost part of the earth."

The previous chapter presented the Biblio-centric view of education. From this philosophy and the redemptive thrust of the New Testament are derived the purposes of Bible college education. This chapter presents the *curricula* that have been developed in Bible institutes and colleges to implement those purposes and to prepare students for the world mission of the church.

*Preach the gospel* suggests the two major elements of the Bible college curriculum, namely, *subject matter* and *communication*. The chief subject matter is the Word of God, and all of the major training programs in Bible colleges aim to develop skills in the several modes of communicating the Word of life. The modes are many: preaching, evangelizing, teaching, counselling, witnessing, broadcasting, singing, even flying missionaries to otherwise inaccessible jungles; but providentially there are training programs in Bible colleges to correspond to the need.

Since the Word is God's saving message to men, it follows that its preachers, teachers and evangelists must have a *thorough* knowledge of its truths to be able to communicate them. Accordingly, the Bible is the chief textbook, and courses in Bible and Biblical theology constitute a major in all Bible school curricula.

In striving for a balance between subject matter and method courses, the same issue that has been a contention in teacher education in the United States has been raised among Bible college educators. At least a few think that the minimum requirement of 30 to 40 hours of Bible is not enough and that too much emphasis is placed on methods. Strengthening this viewpoint, the C. I. Scofield-Lewis Sperry Chafer school maintained that thorough indoctrination in the Scriptures suffices for all forms of Christian ministry. Subject matter is *all* important; methods courses, *un*important. From this principle was derived the single Bible-theological curriculum with a minimum of practical courses in preparing students for all of the major forms of Christian ministry.

Most seminaries and Bible institutes in this tradition have by this time modified or are modifying their curricula in favor of greater specialization in practical preparation. There are now very few Bible institutes and colleges that have only a single Bible theology program. The majority offer a general program along with specialized curricula in pastoral training, Christian education, missions, and ministry of music.

While the gospel and the imperative command to proclaim it have not changed, modern science and technology have greatly affected the media of communicating the gospel. Radio, the mass production of literature, televison, movies, films, and the science of linguistics—all have multiplied the possibilities of disseminating the gospel. But the demand for trained specialists in these fields of communication has in turn called for new or modified training programs in theological schools.

Other factors which tend to affect the pattern and content of Bible school curricula are not so valid. One of these is *tradition*. Next to religion, the force of tradition is most compelling in the field of education. When they are united, as in theological education, tradition can become a strong factor in guiding instructional programs. Once a curriculum is hallowed by time, it tends to be preserved long after it has become functionally obsolete.

Uncritical imitation also affects the setting up of a curriculum. A procedure all too common in initiating Bible institutes or adding new programs is to send for catalogs from several "name" schools and either adopting a curriculum outright or making a composite of several. It is not difficult to identify parent schools in perusing some Bible school catalogs.

However, against these negative factors is the inspiring fact that God is raising up able educational leadership for the demands of this day, not only in Bible college education but among all areas of evangelical education.

## BIBLE-THEOLOGY, PASTORAL PROGRAMS

Nearly all of the programs offered in Bible institutes and colleges fall into four categories—Theological, Christian Education, Missions, and Church Music.

The theological group consists of the general Bible-Theology, the Pre-Seminary, and the Pastoral programs. With few exceptions, all are oriented toward preparation for the pastoral ministry. In content, all have a substantial amount of Bible and Biblical or systematic theology.

Table VI presents the theological programs offered in 36 accredited schools of The Accrediting Association of Bible Col-

TABLE VI

THEOLOGICAL PROGRAMS IN 36 ACCREDITED
BIBLE INSTITUTES AND COLLEGES

| Programs | No. Schs. | Awards | | | | | | | | | | Total |
|---|---|---|---|---|---|---|---|---|---|---|---|---|
| | | ThB | AB | BABE | BBE | BS | BRE | BSL | 4-yr. dip. | 3-yr. dip. | 2-yr. dip. | |
| General Bible-Theol. | 31 | 8 | 16 | 3 | 1 | 3 | 2 | 1 | 1 | 19 | 1 | 54 |
| Pre-Seminary | 7 | / | 6 | 1 | | | | | 1 | | | 7 |
| Pastoral Theol. | 20 | 9 | 9 | | 1 | 2 | 2 | 1 | 1 | 4 | | 25 |
| Total | | 17 | 31 | 4 | 1 | 5 | 2 | 1 | 1 | 23 | 1 | 86 |

leges. All colleges offer one or more programs in this group, but only five offer programs in all three subdivisions. Thirty-one of the 36 schools offer 54 general Bible-theology curricula, 7 offer pre-seminary programs, and 20 offer preparation specifically designated for the pastoral ministry.

All of the Bachelor of Theology programs represent five years of work beyond high school. A few Bible colleges require one or two years of general education to be taken in a liberal arts college or university. All of the other degree programs are four years in length, in which both the general and theological courses can be taken in residence.

The great variety of degrees can be explained by a number of factors. In some states, the granting of degrees is controlled and restricted by governmental authority. A few state boards have been willing to authorize the B.S. degree but not the A.B. for Bible college programs. Some Bible colleges have preferred a bachelor's degree that is descriptive of the Bible major; hence the Bachelor of Arts in Biblical Education, the Bachelor of Biblical Education, and the Bachelor of Sacred Literature degrees. In recent years there has been a trend toward the A.B. degree in states where it is permissible to grant it provided that the curriculum has a substantial amount of general education, including two years of language. In 1960, 53 per cent of the 1,014 baccalaureate degrees conferred by the accredited Bible colleges were A.B.'s and 23 per cent were B.S.'s.

It will be observed that of the total 86 curricula offered in the theological group, 61 are degree programs. The remainder, with two exceptions, are three-year non-degree diploma curricula. Only three of the 36 schools—Moody, Multnomah, and Northeastern—are essentially diploma conferring institutions. Multnomah also offers the five-year Bachelor of Theology program while Moody and Northeastern have only diploma courses. The remaining diploma courses are offered by colleges whose principal programs lead to degrees.

While only seven schools now have a special pre-seminary program, there is a trend toward developing such programs in order to qualify graduates more readily for seminary admissions. A pre-seminary curriculum provides a foundation in Bible and theology, basic work in Biblical languages, and a maximum amount of general education with a minor or even a major in a liberal arts field. Most professional courses in pastoral theology are omitted with the expectation that the student will secure his professional preparation in the seminary.

Among the significant courses found in pastoral training departments are the following: Homiletics, Pastoral Theology, Church Supervision or Administration, Evangelism, Counselling, Worship, Marriage and the Family, Christian Education in the Church, Hermeneutics, Expository Preaching, Hymnology, Ministry of Music, and Denominational Polity.

## CHRISTIAN EDUCATION

Next to the theological group, Christian education and missions programs are offered by the largest number of schools. Thirty-six accredited members of The Accrediting Association of Bible Colleges, and most likely all Bible schools, offer one or more individual courses in Christian education; 32 offer *programs,* either with a major or a minor.

According to the summaries in Table VII, 32 accredited Bible colleges offer a total of 50 programs in Christian education. The 42 regular programs are divided equally between Christian education minors and majors. In addition, seven schools offer a combination of Christian education and sacred music, and one school adds church secretarial training to this combination.

It will be observed that 11, or 22 per cent, of the 50 programs are three years in length; the remainder are degree programs of four and five years.

While this group has only two major types of programs, yet it embraces an amazing span of objectives and courses. The educational work of the church has become greatly diversified in recent years so that it includes not only the Sunday school but youth work, weekday schools, summer camps, leadership training, summer Bible schools, guidance of recreational activities, instruction in family life, etc. These call for able directors of Christian education who can co-ordinate all of these activities into a unified program.

TABLE VII

CHRISTIAN EDUCATION PROGRAMS
IN 32 BIBLE COLLEGES

| Programs | No. Schools | Awards | | | | | | Total |
|---|---|---|---|---|---|---|---|---|
| | | AB | BABE | BS | BRE | BTh | Dip-loma | |
| Christian Educ. Minor* | 18 | 8 | 2 | 3 | 3 | | 5 | 21 |
| Christian Educ. Major* | 16 | 10 | 1 | 1 | 6 | | 3 | 21 |
| Christian Educ. and Music | 7 | 1 | | | 2 | 1 | 3 | 7 |
| Chr. Educ., Music, Church Secy. | 1 | 1 | | | | | | 1 |
| Total | | 20 | 3 | 4 | 11 | 1 | 11 | 50 |

*A Christian education program with a minor normally requires from 15 to 18 semester hours of professional courses; a major requires 24 or more hours.

There are also the numerous extra-denominational ministries to youth by such organizations as Child Evangelism and Youth for Christ that call for trained personnel. In addition, the many home mission institutions and agencies such as Rural Home Missionary Association, Scripture Memory Mountain Mission, and Rural Bible Crusade secure most of their workers from Bible institutes and colleges. Furthermore, the many foreign fields for ministries in the broad field of Christian education call for properly qualified Christian workers. All of these diversified forms of evangelism and teaching call for large numbers of trained personnel. Specialized preparation is needed for many of them.

The Christian Education departments of Bible institutes and colleges are seeking to prepare young people for many of these varied needs. But the wide range of needs and of Christian education courses has led to two weaknesses. First, limited course offerings are spread too thin in an attempt to achieve a large number of objectives. Second, to meet a great variety of needs a Christian Education Department tends to offer numerous fringe courses while omitting basic, foundation courses. The dictum that it is better to do a few things well than many things poorly is relevant to this field.

In 1960 The Accrediting Association of Bible Colleges began a survey of Christian Education programs in Bible institutes and Bible colleges made possible by a joint grant from several evangelical publishers. This investigation is turning out to be the most thorough of any survey made of Bible college education. While it is too early to state the conclusions, some of the findings from extensive research indicate that Christian Education departments not only prepare leaders to serve in the field of Christian education but they serve other departments in supplementing the training of pastors, missionaries, and ministers of music.

It was found that practically all students become involved in the educational program of the church after they leave college; that those who do not major in Christian Education become almost as active in teaching children and directing youth as those who do; that nearly all pastors are engaged in one or several ministries in Christian education even though some have had no special preparation to serve in this field. Following the first phase of research, thirteen regional workshops for the Bible colleges of the United States and Canada were held in which teachers and deans met together to discuss the implications of these findings for the construction of their curricula.

The survey also disclosed that 6,000 regular students in the Bible colleges of the two countries are majoring in Christian Education, and that 80 per cent of the 25,000 students are taking one or more courses in this field. No other class of schools, either liberal arts colleges or seminaries, are preparing so many.

## MISSIONARY CURRICULA

Bible institutes and colleges have made their most significant contribution to evangelicalism in the preparation of Protestant missionaries. It is conservatively estimated that half or more of the 27,000 active Protestant missionaries from North America received their preparation, or a part of it, in a Bible school. 2,700 alumni from Moody Bible Institute and 1,000 from Prairie Bible Institute are presently serving overseas, accounting for 15 per cent of the total Protestant missionary force from the United States and Canada.

Table VIII gives data on the missionary programs given in 29 of the 36 schools accredited by The Accrediting Association of Bible Colleges. The remaining seven members offer one or more individual courses in missions but no program identified as missionary. Among the total of 51 programs offered in the 29 schools, 36 are general and 15 prepare for specialized types of missionary service.

Five Bible colleges have developed a program that combines the regular three years of nurses' training, usually in a nearby affiliated hospital, with two years of concentrated study in Bible-Theology and Missions, leading to a B.S. or an A.B. degree. Two offer specialized preparation for missionary work among Jews. Other programs give specialized missionary preparation in Christian Education, Modern Languages, Biblical Languages, Radio Broadcasting, Aviation, and Vocation. One school, The Bible Institute of Los Angeles, also offers one year of intensive training in medical missions in a separate division known as the School of Missionary Medicine.

In the light of contemporary needs and conditions, educators and missions executives of the Evangelical Foreign Missions Association made a broad study from 1955 to 1959 of missionary preparation. The findings from surveys and con-

TABLE VIII

MISSIONS CURRICULA IN 29 BIBLE COLLEGES

| Programs | No. Schs. | Awards | | | | | | | | | | Total |
|---|---|---|---|---|---|---|---|---|---|---|---|---|
| | | AB | BS | BABE | ThB | BRE | Dip. 3-yr. | Dip. 4 -5 yr. | MA | BD | |
| Regular Missions Minor | 16 | 10 | 5 | 1 | 1 | | 3 | | | | 20 |
| Regular Missions Major | 13 | 7 | 1 | 1 | 1 | | 4 | | 1* | 1* | 16 |
| Missionary Nursing (5 yr.) | 5 | 1 | 4 | | | | | | | | 5 |
| Jewish Missions | 2 | 1 | | | | | 1 | | | | 2 |
| Missions— Education (5 yr.) | 1 | 1 | | | | | | | | | 1 |
| Missionary CE | 1 | | | | | | 1 | | | | 1 |
| Miss. Modern Languages | 1 | | | | | | 1 | | | | 1 |
| Miss. Biblical Languages | 1 | | | | | | 1 | | | | 1 |
| Miss. Radio | 1 | | | | | | 1 | | | | 1 |
| Miss. Broad- casting | 1 | | | | | | 1 | 1 | | | 1 |
| Miss. Aviation | 1 | | | | | 1 | | | | | 1 |
| Miss. Vocation | 1 | | | | | | | | | | 1 |
| Total | 20 | 20 | 10 | 2 | 2 | 1 | 13 | 1 | 1 | 1 | 51 |

*Offered by Columbia Bible College in its Graduate School of Missions. Not accredited by the Accrediting Association of Bible Colleges since it accredits only undergraduate education.

ference discussions as they relate to Bible institutes-colleges are incorporated in a pamphlet, *Preparation of Missionaries in Bible Institutes and Bible Colleges*.[1] The study disclosed that there can well be wide variations in curricula and time required to train missionaries. Requirements of mission boards differ; field needs for specially trained personnel vary. Uniformity is neither desirable nor practicable.

However, there was agreement that a missionary, apart from training for specialized ministries, needs considerable preparation in other areas to serve effectively in a foreign culture. The following course-areas were considered essential: History of Missions, Principles and Practices (including The Indigenous Church), Biblical Basis (Philosophy) of Missions, Anthropology, Non-Christian Religions, Languages (Phonetics and Linguistics), Area Study, and Hygiene and Sanitation. How much time should be given to these course-areas depends on whether a program calls for a major or a minor. Missions executives favored a major, but many educators, facing the problem of balancing maximum content with the limitations of time, favored a minor of from 16 to 18 hours.

Extensive work in linguistics is advocated only for the specialist in language work. Writing is also considered important, but it is for the specialist who is equipped with professional and specialized training.

Among the conferees there was no question that a thorough knowledge of the Bible in all forms of missionary work is indispensable. In the field of general education, the missions executives think that Political Science is important, since missionaries are increasingly confronted with problems arising between government on the one hand and missions, schools and churches on the other. History should include the rise of communism. Sociology is important for an understanding of social institutions, practices and principles. Health should include general hygiene, sanitation, and mental as well as physical health. A thorough knowledge of English with facility in its use is essential as well as some knowledge of another language.

*Effective communication* is the decisive factor in the mission of the church to the world today. With communism poisoning the minds of uncommitted peoples by tons of malicious propaganda; with the vast continent of Africa aflame by revolution; with the dynamic ferment of nationalism and the resurgence of non-Christian faiths, the communication of the gospel faces fiercesome barriers. But Christianity cannot be stopped when the church is emboldened by the power of the Spirit in utterance and witness. For this hour, the evangelist can draw on the new sciences of linguistics and cultural anthropology to assist him in overcoming barriers. He, too, can make use of radio and press to make known the good news of salvation.

To these conditions and opportunities Bible colleges are adjusting their missionary programs and challenging their students. In a timely article by Bernhard A. Helland of Lutheran Bible Institute (Minneapolis), students dedicated to Christ are confronted with this challenge: *Prepare yourself for literary work. Prepare yourself to translate. Prepare yourself to learn another language. Prepare yourself to become a collaborator with some man of a different language, to be his partner in flooding Christian people with literature in their language, as well as in reaching the unconverted with the word of salvation. Prepare to communicate.*[2]

## CHURCH MUSIC CURRICULA

While Theology, Christian Education, and Missions lead the fields in which Bible institutes and colleges offer training, Church Music is a strong runner-up. In the great majority of schools, choral tours, ensembles, gospel teams occupy a much larger place in school life than intercollegiate athletics. All 36 accredited Bible colleges offer some courses in music; 23 offer coordinated programs. Ten of these offer majors in voice, piano, organ, orchestral instruments and choral music.

To illustrate the kinds of music programs offered in Bible

TABLE IX

CHURCH MUSIC PROGRAMS IN 23
ACCREDITED BIBLE COLLEGES

| Program | Schools No. | Awards | | | | | | |
|---|---|---|---|---|---|---|---|---|
| | | BSM | BM | AB | BABE | BSB | Diploma | Total |
| General Music Major | 7 | | | 2 | 1 | 1 | 5 | 9 |
| General Music Minor | 7 | 1 | | 3 | 1 | | 2 | 7 |
| Voice Major | 13 | 4 | 3 | 3 | 1 | | 3 | 14 |
| Piano Major | 13 | 4 | 3 | 3 | 1 | | 3 | 14 |
| Organ Major | 10 | 4 | 2 | 2 | 1 | | 2 | 11 |
| Instrument Major | 7 | 2 | 2 | 2 | | | 2 | 8 |
| Church Music Major | 6 | 3 | 2 | 1 | | | | 6 |
| Theory Major | 2 | 2 | | | | | | 2 |
| Composition Major | 2 | 1 | 1 | | | | | 2 |
| Church Music and CE | 1 | | 1 | | | | | 1 |
| Church Music and Education | 1 | | | | | | 1 | 1 |
| Total | | 21 | 14 | 16 | 5 | 1 | 18 | 75 |

colleges, the 75 different majors and the respective awards in degrees and diplomas which are offered in 23 accredited Bible colleges are presented in Table IX. The actual number of majors exceeds 75 since the category of Instrument Major ordinarily includes a number of orchestral instruments. It is observed that the professional degrees (BSM, BM, BSB) out-number the general AB degrees by 36 to 14. It will also be noted that half of the majors offered are in Voice, Piano, and Organ.

But statistical data do not even suggest the quality of per-formance in many Bible schools. In them, as in other warmly Christian colleges, students sing with a verve that is born of Christian experience. They *communicate* the reality and the glory of their Christ-centered faith whether the setting is in the Western prairies or in a greater metropolitan center of the Midwest.

One of the finest music organizations in the country is the famous Moody Chorale of Moody Bible Institute in Chicago. It has been heard, no doubt, by millions through recordings and concert tours in North America and Europe. Yet I have heard superb choral singing, comparable to the Moody Chorale, in schools housed in frame buildings situated on the open prairies of the Canadian West. In both settings, choral groups, radiant with the presence of Christ, communicated their faith with inspired song.

## PROGRAMS IN NON-ACCREDITED BIBLE COLLEGES

Programs in non-accredited Bible institutes and colleges do not differ fundamentally from those in accredited schools, for their purpose is the same. In both, education is oriented toward preparation for Christian ministries, particularly those of the pastorate, Christian education, missions, and church music. However, there are some minor differences between them. Accredited schools tend to be the older and larger institutions

**TABLE X**

**CURRICULA OF 24 NON-ACCREDITED BIBLE COLLEGES**

| Programs | No. Schs. | BTh | AB | BABE | BSL | BRE | BCE | BMis | BSM | 2-yr. dip. | 3-yr. dip. | 4-yr. dip. | Total |
|---|---|---|---|---|---|---|---|---|---|---|---|---|---|
| **THEOLOGICAL** | | | | | | | | | | | | | |
| Gen. Bible-Theology | 15 | 4 | 3 | | 1 | | | | | 4 | 9 | 2 | 23 |
| Pastoral | 7 | 4 | 3 | 1 | | | | | | | 7 | | 15 |
| Bibl. Lang. | 2 | | 1 | | | | | | | | 1 | | 2 |
| **CHRISTIAN EDUC.** | | | | | | | | | | | | | |
| CE Minor | 11 | | 1 | 1 | 2 | 1 | 1 | | | 1 | 9 | | 16 |
| CE Major | 3 | | 1 | | | 2 | | | | | | | 3 |
| **MISSIONS** | | | | | | | | | | | | | |
| Miss. Minor | 12 | | 2 | 1 | 1 | | | 1 | | 1 | 7 | | 13 |
| Miss. Major | 3 | | | | | | | | | | 1 | 2 | 3 |
| Publication | 1 | | | | | | | | | | 1 | | 1 |
| Construction | 1 | | | | | | | | | | 1 | | 1 |
| Missions-CE | 1 | | | | | | | | | | 1 | | 1 |
| **MUSIC** | | | | | | | | | | | | | |
| General | 7 | | 1 | 1 | 2 | | | | | | 4 | | 8 |
| Voice Major | 1 | | | | | | | | 1 | | 1 | | 2 |
| Piano Major | 1 | | | | | | | | 1 | | 1 | | 2 |
| Organ Major | 1 | | | | | | | | 1 | | 1 | | 2 |
| Instr. Major | 1 | | | | | | | | 1 | | 1 | | 2 |
| Music Secy. | 1 | | | | | | | | | | 1 | | 1 |
| Total | | 8 | 12 | 4 | 6 | 3 | 1 | 1 | 4 | 6 | 46 | 4 | 95 |

and therefore have had greater opportunity to develop their curricula in variety and depth.

As a basis of comparison the curricula of 24 non-accredited schools are presented in Table X. Half are associate members of The Accrediting Association of Bible Colleges and the other half were selected at random from the 250 Bible institutes and colleges of the United States and Canada.

One noticeable difference between the accredited and the non-accredited schools is in the number of courses offered in the four principal divisions. The total in accredited schools is 263, or an average of 7.35 per school, to 95, or four each, in the 24 non-accredited schools. If the miscellaneous courses, apart from those in the four principal divisions are added, the average for accredited schools is 8.2 compared to 4.2 for the non-accredited schools. In other words, accredited schools offer twice as many courses as other Bible institutes and colleges.

There is also a difference in the proportion of degree programs. In accredited schools, 194 programs, or 74 per cent, lead to degrees, while in the non-accredited schools, degree programs account for 41 per cent.

A noticeable difference is observed also in their music programs. All of the 24 non-accredited schools have individual music courses, ranging from one to twenty in number and averaging 9.4 per school. But only six have music programs, two schools having one, three two, and one having eight different music majors. Only the latter has the range of majors generally found in a school of music.

Obviously these differences in curricula development can be accounted for largely by the differences in age between accredited and non-accredited schools. The mean founding year for the 24 non-accredited schools is 1935. They have an average day school enrollment of 130. By contrast, the mean founding year of accredited schools is 1921, and their average day school enrollment is 273.

What is remarkable is that in both types of schools, Bible and Biblical Theology are majors in every program, and that the great majority of the programs offered in the 60 schools surveyed, 94 per cent of the total—fall into the divisions of Theology, Christian Education, Missions, and Sacred Music. These facts point up convincingly that the aim of Bible college education is to prepare students for Christian ministries or church vocations through a program of Biblical, general, and practical education.

## SUPPLEMENTARY CURRICULA

While Bible colleges offer relatively few curricula outside the four major fields, courses have developed to meet specialized needs.

Among these are programs designed to train dedicated Christians to give *assistance* to pastors in the work of the local church. The Lutheran Bible Institutes are training young women as parish workers to assist in visitation, office work and in the educational program of the church. So great is the need for trained personnel in this field that demand far exceeds available graduates. A Layman's Course has also been developed in these schools. Eight Bible institutes and colleges have programs to train church secretaries. Several make possible a combination of secretarial training with Christian education or church music.

As evangelicals are becoming increasingly sensitive to the vast opportunities for Christian service and witness in social work, Bible colleges are beginning to develop programs to train young people for Christian social service. Two programs in this field appear among the 60 schools in the survey.

A recent development among several Bible colleges is instituting programs in teacher education to meet qualifications for state certification. The professional program is combined with a Bible major to prepare the student for teaching in Christian day schools and mission fields as well as in public schools. Three schools, Barrington, Biola, Fort Wayne, have curricula for elementary teaching; three offer programs in music education; and one offers a program in secondary school teaching.

The Bachelor of Religious Education curriculum offered by Piedmont Bible College prepares students for state certification to teach the Bible in public schools.

A few accredited colleges have added liberal arts majors to their programs while retaining the required Bible major. In most instances these courses are only offered in a single school or two: Social Science (2), English (2), History (2), Sociology (1), Education-Psychology (1), Psychology (1), Philosophy (1), American History (1), World History (1), Biology (1), General Science and Mathematics (1), Speech (1), and French (1). It is unlikely that the addition of liberal arts majors will become a trend, for the great majority of Bible college educators share the conviction that liberal arts majors belong to liberal arts colleges and are outside the purpose of Bible colleges. The borderline programs are in teacher education, which may be oriented to either church-related schools or to public schools.

## NEW DIMENSIONS IN COMMUNICATION

The very magnitude of the task of evangelizing the world calls for new dimensions in communication. When William Carey began the modern missionary movement in 1792, the population of the world was approximately 700 million, and it has been "exploding" since. By 1900, it had more than doubled, having reached 1,500 million. By 1950, it was 2,500 million. According to estimates by the Department of Economic and Social Affairs of the United Nations, it will be 3,800 million by 1975 and 6,300 million by 2000 A.D. In other words, in terms of population, the one criteria of earth's size as viewed from the cross of Christ, there are now four earths to be evangelized compared to one in Carey's day. There will be nine to evangelize by 2000 A.D.

The appeals from non-Christian ideologies, religions and cults for the loyalties of mankind also call for stepped up activity in communicating the gospel. Amidst the mongers of hate and the agitators of race violence, the church must articulate its faith in a living Saviour more convincingly than ever. It must make known not only the Christ of personal experience but His relevance to the whole of life. It must seize the initiative in those lands where communism is supplying the bulk of available reading materials to newly literate peoples. Somehow —the message of Christ must get through to the struggling, striving masses.

The Congress on World Missions held at Moody Memorial Church in Chicago in the latter part of 1960, called for a total mobilization of evangelical forces in order to evangelize the world during the immediate generation. Based on a survey of needs among 87 evangelical mission societies, it was estimated that the astounding total of 18,347 missionary personnel is needed.

Bible institutes and colleges "have come to the kingdom for such a time as this."[3]

*Chapter Eight*

# ADULT BIBLE
# EDUCATION

The preceding chapter has surveyed the regular collegiate programs given in the Bible institutes and colleges of the United States and Canada, but adult Bible education is another significant development in the Bible institute movement. It is based squarely on the Scriptural principle that every Christian should know his Bible. One of the first schools, Moody Bible Institute, was begun for the one purpose of giving Bible instruction and practical training to lay workers. The early pattern in which classes met for an hour or two a week for a non-conventional term of fifteen weeks was continued for many years.

Many full-fledged Bible institutes began in churches as evening Bible classes for laymen. As courses were added and the offerings were organized into a curriculum, the programs came to be identified as Bible training schools. The next step up was to become a day school, and eventually a fully developed Bible college. This is an ever-recurring development, for new Bible institutes are founded each year.

Quite a number of regular Bible institutes and colleges which had their origin in evening Bible classes, continue to maintain services for laymen by resident evening schools, extension classes, or correspondence courses. Another type of adult education is the evening Bible institute not related to a day school and operated by a church or group of churches.

## EVENING AND EXTENSION CLASSES

In the 1960 survey of Bible institutes and colleges, a total of 92, or 37 per cent, of the Bible institutes and colleges in the United States and Canada reported separate evening departments. It is not uncommon for Bible schools to offer some of their regular courses during evening hours, but this arrangement does not call for a separate department nor for different academic standards. The evening and extension classes discussed here come within the province of adult education. Usually classes are organized into a separate department or school when they become a sizeable operation.

The total enrollment reported by the 92 schools was 9,058—an average of 98 per school. Among these were 14 Canadian schools with 722 students. Twenty-one member schools of The Accrediting Association of Bible Colleges had evening divisions with a combined registration of 4,765.

Nine schools: Barrington College (Providence), The Bible Institute of Los Angeles, Detroit Bible College, L.I.F.E. Bible College (Los Angeles), Moody Bible Institute, Philadelphia College of Bible, Reformed Bible Institute (Grand Rapids), Toronto Bible College, and Washington Bible College (D.C.) had a combined evening division enrollment of 4,188 and an average registration of 465. They accounted for 47 per cent of the total enrollment in the evening schools of all Bible institutes and colleges.

All of these schools are situated in cities or metropolitan centers. Six are independent of denominational control. It appears, therefore, that the non-denominational institute which is located in a thickly populated center is the most favorably situated for evening classes.

While most schools conduct their evening classes on campus, several have been very successful in conducting classes in the urban centers of the region. For example, Barrington College not only has an evening school at its Providence campus, but in cooperation with Park Street Church in Boston and Calvary Baptist Church of New York City it conducts evening schools in these historic churches. In this way, the school reaches out far beyond the sponsoring church. At Boston, many come from local churches and from points 50 to 60 miles distant. The evening school at Calvary Baptist Church is sponsored by more than a score of churches and Christian organizations in the Greater New York area. A variation from this pattern are the Evening Bible Schools conducted in the United States and Canada for two-week periods by Emmaus Bible School. The correspondence school method is used, and students take a short test at each class session.

Evening schools are usually operated for shorter periods than regular semesters, frequently with two ten- or twelve-week terms commencing in October and ending in March or April. However, some schools, like Moody Bible Institute, have two semesters corresponding to the regular school year. In most schools, classes meet on a single evening with two or three class periods. Generally, a chapel period is included. On the other hand, some schools devote two or more evenings to these adult education classes.

The purposes that brought evening schools into being are similar. They were established to help laymen become better witnesses for Christ and become more effective workers in the church. A better knowledge of the Bible and training in methods of Christian work for Sunday school teachers and officers, lay workers, and parish workers are typical statements of purpose.

As for courses, they fall readily into two categories—*Bible* and *methods*. It appears that the perennial hunger among Christians for the Word of God is not always satisfied in their churches. At any rate, an inspiring experience is to see several hundred people from various churches in a city meet regularly for serious Bible study. The president of a Bible college in a rather large Southern city gave this report: "The Lord has given us an entree into the hearts of many church people of the city by teaching the Word in our evening Bible classes. Among them are many business and professional people. They are eager to learn from the Scriptures. They are also among the most generous patrons of the college."

Most schools offer an evening school curriculum with a sequence of courses extending over a period of two to four years. Completions are awarded by certificates or diplomas conferred in special graduation exercises. Several schools such as Philadelphia College of Bible offer two programs, one suited to the level and needs of the newly-converted and the other to the capacities of more mature Christians. At Philadelphia the General Bible Course for the latter group is offered two evenings each week and requires four years to complete.

Many evening schools offer courses of The Evangelical Teacher Training Association. Both the Preliminary Certificate and the Advanced Certificate can be earned in some schools. Both certificates require six units: (1) Old Testament Law and History, (2) Old Testament Poetry and Prophecy, (3) The New Testament, (4) Child Study, (5) Teaching Techniques, and (6) Sunday School Administration. The Advanced Certificate requires, in addition, the following: (1) Missionary Enterprise, (2) Sunday School Evangelism, (3) A Guide for Bible Doctrine, (4) Vacation Bible School, and (5) Your Bible.

## HOME STUDY

In the 1960 survey of Bible institutes and colleges in the United States and Canada, 32 schools reported home study departments with a total of 259,000 enrollees. Except for two Canadian schools with 102 students, these services are carried on by Bible institutes and colleges in the United States.

However, only ten of the 32 schools have more than 100 enrollees, and only four—Moody Bible Institute, Emmaus Bible School, Lutheran Bible Institute (Minneapolis), and The Bible Institute of Los Angeles—conduct sizeable schools with registrations running into the thousands. In fact, 98 per cent of the reported home study education is carried on by these four schools. They have been so successful in home study education, that a brief account of each follows. They point to the great opportunities and potential in the field of adult education.

Most of the schools with modest enrollments offer a small number of their regular courses by correspondence for limited credit toward the degree requirements of their day school programs. Offerings of this kind should not strictly, therefore, be classified as adult education. However, it is a negligible fraction of all of the work done by correspondence. For the most part these courses are designed for the layman who wants to enrich his life by Bible study and equip himself for lay work in the church.

Most schools offer not only individual courses but a series of courses organized into a curriculum. Completion of a program is evidenced by a certificate or correspondence school diploma.

### Emmaus Bible School

Emmaus Bible School of Oak Park, Illinois, specializes in a unique overseas ministry in its Correspondence School. Although it serves many students in the United States and Canada, one of its chief aims has been to provide study materials for the millions of new literates in underprivileged lands. It has succeeded in adapting courses to the varied capacities of people thirsting for knowledge, beginning with very elementary Bible lessons for the newly literate to advanced courses for those who have a basic education.

In its overseas ministry, the Correspondence School works with and through its missionaries and mission agencies. Its courses are now taught by 130 missionaries. The world-wide dimensions of this service are seen from the fact that courses have been translated into more than 80 languages and distributed in 125 countries.

Emmaus Bible School reports that "by far the most spectacular work has been done in the Philippines," where the Bible School of the Air serves many thousands through the facilities of the Far Eastern Broadcasting Company. Over 13,000 of these correspondence courses are requested in a month, and the total is nearing the half million mark.

The latest report indicates that a total of 1,321,936 courses have been distributed and 344,437 completed since Emmaus established its Correspondence School.

In spite of this outstanding success, the men at Emmaus feel that they have met a very small fraction of the total need. With the conviction that much more can and should be done, they are extending their ministry to new fields as rapidly as possible.

## Lutheran Bible Institute (Minneapolis)

The Correspondence Course Department of Lutheran Bible Institute was established in 1930 and has been growing steadily since, beginning with an enrollment of 270 in the first year to 16,392 at the present time.

The department specializes in Bible study, offering a series of 17 courses. Several are on general topics such as Salvation Made Plain, Life at its Best, Witnessing with the Word, Prayer, and Pillars of Truth, while the remainder deal more directly with portions of the Scriptures. These include Old Testament Personalities, New Testament Personalities, Favorite Psalms, Matthew, Mark, Acts, Ephesians, Philippians, Great Chapters of the New Testament, One Family's Faith Ventures, and Letters from Jesus.

This ministry of Bible instruction is popular with people of many classes. The courses are used by churches for midweek Bible study, Ladies' Guild Circles, home study groups, and by high school clubs, but they are also used by the less privileged in many varied circumstances. Courses are provided free to prisoners in over 70 institutions, and in the last four years, prisoners have earned over 1,000 certificates. One course,

Philippians, has been translated into Braille for use by the Lutheran Braille Evangelism Association.

The ministry of Lutheran Bible Institute goes further into other languages and schools. Two basic courses have been translated into six or more languages. A Bible school in Tanganyika and one in Canada are using the courses to conduct their own home study departments.

Most of those who are studying these courses are doing so in groups. Of the current enrollment of 16,392, only 2,445 are studying individually. The remaining 13,947 are studying in 898 groups. During the past operational year, 1,688 certificates were awarded for courses completed through individual study. Total registrations in both individual and group study from the beginning to the present come to 160,348.

Another feature of LBI's service is personalized instruction and counselling. Students are given counsel through the mail on questions they send in pertaining to the Bible and to personal problems.

## The Bible Institute of Los Angeles

Biola's Correspondence School has a wide range of offerings for home study beginning with four courses for new Christians: Studies for New Christians, Christian Foundations, Bible Foundation Course, and Practical Bible Training.

Most of the courses are related to the Bible such as: Through the Bible by Books and Chapters, Biblical Geography, God's Plan for the Ages, Christ in the Tabernacle, The Prophecies of David, Prophetic Events in the Light of the Minor Prophets, Studies in the Gospels, The Book of Romans, An Exposition of Ephesians, and The Book of Revelation. Biola even has a Bible course for children. Supplementing these are two courses in Christian doctrine: The Great Words of the Gospel, and Fundamental Doctrines of Christianity. In defense of Biblical truth are Non-Christian Religions and Cults in the Light of the Word of God.

Rounding out the program are practical courses in child

evangelism and education. Biola offers both of the programs of The Evangelical Teacher Training Association by correspondence, the one leading to the Preliminary Certificate and the other to the Advanced Certificate.

The most recent report released by Biola gives a total of 6,472 persons currently enrolled in home study courses—a gain of 28 per cent over the preceding year. They are located in 49 states and 20 foreign countries. Since the Correspondence School was established in 1914, over 35,000 have registered for courses.

*Moody Bible Institute*

The Correspondence School of Moody Bible Institute is the oldest of its kind in the Bible institute movement, having been established in 1901.

In the 60 years of its operation, the Correspondence School has developed a wide range of 33 courses in three categories: the *Popular Bible Courses* offered singly or in the following series: Christian Life, Adult Bible, Personal Evangelism, Teacher Training, and Interest Areas; the *Intermediate and Advanced Courses* in three series: Bible Survey, Bible Analysis, and Interest Areas; and the famous *Scofield Bible Correspondence Course*.

The Scofield Course, which the Institute began offering in 1915, is in steady demand. While it has not had a growth and completion rate comparable to those of other home study courses, several hundred enroll each year. During the past five years, the average of new enrollments was 307, and completions averaged 102. Since 1915, approximately 20,000 have enrolled in the course.

In 1960, the Adult Bible Study Program, which incorporates 20 of the regular courses into a well-planned and well-rounded program for home study, was launched. It includes a substantial number of Bible units, two courses in Personal Evangelism, and 5½ units of electives.

About two-thirds of all students in Moody's Correspondence School are enrolled in the Class Study Plan. This procedure is generally used in adult Sunday school classes, Sunday evening training groups, and weeknight Bible study. In 1960, 725 classes were enrolled. When Moody began group correspondence study in 1915, it was an innovation in the United States. Documenting the claims by reference to educational historians, the Director, Herbert Klingbeil, states: "I believe our Class Study Program was established before any class study of this nature was offered by universities in the United States."[1] The latter had their beginning in the mid-twenties.

Moody's Correspondence School has had a phenomenal growth in the past several years. Enrollments increased from 15,935 in 1956 to 32,429 in 1960, while completions rose from 7,715 to 16,589. Classes also increased, from 309 in 1956 to 725 in 1960. More students enrolled in the Correspondence School in 1960 than during its entire first 35 years of operation. Altogether, 379,682 have enrolled for study by correspondence. What indicates solid achievement is the rising completion rate, which rose from 26 per cent in 1944 to 51 per cent in 1960.

Very early in radio-programming, Moody began broadcasting Bible studies. Since 1926, the Correspondence School has sponsored the Radio School of the Bible, which broadcasts two courses each quarter over WMBI in Chicago, WCRF in Cleveland, and WDLM in Moline, Illinois.

*Summary*

This brief account of the four largest correspondence schools points up several features of this type of education. Radio, Braille, translation into various languages, and group instruction suggest the variety of modes that can be used. The range of Bible and practical courses suited to different capacities indicates the breadth of interest among laymen. The phenomenal increase in home study of Bible courses suggests that much greater successes lie ahead.

## EVENING BIBLE INSTITUTES

The evening Bible institute is a special form of adult education. In being sponsored by a church or a group of churches, it differs from the evening division conducted by the full-time Bible institute. "It is distinguished from the Bible class and Sunday school teachers' meeting by its advanced, intensive courses; from Sunday school teacher association meetings by the extended nature of the courses; from ordinary lecture series by the responsibility of the participant as an enrolled student; and from other leadership education programs by the balance it maintains between direct Bible study and courses in practical church work."[2]

Most evening Bible institutes are conducted independently and so patterns and practices vary widely. One homogeneous group is identified with The Evangelical Teacher Training Association, which has standard courses for all of its schools.[3] Homogeneity is also achieved through denominational stimulation and guidance.

A rather recent development of evening Bible institutes has taken place in The Lutheran Church—Missouri Synod. Realizing the need for more trained laymen and recognizing the impressive record of the Bible institute movement, the church, "under the guidance of God and the leadership of its Board for Parish Education, embarked upon a program of evening schools, similar to the evening divisions of Bible Institutes."[4]

The centennial convention of the denomination (1947) encouraged the establishment of Lutheran Bible Institutes throughout the Synod wherever possible to help produce "from among the laity more trained Bible teachers, Bible students, and Christian workers." Beginning with the Lutheran Bible Institute of St. Louis in the fall of 1946, the movement has had a healthy growth. By 1954, some 40 schools were in operation, and by 1961 there were 80 institutes located in 23 states, two Canadian provinces, and the District of Columbia.

In St. Louis, 1,400 persons took courses in the first eight years.
The following report summarizes developments and results:

> Most of these Lutheran Bible Institutes offer 4 or
> more courses per semester, a few as many as 10
> courses. The majority run 8 to 10 weeks, with sessions
> one night a week. Half of the schools operate on a
> one-semester-a-year basis, the other half operate two
> semesters a year. Some notable fruits have been
> achieved, for instance, in devotional Bible reading,
> direct Bible study, in personal evangelism, and in
> teacher training. One school offers 48 courses in a
> three-year cycle, covering six major subject areas:
> Bible — Doctrine — Christian Living — Education —
> Missions — History — Church Administration. We
> gratefully attribute this growth to the grace of God,
> and see in it evidences of the readiness of our Chris-
> tians for advanced training.[5]

After the signal blessing of God on the first institutes, a
week-long workshop was arranged in 1953 at Concordia Teachers College, River Forest, Illinois, to review leadership training
programs both within and without the denomination and to
consider the further development of Bible institutes in the
Synod. Under the able leadership of Oscar E. Feucht, Secretary of the Board for Parish Education, 47 educators worked
together for six full days. The conviction deepened that the
church should have a Bible-centered type of leadership training and that steps should be taken to encourage, systematize,
and promote evening Bible institutes. A principal outcome of
the workshop was a 112-page manual to give guidance in
establishing Bible institutes, particularly in the churches of the
Synod.

## SUMMARY

An understanding of the Bible is not only indispensable in
the education of ministers of the gospel but in the preparation
of laymen for the work of the church. The Word of God alone

satisfies the spiritual hunger of those who are made alive to kingdom realities by the Spirit of God. The demand for Bible courses in America and among peoples overseas as reflected in the remarkable growth of correspondence schools and evening Bible institutes is an index of spiritual interest in the very period, following World War II, which has been characterized by moral declension and materialism. Bible institutes and colleges in their aspirations for academic improvement and educational respectability should never forget their origin. They not only have an obligation to use their resources to train laymen for kingdom work, but they have a glorious opportunity of service as well.

*Chapter Nine*

# FIELD WORK:
# SERVICE IN TRAINING

## RETROSPECT

From the Medieval Period came two contrasting educational movements: scholastic education and trade guild learning. Scholasticism was academic and intellectualistic. It majored on logic, metaphysics, and theology, stressing conceptual, formal learning. Theology was the foremost discipline in the medieval universities, followed by law and medicine. So dominant was intellectualism that universities, including Oxford and Paris, required only book instruction to prepare men for medical practice! This is the ancestry of the theological seminary. It accounts for the fact that until recently the emphasis in seminaries has been on theoretical, conceptual knowledge at the expense of the practical. This imbalance has given ground to the charge that Protestantism has relied unduly on verbalism in the communication of the gospel. Too often seminary products have been mere transmitters of the "letter," falling short of the New Testament pattern in which preaching of the Word is coupled with the presence and power of the Spirit.[1]

The other educational movement was practical and was developed by the medieval guilds. The professional guilds promoted learning for the professions and the trade guilds provided technical training for skilled artisans. Both subordinated theoretical learning to the practical. Students learned individually as *apprentices* from their masters. Until the nineteenth century, craftsmen received practically all of their formal education through the apprentice system.[2]

Both of these systems were transplanted to North America during the colonial era. The earliest colleges, whose chief purpose was to prepare men for the ministry, carried on the scholastic tradition. Preparation for most vocations was secured through apprentice training. For example, before 1840, when the first dental school was established in the United States, a young man wishing to become a dentist would secure his training through apprenticeship.

With this background, the unique combination of formal and practical education which the pioneers of the Bible institute-college movement initiated can be appreciated. With rare insight into the psychology of learning, with daring to break away from convention, and with originality to initiate new patterns of education, they devised programs that included *both formal and practical education.*

Simpson pleaded for "practical training in distinct lines of Christian work." Moody's idea of training was for students to spend their morning hours in the classroom and their afternoon and evening hours in practical Christian service. But some place had to be found for study, and so fourteen years after Moody Bible Institute was founded, Moody's son, William, gave this account of the training program:

> The morning hours are spent in the class-room, and the afternoons and evenings are divided between study and practical work among the unconverted. Rescue mission work, house-to-house visitation, children's meetings, women's meetings, jail work, inquiry-meeting work, church visitation—every form of effort which can be developed in the heart of a great and wicked city is here supplied.[3]

It may well be that Moody was blessed by the fact that he was not a professional educator, for he might have overlooked what was obvious to his sanctified common sense,—that *practice* is an essential element in acquiring communicative skills. However, there were also educators among the pioneers who understood the important place of practical training. One of Simpson's associates in the early years of Nyack Missionary College, F. W. Farr, expressed this educational philosophy in a few terse sentences:

> It is best to know and do it, but it is better to do without knowing than to know without doing. . . . In order that we may know and do, we must be taught and trained. . . . Teaching imparts knowledge and fills the mind. Training imparts skill and shapes the habits.[4]

## CONTINUED EMPHASIS

Practical Christian service as a vital part of education for Christian ministeries has distinguished Bible institute-college education ever since the first schools were established. In fact, realization of its value is growing as Bible college educators are thinking through the learning principles involved. In a recent survey conducted by The Accrediting Association of Bible Colleges, an impressive amount of Christian service performed by students while in training was disclosed. It adds up to a significant part of the total Christian witness. For a recent school year, 23 schools reported 19,198 sermons given; 24 schools reported that Sunday school classes were taught 34,312 times; decisions for Christ came to 13,065. Twenty-two schools reported over three-quarters of a million gospel leaflets and pamphlets distributed and 6,608 times weekday classes for children were held. Eleven schools reported 12,141 sick calls in hospitals. The extent of participation by students in Bible colleges is seen from the fact that in 1958-59, 81.2 per cent of the day students registered in schools of The Accrediting Association of Bible Colleges completed at least one semester of weekly assignments in Christian service. In several schools, participation was 100 per cent for each semester.

## EDUCATIONAL PRINCIPLES

The principles involved in practical Christian work are basic to learning itself and to the genius of Christian experience.

### Method of the Master

Practical training was the method used by the Master Teacher. Jesus did not conduct an educational institution on a campus as we think of an educational enterprise. But He was essentially a teacher: He had a company of disciples or pupils; His instruction was based on clear objectives and the motivation of the learners; the best in modern pedagogy was practiced by the Master 2,000 years ago. His method as a peripatetic teacher was not uncommon in His day.

The record in the Gospels shows clearly that Jesus made extensive use of practical experience in teaching the Twelve. A few months after they came under His instruction, Jesus took them on a preaching tour. Long before they graduated from the school of His personal direction, He commissioned them to go and to preach and to heal the sick. And He backed them to the limit: "He that receiveth you receiveth me, and he that receiveth me receiveth Him that sent me."[5] Jesus knew that *they would learn by doing.*

A. B. Bruce in his classic, *The Training of the Twelve,* says,

> This mission of the disciples as evangelists or miniature apostles was partly, without doubt, an educational experiment for their own benefit. . . . The agents were ignorant; they had few ideas in their heads; they understood little of divine truth; their sole qualification was that they were earnest and could preach repentance well.[6]

### Service in the Present

Christian service is the normal expression of Christian life. As a part of the church with the mission of Christian witness and service, Christian students and teachers are expected to serve Christ in the *present*. Christian service is not merely training for the postgraduate future; it is an outlet for the impulse to share and to serve during student days. It is glorifying God and ministering to human need, not mere practice.

H. Richard Niebuhr has aptly pointed out the peril of stressing the future aspect in field work in *The Purpose of the Church and Its Ministry:*

> All too often "field work" (why not call it "church work"?) is regarded and directed as though its purpose were the acquisition of skills for future use. Students, it seems, should teach Sunday School classes because sometime in the future they will need to organize Sunday Schools, to do "clinical work" in hospitals because they will learn something beneficial for their later practice as counselors; to practice preaching so that in other times and other places they may proclaim divine righteousness and mercy. When such considerations are urged upon them an inner contradiction comes to appearance; a kind of professionalized self-love has been substituted for love of God and neighbor. The children in the Sunday School class, the patients in the hospital, the hearers of the "practice sermons" have been put into a secondary place; they have become means to a personal end.[7]

### Necessity of Practice

Service skills are acquired by practice. No one questions the necessity of combining practice with theory in learning to play the piano, fly a plane, nurse the sick, or acquire a language. When it is recalled that nearly all the skills required in the various Christian ministries whether at home or abroad are communicative skills, it becomes obvious that theoretical instruction alone is far from adequate. It takes a combination of theoretical instruction and practical experience to learn a communicative skill whether it is preaching, singing, teaching, counselling, or witnessing.

It follows that theoretical and practical learning should be integrated. As components of the learning experience, they should complement and reinforce each other by effective co-ordination.

## Confrontation with Reality

In Christian service the student is confronted with reality. He is brought into a vital relationship with people—their sins, their struggles and conflicts, their sorrows and aspirations. He learns to know differences and likenesses in people. Only by actual experience can he learn the truth once expressed by a farmer to William James: "There is not much difference between people, but what difference there is is very important."

Through field work, what the student learns in the classroom about social life and problems becomes alive with reality. As pointed out by the Association of Seminary Professors in Practical Fields, "the days of preparation in the theological school too easily become 'ivory tower days.' There is a marked tendency to follow the liturgy but ignore the market place, to embrace theology but shun its social implications. This variety of ivory tower callousness can be successfully treated if the theological student will combine with his academic preparation a project in field work. . . ." [8]

## Personal Development

Field work contributes to the personal development of students. Bible college education is concerned with the total development of the student. Accordingly, all experiences in the life of the school can and should contribute to his spiritual, social, and intellectual growth. And since development of personality takes place not only in personal experiences, but in social interaction, it is obvious that field work provides rich opportunities for growth into Christian maturity. Field work takes the student away from the shelter and exclusiveness of the ivory tower. It takes him to streets, homes, missions, hospitals, and prisons to mingle with the "other half of the world." It puts him *in rapport* with the minds and hearts of people as

he seeks to present Christ as the answer to their innermost
needs. It involves working relationships with pastors and other
Christian leaders. Often, too, it calls for team work with fellow
students in which praying and planning and ministering are
done together.

In field work, therefore, the student's sympathies are deepened and broadened. He learns consideration for others, for
his fellow students and his supervisors. He grows in self-understanding both in recognizing his limitations and developing his
abilities. He has the opportunity of achieving a disposition of
friendliness and good-will toward others.

*Learning by Expression*

Christian service completes the four steps of the learning
cycle: communication, reception, assimilation, and expression.
The last step is particularly significant in Christian education,
which calls for moral responsiveness. Unless the impulse to
share is released, unless awareness of human need results in
action, knowledge is not only incomplete, it is abortive. "Im-
pression without expression ends in depression."

A great teacher, who again was not a professional educator
but whose mind and heart were shaped by divine processes,
gave first place to *knowledge* as the means by which the grace
of God is released in human lives. The Apostle Peter stated
that "all things that pertain unto life and godliness" come
"through the knowledge" of Jesus Christ.[9] But knowledge to
be fruitful must be put into action. Therefore, Peter advises
that the virtues of temperance, patience, godliness, brotherly
kindness, and charity be added to knowledge. Only if these
traits abound in believers, are they neither "barren nor un-
fruitful in the knowledge of our Lord Jesus Christ." [10]

To these basic principles can be added a number of by-
products of field work. It stimulates interest in courses of
study, tending to make theoretical studies more meaningful. It
helps the student to see his own inadequacies and his need for
thorough preparation on the one hand and to appreciate the

infinite resources of grace on the other. Through the whole faculty becoming involved in the administration of field work, it tends to keep instruction functional. Classroom procedures will be focused on the personal development of students and their improvement for effective ministries. Through field work, the institution and its personnel are related to the evangelical community and its life.

## A NEW CHAPTER IN FIELD WORK

For 75 years practical Christian service followed a routine pattern in Bible institutes and Bible colleges. Assignments were made by a Christian service director, and the student made periodic reports on the number of Sunday school classes taught, the number of mission services attended, the number of decisions for Christ, etc. With few exceptions, there was no evaluation made of the student's performance, and there was no coordination between classroom instruction and field experience. More unfortunate still, very little thought was given by Bible college educators to the objectives, principles, and effective methodology of field work. Until a few years ago, so far as can be ascertained, there had been no conference for Christian service directors to seek improvements in this vital aspect of Bible college education.

However, a new chapter is being written by Bible college educators as they have come to realize the untapped learning potential in field work. Some schools have completely revamped their programs and many have initiated new procedures and techniques. It is evident from the study being given to field work in workshops and seminars that traditional patterns are passé, and a fresh look at Christian service programs is resulting in new ideas and practices.

### Weaknesses in Christian Service Programs

The 1958 survey revealed the following weaknesses in Christian service programs:

1. *Lack of formulating the educational principles involved*

*in Christian service.* For example, approximately half of the schools surveyed had not spelled out their aims in Christian service activities. Several expressed them only in general terms. Only a minority had carefully prepared statements. Since objectives provide the basis for sound planning, selection of field experiences, and evaluation of performance, their importance is obvious. In a few schools it was found that Christian service is not even a faculty concern. Policy and procedures were determined by the "administration."

2. *Lack of sound organization.* In organization, the widest differences were found. At one extreme, among a few schools no organized program could be reported. Christian service was encouraged, but participation was voluntary. No reports were required and no records kept. On the other hand, some schools had programs characterized by thoughtful planning, effective correlation, careful supervision and guidance, able administration, careful reporting and recording, and periodic evaluations.

3. *Lack of coordination.* This was one of the most common weaknesses discovered. It has been common practice to delegate the responsibility for Christian service activities to the "Christian Service Department," which functions wholly independent of the academic program. By thus compartmentalizing field work, it is not coordinated with related courses of study. The instructor of pastoral training, for example, assumes no supervision for the practical work done by his trainees, which may or may not be related to their vocational objectives. By this arrangement, it is possible for a student to go to a school to prepare for the pastoral ministry, but because he is blessed with a rich tenor voice, his field work is limited to singing on the varsity quartet. It was found that in a few schools, Christian service is not even conceived as essentially educational; its primary function is serving public relations. Accordingly, it is supervised by the public relations department.

A lack of coordination was also found between the schools themselves and the churches and institutions served by their students. As a result, leaders of the church who engaged the help of students did not understand the aims and policies of the school, and the college administrators did not understand the problems created by their students having to conform to school schedules and regulations.

4. *Lack of adequate personnel.* Probably the most common weakness of all is the lack of adequate personnel to give leadership and supervision to the Christian service program. Inadequate personnel means inadequate supervision of the work done by students, ineffective coordination, and faulty keeping of records. In the great majority of schools a regular faculty member is appointed to give part of his time to directing the program, and with a modest amount of secretarial help he is expected to do what is necessary to operate the department. By contrast, the exceptional program of Columbia Bible College may be cited. For its 400 students, it has a soundly-developed, well-organized program that requires the full-time services of seven persons and the part-time assistance of five others. With this force, it is possible to give considerable time to checking lesson plans and sermon outlines, to observe performance, and to counsel students individually.

## Workshops and Seminars

As an outcome of these findings, The Accrediting Association of Bible Colleges arranged a series of regional workshops in 1959 in which Bible college educators met together to seek answers to the question: How can more training values be derived from field work experiences? The eight seminars held in Philadelphia, Columbia (S.C.), Chicago, St. Paul, Kansas City, Portland, San Francisco, and Azusa (Calif.) brought together 227 educators from 77 schools. These were followed by a national workshop held in Chicago for a two-day period in October, 1960.

These conferences have already been fruitful in strengthening field work programs. They have provided a forum for the exchange of ideas and techniques. They have provoked study regarding the aims of field work; the need and means of coordinating theoretical and practical instruction; methods of evaluation and supervision. They have led some schools to examine and then to reorganize their whole Christian service programs. A year afterwards, schools of the Accrediting Association reported initiating an average of two definite measures aimed at improvement.

Concurrently, the Accrediting Association itself decided to evaluate its own criteria on Christian service to see whether they were adequate. It became apparent that some criteria needed to be clarified and made more explicit. Thereupon a revision was submitted to member schools for study. After further modifications it was incorporated into the 1960 edition of the Association's *Manual.* Since these criteria represent the current thinking of Bible college educators, they are presented as descriptions of a sound program.

### CRITERIA [11]

1. The twofold idea that Christian service assignments are first actual service for the glory of God and then an integral part of the educational program should dominate the thinking and planning of the whole faculty.

2. The whole faculty should see Christian service training as one phase of the total educational program devoted to the student's development in terms of his personal growth and vocational skills.

3. Objectives of field work aimed at the student's growth, maturity, and skills should be well thought out, clearly expressed, and made known to all concerned.

4. Since field work is a part of the educational program, it should be under the control of the faculty, which will determine policy in relation to such matters as objectives, integration, academic value, and controls.

5. Departments that provide training for specific ministries (missions, pastorate, Christian education,

sacred music) should assume the responsibility for assigning, supervising, and counselling their trainees in coordination with the Christian service department.

6. The Christian service department should be efficiently organized under the leadership of a qualified director who is an educator with regular faculty status, and who has reasonably adequate staff assistance and office facilities. A faculty Christian service committee composed of the director, the chairmen of the training departments, the academic dean, and one or more of the student deans is a practical arrangement for the sake of planning and achieving coordination.

7. Field work should be effectively coordinated with course work, particularly in those areas where students are training for specific Christian ministries.

8. Assignments should be made in accord with the general needs and basic education of students (usually in lower division), their vocational objectives (usually in upper division), and available opportunities. Assignments should not be made on the basis of what students can do well through previous experience nor what uses the promotional department wishes to make of them. Needs will include growing maturity, balance of experience, and preparation for their varied callings.

9. There should be effective coordination between the Christian service department and the organizations that engage students through individual and group conferences so that the college understands the problems of the agencies and the agencies become fully acquainted with the objectives and program of field work so that some of the Christian leaders, at least, can intelligently and effectively cooperate in training students.

10. There should be sufficient supervision through pre-checking lesson plans, programs, sermons; through observation of performance; through reports from

students themselves, student leaders, and employing agencies, so that reasonable guidance can be given to students individually and in groups.

11. A system of regular reporting and evaluation should be conducted. Evaluations should be made in time to be useful in counselling.

12. An efficient system of recording should be maintained. Summaries of the students' development and the quality and quantity of performance will be placed in the permanent records.

13. Only field work that is coordinated with course instruction and the student's vocational objectives and which is closely supervised should be given academic credit.

14. There should be sufficient controls to maintain a wholesome balance between study and field work.

## AIMS

Some objectives of field work are general and obtain for all schools with varying emphases given to each. In addition, each school has individual objectives growing out of its local situation and the types of training it offers. Very few schools, for example, offer such highly specialized training as missionary aviation, which calls for corresponding specialization of aims in field experience. Special objectives might well grow out of a denominational relationship in which field work is coordinated with the home missions program of the parent body.

However, some aims of field work can be given that are generally applicable. The following were rated by Christian service directors as *very important* or *important:*[12]

1. To broaden interests and knowledge of the church

2. To develop qualities of Christian leadership (learning to accept responsibilities, to face tasks and difficulties with faith and courage, to plan and to organize programs, to accept criticism, etc.)

3. To gain experience in working cooperatively with others

4. To stimulate interest and to develop skills in evangelism

5. To mature in spiritual and personal development

6. To acquire skills for student's particular calling

7. To know how to deal with people and their problems

8. To develop skills in expression and communication

9. To provide an outlet for impulse to witness, to serve

10. To deepen sympathetic understanding of people and their needs

11. To discover personal inadequacies so that they can be dealt with before students leave school

12. To keep courses from becoming academic and theoretical

The basic aim here as in all Christian activity is to glorify God. Among lesser but important spiritual aims are the following:

1. To respond to the constraining love of Christ

2. To discover the joy of Christian service

3. To learn to live for Christ and others rather than self

4. To learn to look to the Lord for guidance and enduement

5. To learn the meaning of interdependence in the body of Christ

6. To learn to react in a spiritual rather than a carnal way toward defects in Christian organizations and their personnel

*Internship and Counselling*

Intern training is a special form of practical Christian service. It is a period of supervised training in which a student gives his whole time to a Christian ministry either before or after graduation. Not many Bible colleges have inaugurated programs of this type, but their number is increasing. There has been a growing awareness that more practical experience is needed for certain ministries than the ordinary Christian service program affords. Missionary Internship has discovered that numbers of accepted candidates for the mission field have much to learn in terms of adjustment, social adequacy, and spiritual victory in their lives. In fact, some discover in themselves unresolved emotional conflicts that incapacitate them for effective service.

This awareness of the needs of students has led Bible college educators to re-evaluate their programs with two outcomes: More importance is attached to expert counselling of students in their field work, and more schools are instituting intern training supervised by the school in cooperation with employing organizations.

## CONCLUSION

This new chapter in Bible college education in which steps are being taken to provide better training in terms of personal development and professional skills comes at a critical time. If Bible colleges seriously aim to prepare students for effective service in this revolutionary complex age, they must strive for the best possible training. Second-rate educational programs in which students are put through a sequence of routine courses on the assumption that a collection of credits and a degree qualify them for Christian work are wholly inadequate. The very aims and emphases in Bible college education demand the best.

*Chapter Ten*

# TEACHING
# THE BIBLE

What methods are used in teaching the Bible have much to do with releasing its life and power in the learner.

The concept of divine inspiration and authority of the Bible has important implications for the teaching-learning process. When the Bible is regarded as the Word of the Living God through which He speaks to the hearts and minds of men, an entirely new dimension is added to education. It involves more than teacher-student interaction; it embraces interaction of three persons—Spirit, teacher, and pupil. This is the mystery and the power of education that is truly Christian.

Generally, Christian education and theological education in particular have not adjusted their methods to this larger dimension. The rational approach has dominated theological education since the time of scholasticism, which gave rise to the first theological faculties of the medieval universities. Frequently rationalism excluded any other approach. While there have been Christian educators who understood the extra-rational factors, it cannot be said that a unique pedagogical system has been worked out by Christian educators predicated on the special nature of communication inherent in the Word of God. Nor can it be claimed by Bible institutes and Bible colleges that they have followed through on their belief in the plenary inspiration of the Scriptures by employing instructional methods that are in accord with their faith. Much more time has been given to defining and defending the dogma of plenary and verbal inspiration than to tapping the dynamic, creative potential for learning in the resources of grace. Theological education has been prone to take its cues from non-Christians all the way from Aristotle to Dewey.

Before considering the unique learning factors in Christian education, it should be pointed out that the Bible is an objective body of literature which can be studied as any other great literature. It includes narrative, history, epic poem, hymn, epistle, biography, and as such it is subject to the canons and laws that govern all great literature. It can therefore be studied by books, by textual analysis, by synthesis, by induction, by topics. It may be studied for information, for understanding, for insights, appreciations, and wisdom as any other classic might be studied. Ghandi read and studied the New Testament but that did not lead him to become a Christian. For him the New Testament was a body of religious literature no different in kind from the Upanishads. More than one man has pursued years of Christian training from catechetical instruction through seminary studies only to discover that all of his education was theoretical, not related to life. The Word had not become the voice of the Spirit speaking to *him*. Even Biblical studies had not opened his eyes and transformed his being because the approach to them was no different from that used in studying Plato or Virgil or Shakespeare.

## UNIQUE ELEMENTS IN BIBLE STUDY

### Moral Imperative

There are many implications for education from the fact that the Bible is the inspired, authoritative Word of God. First, it is the voice of *soverign authority* speaking to the conscience and calling for *moral response*. The Bible is not only the Word of God to mankind but to each individual, and to none more so than to teacher and student. Before the teacher is qualified to teach, he must himself respond to the divine Voice speaking to *him. He* must "walk in the light." Theoretical knowledge must become experiential knowledge. The Greek has a particular word for this kind of knowledge— *gnosis.* The epistles of the New Testament at times use a more emphatic form, *epignosis,* meaning full knowledge gained by experience. And this same depth of knowledge is for the student also. In studying the Bible, *his* heart and mind should be open and expectant to the Spirit of God speaking to him. Only when study results in communion with God does it bring *epignosis.* And that may be knowledge of God's will, awareness of need, insights into the provisions of grace, or deeper understanding of the mystery of the Godhead.

Responsiveness to the will of God as communicated in His Word is a unique and extremely important condition of learning. A readiness to do the will of God is the prerequisite to spiritual understanding. It is the key that unlocks the treasure of divine mysteries. It is the condition of certainty in knowledge. Jesus said, "If any man will do his will, he shall know of the doctrine, whether it be of God, or whether I speak of myself." [1]

Motivation is a very important factor in learning, but it is not the only one. To it must be added the equally important factor of *moral* responsiveness. It follows that the teacher of Bible should seek this kind of response among his students. There come times when the claims of Jesus Christ can and should be pressed upon the minds and hearts of students and when a Scriptural principle can be applied directly to an immediate situation. The teacher must seek to cultivate reverential and receptive attitudes in the study and discussion of the Word. He must also be sensitive to positive and negative attitudes in students knowing that wrong attitudes hinder and right attitudes foster growth "in grace, and in the knowledge of our Lord and Saviour Jesus Christ."[2] Dr. Howard Tilman

Kuist once commented, "There comes a time in Bible study when we can go no further until we have acted upon the truth we already know."

## The Interiority of Knowledge

Inner, experiential knowledge through divine-human interaction is another unique principle in Christian education, but it is frequently ignored today.

Dr. Lois E. LeBar summarizes a survey of educational practices as follows: "Thus we see that throughout the ages teachers have most often considered their task to be that of exposing pupils to factual content and of getting them to give back in words this outer knowledge. They have relied almost wholly on communication of facts."[3] Modern educators, such as John Dewey, have stressed experience in learning but purely on the horizontal plane. Learning issues from a person interacting with his environment. Dewey repudiated Christian theism—the validity of knowing a personal God who has revealed Himself and His will for mankind. Consequently, there was no place for divine-human interaction in his philosophy. In fact, the great bulk of American education is based on purely horizontal presuppositions. The vertical relationship is either ignored or regarded as irrelevant.

The "interiority" of knowledge in Christian education rests on the "interiority" of experience through a vertical relationship. The experience centers in Christ; it *is* Christ, the Living Word. The medium of communication is the written Word, which reveals the Living Word. Jesus spoke of His relationship to His disciples in terms of LIFE—life sustained by mutual indwelling: "Abide in me, and I in you. As the branch cannot bear fruit of itself, except it abide in the vine; no more can ye, except ye abide in me." [4] But Jesus also stressed the vital importance of the spoken and written Word as the medium of communicating His living presence: ". . . the words that I speak unto you, they are spirit, and they are life."[5] Dr. LeBar described the mutual functions of the Word, both the written Word and the Living Word, as follows:

> The Word of God is originally outside the learner, but is to be taken inside to become the life of the pupil. In order to effect this transformation, the Word must be personally, actively, continuously appropriated by the pupil. . . . Life is changed to the extent that Christ is taken inside and becomes THE inner factor.[6]

But aims in Christian education do not stop with an initial experiential knowledge of Christ. That is only the seed of the Word springing into life; it is meant to grow to maturity and to bear fruit. "First the blade, then the ear, after that the full corn in the ear." Interiority is to be expressed externally in daily Christian living. All the while the sensitive, creative teacher observes the pace of growth in his students, adjusts the depth of truth to their capacities and needs, and under the guidance of the Holy Spirit leads them toward the supreme goal of Christlikeness.

*Principle of Immediacy*

Protestantism has gloried in its great faith that the individual has direct access to God by prayer and faith. By the same token, God's grace is released directly and is not restricted in its flow to the seven pipes of a sacramental system that can be manipulated only by an official priesthood. Protestantism has also held that the Bible as the Word of God is the chief means by which God communicates His truth and grace for salvation and edification. "According as his divine power hath given unto us all things that pertain unto life and godliness, through the knowledge of him. . . . Whereby are given unto us exceeding great and precious promises." [7] In keeping with this principle Luther translated the Bible into the vernacular so that *the common man might hear the voice of God speaking directly to him through the Word.* And for this principle, Luther had Scriptural warrant. The New Testament was written in the vernacular rather than in literary Greek. Most of the epistles were addressed directly to assemblies of believers. "Let the word of Christ dwell in you richly in all wisdom" was a privilege urged upon "the saints and faithful brethren" at Colosse. Certainly if every believer is to be exposed immediately to the Word of God, the theological student is not exempt. In fact, he should rely even more on direct study and meditation on the Bible.

But the long history of God speaking through the written Word to the hearts of men is a tragic record of human obstructionism. Teachers have often been tools of Satan to obscure the truth "lest the light of the glorious gospel of Christ, who is the image of God, should shine unto them." Blind leaders of the blind shut out the light of saving truth before it dispelled the darkness of sin. This was done by teaching elaborate interpretations instead of the plain truth of the Scriptures.

In Christ's day the common people did not have direct access to the revealed Word. The Scriptures of the Old Testament had become overlaid by the accretions of the centuries in the form of highly ingenious commentaries. So involved had these become that only specialists could interpret the interpretations. Thus, instead of teaching the simple Word as revealed to Moses and the prophets, the scribes expounded the "traditions of the elders." One of the most terrible indictments uttered by the Son of Man was directed against these teachers, who considered themselves to be exponents of pure orthodoxy: "Woe unto you, lawyers! for ye have taken away the key of knowledge: ye entered not in yourselves, and them that were entering in ye hindered." [8]

So it was before the Reformation. The Bible was hidden from the common man. There were even priests who knew little of its contents. They were mechanical voices chanting the dogmas of the church and the traditions of the Fathers. The multitudes were denied the light of the word of salvation. And the supreme task of the Reformers was to place in the hands of the common man the Bible in his own tongue, thereby re-establishing its pre-eminence as a moral guide and the font of spiritual life.

But unfortunately the Reformers did not overcome once and for all the persistent tendency to teach human opinions and farfetched interpretations about the Bible instead of the Bible itself. Many a seminarian has been more exposed to the volumes written by authorities and commentators than to the Bible itself. He may have spent more time on the documentary hypothesis of Wellhausen than on a direct study of the Pentateuch itself. Even Bible institutes and Bible colleges have not been guiltless in the common malpractices of teaching something less than the Bible in Bible courses.

## Spiritual Illumination

In the Christian teaching-learning situation there is a second teacher, the Holy Spirit. Jesus promised that the Holy Spirit would take His place after His departure to become their divine Teacher: ". . . when he, the Spirit of truth is come, he will guide you into all truth: for he shall not speak of himself; but whatsoever he shall hear, that shall he speak." [9] "The Holy Spirit's teaching is defined as guiding and declaring, one term emphasizing the pupil, the other the content. He is God's gracious provision for doing that delicate work of making the outer Word an inner experience. He first convicts the learner of his need, leads him to seek the solution to that need in the written Word, illumines the Book to make Christ real, quickens the conscience to produce decision, and prompts practice of the truth that has been discovered." [10]

Another aspect of illumination is the Holy Spirit's work of making significant and real the deeper truths of revelation that are beyond ordinary comprehension. The Apostle Paul declared in I Corinthians 2:10, 13, "God has revealed to us through the Spirit. For the Spirit searches everything, even the deeps of God. . . And we impart this in words not taught by human wisdom but taught by the Spirit, interpreting spiritual truths to those who possess the Spirit" (RSV).

The teaching ministry of the Holy Spirit is significantly related to both teacher and student. When submissive to His leadership, the teacher will be given daily guidance in his work, spiritual discernment in dealing with his students, a creative imagination for the art of teaching, and a joyous inspiration to do his work effectively for the glory of God. "The Institute instructor must frequently urge his students unto and guide them in cordial prayer for the Holy Spirit's enlightening, quickening, and sanctifying influence." [11]

### Faith

From one point of view *faith is the most important of all principles in Bible study*. Without faith, Bible study can be one of the dullest of all disciplines. Without faith the Bible is a closed book with no relevance to an individual's inner needs nor to contemporary social needs.

Faith has been defined as man's total response to God. It is the response of total personality—mind, affections, will. Andrew Murray noted two phases in faith. First, it waits for *God Himself* to speak His word, and then does the *thing He has spoken.*[12]

This principle is of vital importance in Biblical study. A study of the Bible can well make use of all of the tools of scientific exegesis and the wealth of factual data on hand. Never before have there been such refined and massive contributions available from philology and archeology. But the rationalistic approach without faith does not lead to an experience of spiritual reality. On the contrary, it leads toward the desert wastelands of arid intellectualism. It approaches the text with a questioning and a doubting mind. A statement must be rigorously tested before it can be accepted as authentic. The approach in Biblical studies without faith is no more productive of certainty here than in any other field. At best it can arrive only at "warranted assertibility," not at certainty of belief. In the end it produces skepticism and despair.

Professor Robert A. Traina points out the place and the limitations of rationalistic interpretation:

> The rationalist attempts to expound the Scriptures in such a way as to make them understandable and acceptable to the reason. . . . Rationalism reminds us that exegesis must involve the use of reason, and that there should be a sincere attempt to comprehend the message of the Bible. However, the rationalist needs to be made aware that man's reason is finite, and that the Scriptures can therefore never be emptied of their mystery. Man is more than reason, and he must approach the Scriptures with all that he is.[13]

These, then, are the unique elements in the teaching-learning process of acquiring Biblical knowledge. It does not follow that the Bible teacher relies on these alone. He needs to be a specialist in both natural and spiritual processes. He makes use of all the knowledge and techniques from modern educational psychology that lend themselves to his discipline. He will make use of the conventional methods of Bible study that are suited to his aims. Dr. Merrill C. Tenney lists eight approaches to the mastery of Bible books besides the devotional:

1. The *synthetic* approach, which concerns itself not with detail, but with the central message of the book.

2. The *critical* approach, which seeks to ascertain the reliability of the book and its relation to the day and conditions in which it was professedly written.

3. The *biographical* approach, which draws from the book information concerning the author and his associates, and to analyze this information in its relation to the main theme of the book.

4. The *historical* approach, which reproduces the historical and geographical setting of the book, and attempts to show how these affect its interpretation.

5. The *theological* approach, which concentrates on the doctrines of the book and explains its spiritual emphases.

6. The *rhetorical* approach, which takes note of syntax and figures of speech employed to convey doctrinal teaching.

7. The *topical* approach, which extracts from the book all references to a given topic.

8. The *analytical* approach, which engages in detailed examination of the text through analysis of its grammatical structure, and indicates the meaning of that structure through the formulation of a detailed outline.[14]

## BIBLE STUDY IN
## BIBLE INSTITUTES-COLLEGES

To what extent have Bible institutes and Bible colleges made use of the unique principles of Bible study? How are they to be rated from the standpoint of sound instructional methods, particularly in their speciality—Bible instruction? If the best in modern educational psychology is added to moral responsiveness, faith, and the Spirit's illumination, students should excel in achievement. But do they? In a word, have Bible institutes-colleges made full use of their rich resources?

The Bible institute movement is indebted to several outstanding Bible teachers who sensed a need for *a return to direct Bible study*. It was the conviction of these perceptive men, among whom were Dr. James H. Brooks and Dr. A. T. Pierson, that the seminary was prone to offer mediumized education through recourse to human authorities. Students studied the Bible through books about the Bible. While not disparaging the rich heritage of the past nor the refined tools of the present, they nevertheless felt that there should be a direct approach to the Bible by firsthand study. In other words, they sought to restore *immediacy* in Bible study when they lent their encouragement to the establishment of Bible schools.

But the kind of schools they envisioned were only partly

realized in their lifetime. Even today their vision has not been fulfilled. The record is spotty with brilliant teaching interspersed with some that is mediocre and some that is unworthy of being called Bible teaching. Compensating factors, however, have saved inferior pedagogy from failure. Bible institutes-colleges have dedicated faculties, including men of outstanding ability and spiritual stature. By their exemplary lives, rich in the Christian graces, they have unconsciously influenced their students toward Christlikeness. By their mature wisdom, they have emphasized the right things in the classroom. And for the most part, Bible school students also are dedicated to Christ. They are motivated by a serious purpose to prepare themselves for His service. Furthermore, Bible classes are not given to skeptical inquiry but to reverential regard for the divine Author who speaks through the Word. Evidence that Bible teaching in Bible institutes-colleges has enjoyed a measure of success is the fact that thousands have left the halls of these institutions to become able exponents of the Scriptures.

But without question the teaching of the Bible in Bible institutes-colleges could be more effective than it has been. The resources from both educational psychology and the Christian faith have only been partially utilized. In some cases not only have the unique principles of acquiring Biblical truth been neglected, but wrong methods have been substituted that obscure light instead of transmitting it.

## Teaching Points of View

A common tendency is to teach special points of view instead of the Bible itself. Let us trace the process as it unfolds from principle to method, and from method to result. A school is committed, let us say, to British-Israelism. It holds that the British are one or more of the "Lost Tribes," and that they have an important place to play in the events of the end time. Now from this point of view, all of the prophetical Scriptures are seen. The outlook over the whole vista of inspired truth is through the colored glasses of British-Israelism.

Only teachers who hold this interpretation are permitted to teach in this school. It becomes their task to get students to see their point of view and to become able exponents of this theory. As a consequence, Bible teaching is not an attempt to permit the Bible to speak for itself and to unfold before the open mind and heart its glorious realities. It is rather an attempt to make it fit the interpretation of British-Israelism and to make it say what the teacher wishes it to say. Texts must be sought and interpretations defended that are taken to support this view. The *a priori* rather than the *a posteriori* method is used. The product of this process is a graduate who is indoctrinated in the tenets of this school and who goes out to poll-parrot what he has been taught.

In the end, this process, unless arrested and corrected by an open-minded examination of the Scriptures, produces a cult. Defences are added to defences until the involved interpretations are wholly unintelligible to the uninitiated. The movement becomes esoteric, and it may even be stoutly maintained that British-Israelism is the one and only key that unlocks the Scriptures. Without it, one can't hope to find the truth of God's message for our age. Fellowship with the larger body of Christian people is disrupted, for in the very nature of the case it can foster fellowship only with those who rally about this special point of view. Attitudes of bigotry and superiority are apt to develop in reference to the unenlightened.

Whether the special point of view is British-Israelism, hyper-dispensationalism, or hyper-Calvinism—and the number is legion—special points of view always obscure instead of reveal light. They lock rather than unlock the Scriptures. This follows from the fact that the overemphasis of a single truth at the expense of correlative truths makes for distortion of the body of truth. All heresies have begun by the overemphasis of a single truth. Accordingly, there must be a balance of emphasis in the treatment of Scriptural truths. "*All* Scripture . . . is profitable for doctrine, for reproof, for correction, for instruction in righteousness: That the man of God may be perfect, throughly furnished unto all good works."[15] The corrective to special points of view is the direct, open-minded approach to the whole Bible itself. "The Bible is its own best commentator."

## Deductive Teaching Versus Inductive Study

When men like Brooks and Pierson sensed the need of Bible study that exposed the student directly to the Word of God, their perceptions were entirely correct. There was then, as now, excessive study of books about the Bible, sometimes to exclusion of the Bible itself. It was not even given the opportunity of becoming the voice of the Spirit speaking to the heart of the student. But Bible institutes and colleges did not succeed in cancelling out interpositions when they disposed of texts about the Bible. They simply changed the interposing form. Mimeographed notes or polished lectures to be taken down in notes took the place of texts and collateral volumes. All too often the student had no more to do than to memorize by rote mimeographed syllabi or notes from lectures. He was then graded on his ability to memorize the "finished" deductions offered him. Little encouragement was given him to go to the Word to make an examination of the facts for himself. As a consequence, he did not experience the joy of discovering truth for himself. But more serious for his development and his future usefulness was his failure to mature as a Bible student in his own right. Simply memorizing the propositions formulated by the teacher gave little or no opportunity of acquiring exegetical skills. The instructor spared the student from deep thinking by doing all of the serious thinking himself, but in so doing his kindness blunted the curiosity and initiative of his students.

There are many methods in Bible study, and the versatile teacher will suit method to subject matter, to available time, and to the needs and maturation of his students. There is a place for deductive teaching as well as inductive. But the method that is as productive as any and which is based on the principle of immediacy, *induction,* has been used the least in Bible institute-college education.

There have been notable exceptions. Some Bible teachers of distinction have stressed direct, inductive study of the Bible. Among the pioneers were two members of the Nyack Missionary College faculty, Rev. W. C. Stevens and Miss Ruth Miller. Although inductive methods are used today at Nyack, it appears that the early attempts of Mr. Stevens and Miss Miller to introduce them were somewhat premature. Leaving Nyack, they went to Kansas City, Missouri, in 1918, and founded Midland Bible Institute, which continued until 1923. From there Miss Miller went to Three Hills, Alberta, to become one of the first teachers of Prairie Bible Institute. There, she contributed much to initiating a pattern of Bible study by which "the student, by personal firsthand research, but under careful guidance, is pushed into rich original findings . . . putting the student into direct contact with God through His Word." [16]

Another pioneer was Wilbert Webster White, who, while preparing for a teaching career at Yale University, came under the influence of William Rainey Harper. "He had caught the enthusiasm of Dr. Harper, who was convinced of the need of reform in theological education in relation to the English Bible."[17] Armed with the conviction that the study of the English Bible should occupy a central position in the theological curriculum, White began his teaching career, first in a seminary and then at Moody Bible Institute. After two years at Moody he left to pursue a new venture—the founding of The Bible Teachers College in Montclair, New Jersey, in 1900.

Two years later the college was moved to New York City and renamed The Biblical Seminary in New York. Dr. White had in mind a theological school which would give a central place to the English Bible and at the same time meet acceptable academic standards. The Seminary has exerted a far-reaching influence in Biblical education. Several of its professors, including Howard Tilman Kuist and Robert A. Traina, have made extensive refinements in the inductive method. The Seminary has given training in direct methods to scores of Bible teachers, who in turn have introduced this approach to other schools. Foremost among Bible institutes and Bible colleges that have been influenced by Biblical Seminary are the several Lutheran Bible institutes. They have been very successful in adapting the methods worked out by Biblical professors to a Bible institute situation.[18]

There have been other defects in instructional methods that have reduced instructional effectiveness. In some schools undue reliance is placed on inspiration, emotional or spiritual experience at the expense of mastering fundamentals through sound methods of instruction. The opposite deficiency is observed in other schools,—undue reliance on the rational or scientific approach. Not infrequently, too, educational theories and practices have been introduced that are completely alien to Christian principles. However, it can be reported that gradual improvement is going on in methods of teaching the Bible.

Reformation in most schools is long overdue. Many students now coming to Bible schools are ready for greater demands being made upon them. The times call for more thoroughly trained men and women to propagate the gospel. If universities and colleges are placing increasing responsibility on students for their education, when it is common to expect more of pupils at all levels, Bible colleges ought to be in the forefront of developing intellectual maturity and self-reliance in the pursuit of knowledge. Deep involvement of heart and mind in theology is not inconsistent with the response of faith. The Apostle Peter's word is apropos, "Wherefore gird up the loins of your mind." Dr. Samuel Zwemer's comments on this passage are also timely: "No man should think so much, so hard and so highly as a Christian because he has so wide a range of thought open to him," and "Deep thought produces deep theology and deep piety."[19]

Bible institutes and colleges need only to implement their

own principles of education more fully to meet this demand of our times. Historically, they have given a prominent place to direct study of the Bible while other types of higher education have tended to stress the critical approach and to give more place to volumes written by oft-quoted theologians and critics than to the Bible itself. If serious demands upon students are coupled to the attitudes of reverence, moral responsiveness, and faith, the teaching-learning process cannot fail.

*Chapter Eleven*

# DEVELOPING
# CHRISTLIKENESS
# IN PERSONALITY

The concept of "education for the whole man" or "development of total personality" is widely accepted as an educational aim in America. While first place is given to intellectual disciplines, yet because students have physical, emotional, social, moral as well as rational needs, educational aims must take into account all phases of the personality. There is, of course, much disagreement among educators regarding the emphasis that should be given to the non-intellectual aspects of education. Extremists are found on both sides, but there should be no question about the importance of moral and spiritual factors in Christian education.

But what are the true dimensions of personality? Here concepts become fuzzy and no more so than in religious education. Even in so-called Christian education, the Biblical concept of personality is often watered down by liberal and loose thinking. When the concept of personality is vague, the educational aim lacks of precision also. And if the aim is nebulous, no well-ordered program of education can be organized.

In education based upon the revealed and authoritative Word of God, man's true selfhood is not only sharply defined but its dimensions far transcend any concept of man formed by human speculation. In fact, the idea of a human being with moral and rational faculties created in the image of God could only have been born of God.

The Scriptures teach that man's fundamental makeup was in the likeness of His Creator: a being with rationality, sensibility, self-consciousness, self-determination, and moral purity. When man fell in sin, he not only became estranged from God, but all of his God-given powers were affected and turned to "fulfilling the desires of the flesh and of the mind."

What was undone in the fall, God more than recovered in redemption. Christ not only "died for the ungodly" to effect reconciliation but to confer on redeemed man the great privilege of unique sonship. "Therefore if any man be in Christ, he is a new creature."[1] In the new birth, the believer becomes a son of the Living God, "a partaker of the divine nature," a member of the heavenly household. Nowhere does the New Testament become more eloquent than in exalting the nature and rank of the sons of God. "The Spirit itself beareth witness with our spirit, that we are the children of God: And if children, then heirs; heirs of God, and joint-heirs with Christ."[2] "Behold, what manner of love the Father hath bestowed upon us, that we should be called the sons of God."[3]

The concept of human dignity is basic to the principles of freedom and justice which distinguish the Western democratic tradition. But human dignity is usually considered in a social context. Even writers on American government either ignore or only casually mention the fact that the founders of the American tradition derived their esteem of man from his standing before God. For the Puritans, the Christian concept of sonship was the true measure of human dignity.

The Bible not only presents the outline of sonship but it delineates its meaning. In a word, the portrait is *Christlikeness*. God purposed from eternity that His children should "be conformed to the image of his Son."[4] And Christlikeness is spelled out on every page of the Gospels. There, the Son of Man lived an exemplary life, exhibiting the character of both a holy

God and perfect man. In the Beatitudes, Christlikeness is spelled out in words—on the Cross, in deeds. Accordingly, the Christian ideal is not vague and undefinable. In the Incarnation it was made concrete for the common man's understanding.

Supremely, therefore, the aim of Bible colleges is to bring students into conformity with the image of Christ. With few exceptions, they limit admissions to those who confess Christ as their Saviour and who give evidence of having become "new creatures" in Christ. Some further limit admissions to those who seek preparation for a Christian ministry. In either case, the "new birth" is a prerequisite to learning and the aim of the college is to develop maturity in terms of Christlikeness. While Biblical education may also transmit the fundamental knowledge, skills, and techniques that are needed by the dedicated Christian to serve effectively to bring others to Christ and to help them attain their highest levels of life and service, the prior aim is to set the conditions by which the student may become "a perfect man, unto the measure of the stature of the fullness of Christ."[5]

## DELINEATING CHRISTLIKENESS

It has been alleged that such terms as *Virtue* and *Christlikeness* are too ethereal to serve as educational goals. It is admitted that character aims as frequently expressed in the literature of Christian education are too general to be useful in selecting and organizing learning experiences. But this need not be. Certainly the concept of Christlikeness, which has as many facets as life itself, can be broken down into specific educational aims that will serve in every department of learning.

The first place where Christlikeness is delineated is in the Gospels, where the pure ray of divinity passes through the prism of the Incarnation to reveal on the canvas of history the myriad hues of Emmanuel's character. Horne found these qualities of Christ in the Gospels: loyalty, courage, prudence, dignity, social efficiency, love of nature, love of children, friendliness, pleasure in social life, passion for service, love, self-control, self-sacrifice, self-respect, sincerity, joyousness, intensity, gratitude, reverence, modesty, dependence, prayerfulness, artistic feeling, justice, love of truth, sense of mission, alertness, positiveness, and physical strength.[6]

These are the very qualities that we want to see reproduced in our students. They add up to Christlikeness. They can become educational goals for teachers, counsellors, deans, administrators, staff personnel, work supervisors, Christian service directors—all who seek to guide students to spiritual maturity.

## PROBLEMS IN PERSONAL DEVELOPMENT

Few would question the importance of the spiritual, personal, social, and intellectual qualities of Christlikeness in anyone who is called into a position of Christian leadership. It is generally agreed among perceptive Christian leaders that the critical problem is *spiritual,* for desirable social and intellectual qualities stem from a right relationship with God. When a life is completely dedicated to Christ and filled with the Holy Spirit, the whole of the personality is affected. Right social attitudes are generated by love; desire to know the truth is stimulated by the Spirit of God; critical faculties are sensitized by the Spirit's presence; distractions from within and without are overcome by Christ's mastery.

At one of the annual retreats of missions executives of the Evangelical Foreign Missions Association at Winona Lake, Indiana, the discussion centered on the most desirable attitudes of missionary candidates. It was agreed that the most important is the spiritual, and the most common deficiency today is *spiritual inadequacy,* in other words *how* to bring about Christlikeness in the lives of students preparing for church vocation. Here many insuperable problems, apart from God's grace, confront the Christian educator.

### Immaturity

Veteran educators agree that the youth coming to Bible colleges today are less mature than those of twenty-five or thirty years ago. More students come from broken homes. Fewer have had the blessings of a wholesome and thoroughly Christian home life. Young Christians are still suffering from the type of evangelism that offers everything, even fun, by an easy "believism" without the call to repentance and self-denial.

Due to the laxity in standards of the American high school and the flabbiness in our culture, many freshmen come with undisciplined minds and serious educational deficiencies. "They don't know grammar," "They don't know how to spell." "They don't know how to write," "They don't know how to study," are comments frequently heard from teachers of college freshmen. However, the critical events of our time are having a sobering effect on American education.

When Bible college educators face up to their educational responsibility in terms of developing maturity, their task becomes appalling in its dimensions. They are expected to admit freshmen who are immature emotionally, spiritually and intellectually, and in a few short years turn them out with a degree of maturity that will qualify them for positions of Christian leadership!

## Disintegrating Forces

Gone forever is the day when a youth could grow up in the security of a local community where his attitudes and ideals were shaped by the influences of home, church, and neighborhood. Now by means of radio, television, popular magazines, motion pictures, ease of travel, the typical American youth is battered daily by a thousand competing stimuli, most of which accent sex, affluence, and violence. It appears that the commercial interests that control most modern media of communication never heard of the Platonic philosophy that responsible leadership aims to turn mankind away from baseness, "to lift up the wing of the soul," nor of the Pauline injunction ". . . whatsoever things are honest . . . just . . . pure . . . lovely . . . of good report; if there be any virtue, and if there be any praise, think on these things."

It has been observed that the external chaos in the world mirrors the chaos within men's lives. Far too many suffer disintegration of personality, adding to the appalling totals of society's mental casualties. When a Christian youth, therefore, achieves integration of personality through complete devotion to Christ, it represents an extraordinary victory over "all that is in the world, the lust of the flesh, and the lust of the eyes, and the pride of life."[7]

In seeking a solution to the problem of achieving Christlikeness in the midst of a pagan culture, Bible college educators do not take refuge behind the walls of monasticism. In keeping with their concern for human need, the first Bible schools in this country were established in large cities, where need on every hand afforded numberless opportunities for Christian ministry. Cities, too, provided work opportunities for their students. Following this precedent, most Bible colleges today seek to carry out their holy mission in the stream of urban life. In so doing, they can trust that Christ's petition will be answered in them: "I pray not that thou shouldest take them out of the world, but that thou shouldest keep them from the evil."[8]

Christian educators, as an outcome of the deterioration of moral standards, cannot assume that even Christian young people are sensitive to right and wrong. They well know that the insidious temptations which Christian youth face today are aimed at destroying spirituality and elevating sensuality as the norm of behaviour. Many a time they discover that practices which are identified as gross sins in the Scriptures are looked upon as excusable if not healthy indulgences.

### Affluence

Modern conveniences and gadgets can become aids but more frequently they become hindrances. Students today must have, so they think, so many "things" that architects plan larger dormitory rooms than formerly. The danger lies in gadgets becoming distractions. Students become so engaged in operating them and paying for them that intellectual pursuits take a secondary place. Often, too, indulgence in too many calories impairs student efficiency. We can seriously ask whether the call of the Master to learners to deny self has not been displaced by the appeal to satisfy self even in Bible colleges.

## Shifting Responsibility

Another hindrance in solving the tremendous problem of maturity is the false view *that the responsibility for the personal development of students is the exclusive function of student deans.* Classroom teachers are responsible for the transmission of subject matter. To them belongs the field of intellectual pursuits, scholarship, and erudition. Such matters as personal and spiritual problems are referred to student deans and counsellors. In some colleges and institutes the important work of guiding students to moral and spiritual adulthood is not accorded the same esteem as formal teaching. Student deans are not even members of the faculty, which is composed exclusively of teachers.

Let it be said with all emphasis that the responsibility for bringing about Christlikeness in students *is the obligation of the whole faculty,* including every teacher and every counsellor. It is too big an undertaking to be carried out by a few. Furthermore, neither the Hebrews nor the New Testament Church differentiated between a teacher of ethical living and a teacher of subject matter. The teacher taught both truth and its application. It follows that student deans and counsellors are also instructors—teachers in the art of exemplary living. It follows too that professors who limit their teaching to mere transmission of conceptual knowledge fall far short of the pattern of instruction exemplified in the Scriptures and above all by Jesus Himself.

This writer saw an extraordinary example of Christian maturity in a seventeen-year-old youth; however, not in affluent United States but among the Eskimos far up in the grim country of the Canadian North. Alpok, the product of a Christian mission, had few "things"—some books, a couple of dogs and a gun. During the short summer, he lived with his brother and parents in a crude caribou hide tent. During the long winters, they lived in igloos. But Alpok was an extraordinary Christian. He was spiritually and socially sensitive. He was rich in the Christian graces of humility, kindness, gentleness, graciousness. He had the God-given gift of an evangelist, and he had no difficulty in sustaining rapt attention for an hour and a half while preaching the Word to his fellow men. What a difference between Alpok and most students of superior privilege whose spiritual development suffers from involvement in material things and social affairs.

## REALIZING THE GOAL

No doubt there is consensus that many formidable influences impede the deepening of spiritual life in Bible colleges. But what can be done to cultivate the spiritual life so that students become dedicated, Spirit-filled, radiant, victorious persons?

1. There must first of all be a *complete recognition of the all-sufficiency of God's grace and the insufficiency of human resourcefulness.* Even when a student dean is armed with the latest diagnostic tests, counselling techniques, and psychological know-how, his finest efforts will fail unless he depends above all else on the resources of grace. Christlikeness is produced by the Spirit of God: "The fruit of the Spirit is love, joy, peace, longsuffering, gentleness, goodness, faith, meekness, temperance. . . ."[9] Significantly these graces of the Spirit are *fruit*—the product of a living process.

Just as productivity in the natural realm depends upon understanding and conformity to natural laws, so spiritual ends can only be attained by following the principles of the kingdom of God. Those that would lead their students to a realization of the supreme good of Christlikeness must themselves obey the laws that govern spiritual processes. That means seeking first the kingdom of God, walking in the Spirit, exercising faith, employing prayer, abiding in Christ, and constantly yielding to the will of God.

2. *Of equal importance is the integrity and creativity of teachers.* Since the meaning of Christlikeness is "caught rather than taught," it must first be experienced in teachers of youth—instructors, leaders, counsellors. They must be persons of complete integrity, selfless devotion, sympathetic understanding, and enthusiasm born of dedication.

Teachers with these qualities will likely have the creative gift of awakening latent capacities, stimulating an enthusiasm for learning, igniting a spark that causes the mediocre student to catch fire, and raising sights of achievement and usefulness.

One of the students of Dean Gauss of Princeton, perhaps the best known dean in America, attempted later in life to analyze the enormous power of the dean's influence but could only say: "How he did it I shall never know, but of course his own integrity was a constant example to follow. 'He made you want to do the right thing, and the right thing is what Dean Gauss would want you to do.'"

3. Along with the influence of exemplary instructors is *the influence of the student body.* Studies indicate that "bull sessions" in dormitories generally influence attitudes more than sermons from pulpits. The crucial factor is to what extent the upperclassmen are in accord with the spiritual objectives of the college. If the majority are under Christ's lordship, infusing campus life with spiritual reality and vitality, it is surprising how soon freshmen "catch on."

Administration and faculty must constantly be sensitive to the morale of a student body. Even among Bible colleges there are wide differences in the degree to which the policies, regulations, and standards are accepted by students. Hostile attitudes toward "rules" are usually indicative of deeper resentments that not only disrupt Christian fellowship but which nullify the social forces that aid spiritual growth.

4. *A planned program to cultivate and to deepen spiritual life is essential* and is characteristic of Bible schools. From the

time of Moody and Simpson, Bible schools have had formal arrangements for worship, meditation, and missionary challenge. Daily quiet periods for private devotions, regular chapel periods given to worship, spiritual emphasis weeks, missionary conferences, special days of prayer—are the kind of events that are found in nearly all Bible colleges. Then there are the many informal occasions for prayer in meetings of dormitory and activity groups.

Since cultivation of the spiritual life is the central theme of Christian education, The Accrediting Association of Bible Colleges has given a prominent place to it in its criteria of excellence. This is an unusual procedure among accrediting agencies. The *Manual* of the Association states: "Foremost in the total development of students is the cultivation of Christian life and experience. Accordingly, the provisions made for the culture of the spiritual life are considered in the evaluation of the educational program."[10]

5. *The use of social controls is another means of developing Christian character,* but there are wide theoretical and practical differences among Bible colleges regarding their efficacy. The first Bible schools maintained rigid controls by rules. But today there are very few institutions, for example, that solve the boy and girl problem by simply prohibiting dating. At the opposite extreme are a few schools that have followed the modern trend of eliminating all authoritarian controls leaving discipline to the decision of students and the "self-directive" guidance of counsellors. The great majority of Bible colleges are found in the broad zone of moderation.

These colleges hold that some controls are necessary; that most freshmen are too immature to be placed wholly on their own; the welfare of serious students must be protected; the name of the institution must be safeguarded; irresponsible students must be spared the consequences of their follies. These considerations justify controls in relation to the immature and the irresponsible, but there are constructive as well as protective values to controls. They are not incompatible with growth, as some assume, but in combination with the exercise of responsibility, they can be useful aids in personal development.

The service academies illustrate this combination in the training of youth. Military discipline is severe. The cadet is taught to subordinate impulses and selfish desires to duty. But through the system of military rank and promotions, he is given more and more responsibility, with the opportunity of becoming a leader of men before he graduates. When the cadet arrives at the top echelons of command he wields great authority. In this self-indulgent age that has repudiated all external authority Bible college educators may well learn that the same combination of discipline and responsibility builds Christian manhood for spiritual warfare.

6. This brings us to *the importance of developing a sense of responsibility in students*. Bible colleges have sometimes been justifiably accused of retarding growth by failing to delegate responsibility to students. For example, too little has been done to develop self-initiative in study. Students are not given the opportunity of becoming students in their own right. Too little is demanded of them, and throughout college they are treated to spoon-feeding in the classroom.

Opportunities must be provided for students to mature by conferring responsibility in the management of dormitory life and campus affairs, by sharing in the planning and direction of Christian service activities, by giving leadership to student organizations and projects, by contributing their thoughts and ideas to the making of policy in certain areas of administration, and by sharing the responsibility for conferences and public relations events.

## RECORD

No record of nurturing Christian life and achieving spiritual maturity has ever been perfect—even in Apostolic times. So long as persons have the capacity to respond affirmatively or negatively to the Truth, there is the possibility of tragic failure as well as glorious success. While the Bible college record has its blemishes, yet it is true that from their halls have gone many thousands of devoted young people who have become exemplary Christians and successful church workers. Many have been willing to make great personal sacrifices for the cause of Christ.

A distinguished Bible college graduate, Billy Graham, told of the vital influence that a Bible college education made on his life. Responding to an invitation from the 1957 senior class of Trinity College, he paid the following tribute to his Alma Mater:

> There are many things that Trinity did for me. First, it helped give me a sense of direction. I was a confused, bewildered and uncertain youngster when I came there. During my stay I answered the call to preach and for the first time knew what it was to depend on the Holy Spirit for daily direction.
>
> Secondly, Trinity taught me the Bible. The fundamentals of Biblical theology that I learned there are still basic in my preaching and teaching. Down through the years the Lord has blessed the knowledge of the Word of God which I acquired while at Trinity. I learned the importance of the Bible and while there, came to believe with all my heart in its full inspiration. It became a rapier and a sword in my hand that I have used as a hammer as well as a sword to break open the hearts of men and to direct them to the Lord Jesus Christ.
>
> Thirdly, while at Trinity I learned something of the crucified life. I learned what victorious living meant through many personal experiences and the things I was taught in the classrooms. I learned something of the Spirit-filled life. I am convinced that the greatest need in America today is not new institutions or better methods, but Christians who know what it means to live in daily communion with Christ.

Fourthly, Trinity gave me my beginning in evangelism. Opportunities to preach in Tampa and surrounding areas were mine. My first sermon was preached while a student there. I was encouraged at all times to preach wherever possible.[11]

*Chapter Twelve*

# FORCES AND
# ISSUES

The Bible institute-college movement faces many issues precipitated by the impact of contemporary social forces. Tensions between the movement and the social order are inevitable, for the genius of Biblical education is not of this world. Its source is in God as revealed in the Holy Scriptures. Its basic principles are derived from the revealed truths of Creation, Redemption, Divine Purpose. Even its motivations are other-worldly, for it was the constraining love of Christ in the hearts of the founders that prompted them to establish the first institutes. On the other hand, the redemptive mission which Bible colleges seek to carry out takes place in the temporal world of man. Bible colleges must fulfill their mission as social institutions in interaction with society.

Since the very bases of worldly culture and Christ's Kingdom are antithetical, conflicts are inevitable. Some educators hope to solve the problem by accommodating Biblical education to the mores and ideals of the surrounding culture, but the price is unthinkably high. It is nothing less than the extinction of the holy, living flame of redemptive concern which gives life to the Bible college movement. The purpose of this chapter is to point out some of the more important issues confronting Bible college educators and to suggest measures to resolve them.

*Forces of Declension*

The first problem is that which every Christian movement since Pentecost has faced,—*overcoming the forces of declension.* How can evangelical faith, spiritual vitality, Biblical emphasis, and the devotional life be maintained in a society that places a premium on materialism, conformity, professional success, and social prestige? A few say frankly that it can't be done. Every generation must start from scratch and establish its own schools because decline is inevitable. Others, of course, disagree, even though they recognize the persistence of the forces of decay and are sobered by the history of American Protestant education.

In Guy E. Snavely's important work on *The Church and the Four-Year College*,[1] a clear pattern of defection is apparent in the evolution of Protestant colleges. Christian motivation was dominant in the founding of each of the nine colleges during the colonial period. Of the first 120 colleges about 100 were established under church auspices. Initially they were conservative in theology, and dedicated to evangelism, and training of church leaders.

It is apparent that the first step in declension was not liberalism. Orthodoxy was maintained but only in its conceptual form. The loss was in life, in spiritual dynamic. "Inert ideas," as Alfred North Whitehead called them, were substituted for reality. Christianity in form was maintained but its Spirit-generating power was fatally lacking. When human reason displaced faith in revelation, other steps of decline followed. Since rational religion tends in time to become no religion at all, colleges became secular with only minimal attachment to the Christian faith and their sponsoring churches. In time, a nominal attachment was eventually followed by the complete severance of church ties.

In spite of the prevalence of this trend, there have been exceptions. Many educators in the Bible institute-college movement stoutly defend the thesis that by the grace of God it is possible to overcome the tendency toward spiritual declension. The triumphant resources of divine power, they believe, are as available to a Christian enterprise as to the individual Christian. To believe otherwise is to yield to fatalism.

But several conditions must be met if stability of purpose and continuity of spiritual life are to be maintained. A school cannot be left to indecisive leadership nor to a faculty of Laodicean Christians. It requires vigorous leadership, teachers who combine warm devotion with scholarship, clearly defined aims in terms of sound Christian education, a conscious commitment by the board, the administration and faculty to the values and objectives of Biblical education, and a determination to give first place to spiritual values and cultivation of the spiritual life. There must be a constant guard against the insidious forces of decay, and the whole institution must be infused with positive attitudes born of faith and a sense of mission.

There are several encouraging factors in the present situation. There is the demonstrated record of stability of quite a number of Bible institutes and Bible colleges. Significantly, the two oldest schools, Nyack Missionary College and Moody Bible Institute, both continue to be dynamic institutions holding to the distinctives of Biblical education. The academic recognition given to sound Bible schools makes it unnecessary for them to change their character in order to achieve academic standing. The Accrediting Association of Bible Colleges has incorporated the vital qualities of Biblical education into its criteria. By so doing, it not only gives emphasis to cultivation of the spiritual life but recognizes that it is an essential element of the educative process.

*Moral Standards*

Another problem is created by *the trend toward cultural accommodation* in relation to moral standards. Is it possible to develop the qualities of purity, self-discipline, self-denial and altruism in a cultural environment that stimulates sensualism, avarice and every form of self-indulgence? Protestantism has not been given to training its servants in cloistered monastaries isolated from society. But to conduct an educational enterprise that seeks to mold lives to holy standards and a pattern of Christlikeness amidst the swirling currents of urban life is a superhuman undertaking. Only God's grace is sufficient.

It is generally recognized that many Christian young people today, even from evangelical homes and churches, have been seriously affected by the low standards of morals that have gained acceptance among youth. But this condition presents opportunity as well as responsibility for Bible schools. Through the cleansing power of grace, they can and should be centers of holy, radiant Christian influence. For students, they can be oases of life in a spiritual wasteland. Colleges have an advantage over churches in that through institutional controls they can set the conditions that are conducive to developing Christian character. They should maintain standards of decency, purity and refinement for a generation of youth continuously exposed to vulgarity and sensuality.

To accomplish this, Bible college educators will have to exploit the unique educational principles of the Word of God and they will need to tap the higher resources of grace. Their chief reliance must be on the fullness of life in Christ. This dynamic of life centered in Christ can become a unifying and transforming experience even among twentieth-century youth.

## Distinctive Function

A further problem is that of *maintaining the distinctive function of Bible colleges in the face of pressures to broaden their services.* This trend has precipitated the Bible-college-liberal-arts issue in the movement.

There is no question about the need for evangelical liberal arts colleges. They occupy an honored and highly useful place in the pattern of Christian education. Neither is there a question about the propriety of a denomination taking the facilities of one of its Bible colleges and using them to conduct a liberal arts college in order to increase its services and economize its resources. Behind a change of this kind is the policy decision of a responsible body exercising its perogatives.

In the past few years, several denominational bodies have taken this action, converting Bible colleges into liberal arts colleges. But the situation is different when a Bible college yields step by step to pressures to broaden its offerings without deliberately thinking through its aims and charting its course by purposeful action. Its traditions constrain it to function as a Bible college specializing in the preparation of students for Christian ministries while social pressures induce it to become a general college. When no policy decision is made, the issue is left to the force of competing pressures.

This problem will be faced increasingly by Bible colleges in the decade ahead when pressures can be expected to mount with the doubling of the college-age population. There will be many practical inducements to broaden the curricula of Bible colleges and even to change their essential function. A liberal arts major and curricula preparing for lucrative professions are more popular than theological programs. The practical advantages are many: increased operational income, higher prestige of the liberal arts, eligibility to foundation grants, wider academic recognition as well as being able to meet the requirements of graduate schools and satisfy the needs of the community.

At this point, the Bible college at the highest level of policy-making must decide what its primary function is. If it seeks to meet both the requirements of a general college and a Bible college, it will likely turn out to be neither fish nor fowl, neither a first-class general college nor an effective Bible college. It is very questionable whether a liberal-arts-Bible-college combination makes for institutional stability. One or the other will tend to dominate and stamp the institution with its emphasis. History indicates that a dual college usually becomes a liberal arts college. The record also indicates that when "Bible" is maintained as one among a number of departments, it tends to be overshadowed in size and prestige by departments in the arts and sciences. Furthermore, the element of vital Christian fellowship, the emphasis on the devotional life, the place given to Christian service, the unity and morale generated by common purposes tend to be dissipated on a campus that fosters the varied interests and activities of a general college.

What is the attitude of Bible institute-college educators toward this issue? Generally, it can be affirmed that the great majority have deep convictions that the Bible college has an important and distinctive function, and that it can only fulfill its mission effectively by remaining specialized. Accordingly, quite a number of Bible colleges, as a matter of policy, refuse to add majors outside of those directly related to church vocation. In general, this is the policy of the two score Bible colleges of the evangelical movement in the Christian Churches. If more liberal arts colleges are needed, they should be established as such. In Canada the more than 50 Bible institutes and Bible colleges are in no danger of becoming general colleges because conditions are not conducive for churches to develop liberal arts colleges. As pointed out earlier, in most Canadian provinces, education in the arts and sciences is controlled by the provincial universities.

Several evangelical denominations are seeking to solve this problem by a multiple type of institution. The Bible college is maintained as a distinct unit with an administrative head and a distinct faculty. By this arrangement it is expected that the unique elements of Bible college education will be preserved by a faculty whose chief concern is to prepare students for Christian ministries. General education and liberal arts programs are offered in a separate unit, which also has an administrative head and a separate faculty.

In the United States, the regional accrediting associations, which heretofore have accredited only general institutions, are now one by one adopting the policy of extending their services of accreditation to specialized colleges. It therefore becomes unneccessary for Bible colleges desiring regional accreditation to become general institutions. They can now qualify for regional recognition as Bible colleges, although it will take time for policy to be implemented, for regional associations have had little experience in evaluating Bible colleges, and it will take time to establish special criteria to evaluate their unique elements.

## Need for Bible Colleges

*Will the long trend toward higher educational levels eventually eliminate the need for undergraduate schools to prepare students for Christian ministries?* Will the newer denominations find that Bible institute-college training becomes inadequate for ministerial preparation as their churches become more sophisticated? Will the rising levels of literacy in underprivileged lands exclude the missionary with less than graduate preparation in a professional field? Will the increasing demands made upon Christian leadership whether in Christian education, the pastorate, sacred music, or missions raise the minimum level of preparation to at least the first graduate degree beyond the bachelor's? If so, what will happen to Bible institutes and Bible colleges?

That the general educational level is rising is, of course, an acknowledged fact. It is a universal trend. A college diploma is as common today as a high school diploma was 50 years ago. It is true, too, that the demands are growing among many of the "Third Force" groups for better trained men in the ministry. Certainly, among mission boards, including independent faith missions, the demands increase for better prepared candidates.

But Bible schools have not been static. Far from being reactionary, they have, as a class, been sensitive to changing conditions at home and abroad. Whereas the first schools had few high school graduates in their student bodies, now they have few who have not completed high school. For example, in Moody Bible Institute there is not a single non-high school graduate among its 1,000 day students, and nearly half of these have had college studies. Scores of schools that were conducted with little regard to academic standards 25 years ago, are now seeking to raise their programs to recognized standards of excellence. Furthermore, quite a number of Bible colleges have developed undergraduate programs designed to prepare students for post-college studies.

But the most convincing answer regarding the validity and the place of undergraduate preparation for Christian ministries is the simple but inescapable fact that seminaries and graduate schools do not prepare nearly enough men and women to man the thousands of posts of Christian service throughout the world. Even when admitting candidates with less than graduate preparation, many mission boards are facing an acute shortage of recruits. The United States military academies turn out only a fraction of the trained men needed for the armed forces. Many other schools are needed to train noncommissioned officers, technicians and also commissioned officers. Likewise, the Christian forces need many trained men and women—professional and non-professional, lay and ministerial—for the Christian crusade in the technological age.

## Opportunities for Graduate Studies

Since an increasing proportion of Bible college graduates pursue advanced studies, the problem of opportunities for graduate studies arises. Stated simply, where shall Bible college graduates go for advanced studies? Some Bible colleges have good relationships with their state universities whereby students with proper prerequisites are admitted to graduate schools, particularly in education and music. But most Bible college graduates seek further preparation in the theological fields. Some have had their sights raised while in Bible college; some have deliberately gone to a Bible college for their pre-seminary education.

It is freely admitted that not all Bible school graduates are ready for the seminary. Those who have taken three-year programs beyond high school do not have the required general or liberal arts education. Even some who graduate from four-year programs lack the breadth of general education required by seminaries because their programs are too highly specialized. Some come from schools of unknown or questionable academic quality, while some do not achieve high enough grades to be encouraged to pursue advanced studies. But there is a considerable number of qualified graduates who are confronted by the problem of where to go for advanced study.

That such students make good in seminaries was disclosed in the investigation on the readiness of Bible college graduates for advanced studies conducted in 1960 by The Accrediting Association of Bible Colleges in cooperation with eleven seminaries. The scholastic records of 127 seminary graduates who took all of their undergraduate work in Bible colleges compared favorably with those of 154 men who took their undergraduate work in liberal arts colleges and universities. The Bible college graduates achieved a mean Grade Point Average of 2.12 at the seminary compared to 2.10 for the liberal arts and university men.

The investigation also disclosed that both Bible college graduates and those from church related colleges did better than graduates from secular universities and those who majored in engineering, chemistry and similar programs.

This points up the importance of college programs that condition students for seminary studies by courses that are *pretheological* in nature. Among the subjects which the American Association of Theological Schools lists as a desirable minimum which a student should have before beginning study in seminary is religion. Specifically, it is stated that "a thorough knowledge of the content of the Bible is indispensable, together with an introduction to the major religious traditions and theological problems." Greek and Hebrew are among the language tools recommended for "scholarly research," but many theological educators hold that these languages are indispensable for exegesis of the Scriptures, and the student should be required to secure a working knowledge of one or both of them before entering the seminary.

However, the American Association of Theological Schools, the one accrediting agency for Protestant seminaries, does not *require* the pre-seminary studies it recommends. The only admission standard that must be followed is that no less than 85 per cent of admitted students be from regionally accredited colleges. This has made it possible for many men with little work in the humanities and with no studies in the Bible and Biblical languages to be admitted to seminary. Some even major in engineering, business administration, and chemistry, but because they hold a bachelor's degree from a regionally accredited college or university they meet the critical requirement for admission. It should be added that some seminaries do require such men to make up deficiencies before or soon after they are admitted. Several denominations like the Missouri Synod of the Lutheran Church operate colleges for the one purpose of preparing their men for the seminary. The work required is as much pre-theological in content as is a pre-medical program in medical education.

The requirement of graduation from regionally accredited colleges has limited the number of seminaries that are open to Bible college graduates. Other selective factors further limit opportunities for Bible college graduates to pursue theological studies in graduate schools. They prefer seminaries with whom they have a theological affinity, and, if available, those with which they are denominationally related. Among conservative seminaries, the students tend to choose those that are in accord with their own theological views, particularly in relation to Calvinism and Arminianism. Fortunately, there are some conservative seminaries of varying theological hues that freely admit qualified Bible college graduates.

However, internal demands coupled with limited external opportunity have led several accredited Bible colleges to establish seminaries or graduate divisions. In 1947, Columbia Bible College instituted its Graduate School of Missions. The Bible

Institute of Los Angeles in 1952 inaugurated a standard three-year theological seminary. Central Bible Institute began its Graduate School of Religion in 1957. A graduate missions program was begun in 1960 at Nyack Missionary College named the Jaffray School of Missions. A regular seminary program is also offered by Lincoln Christian College in its Graduate School. Several non-accredited Bible colleges have also begun seminary programs or graduate divisions in recent years.

This whole problem of ministerial preparation beginning with college is now undergoing critical study. A study was recommended by the American Association of Bible Instructors, some of whom "advocate that pre-seminary students should be able to fulfill some of their basic requirements while still in college, so that they can take advanced courses during postgraduate seminary teaching." Aided by a grant of $85,000, this organization in cooperation with the American Association of Theological Schools is making a study of pre-seminary education in the colleges and universities of the United States and Canada.

At the same time, the Education Commission of the National Association of Evangelicals appointed a committee to make a broad study of pre-seminary education in the framework of evangelicalism. It is evident that many Christian educators share the conviction that sound ministerial preparation should follow a well-planned sequence from the first year of college to the end of seminary.

A new and more realistic approach led by educational statesmanship could go far toward removing the ambiguities and inequities in a theological education. The B.D. seminary program follows college but it is not always considered of graduate quality because it must include basic, elementary studies that should be taken in college. Accordingly, the seminary includes those pre-professional courses that in other professions are taken in college. This situation creates another irregularity in the pattern of graduate studies. It is possible to secure a university Ph.D. in three years of post-college work, but it takes at least six years to complete a Th.D. program in a seminary. It is obvious that educational leadership with imagination and courage is needed to devise new and more realistic patterns of theological education.

## Qualified Personnel

One of the most critical problems that confronts Bible colleges is that of securing fully qualified personnel. "Where do you get teachers qualified to teach in a Bible college?" was asked by a perceptive educator upon his first visit to a Bible college campus. The qualifications called for are many and each tends to eliminate the number of candidates. Teachers in Bible institutes-colleges must first of all be persons of Christian maturity and exemplary character. They must be thoroughly dedicated, for the Bible college offers no inducements to the self-seeker. They must understand and be in complete accord with the objectives and distinctives of Bible college education. They must have a definite concern for the total welfare of their students and must be the kind of Christians who will on occasion pray and counsel with them. They should have ability and competence to teach. They should be masters of their teaching fields; at least those who teach skills should have practical experience. Finally, their knowledge should be integrated in Him who is the sum and center of all truth. Teachers with these qualities are essential both in the educative process of shaping lives into Christlike personalities and in preserving the integrity of a Christian college.

But where are the graduate schools suited to prepare teachers at the highest level of professional competence, particularly for teaching general education or liberal arts courses? As matters now stand there are few opportunities to pursue graduate studies in the natural sciences, the social sciences and the humanities outside of secular universities. But their naturalistic frame of reference and the value system that goes with it are completely alien to the climate and the presup-

positions of Biblical theology. What then, does the prospective
teacher do with the problem of antithetical knowledge?

If his own knowledge is grounded in Biblical truth and
systematized with the Christian world view, and if he has the
critical ability to identify and to evaluate the presuppositions
of knowledge systems, he will screen whatever is presented
in the classroom and integrate tested facts into the Christian
system. Unfortunately, not all have the competence to do this
on their own. Some never achieve integration, and they tend
to pass on to their students their unresolved intellectual conflicts. Some will compartmentalize their knowledge and will
teach sociology or psychology in one frame of reference, then
shift to an entirely different frame of reference when teaching
a Sunday school class.

A Bible college president who wanted to be certain that
his teachers have a Biblical philosophy, conducts a weekly
seminar for new teachers on Christian philosophy and the
significance of Bible college education. Some presidents hold
that Bible colleges must "grow their own." They first pick out
students of outstanding ability with teaching aptitudes and
then guide them in their preparation for a career of teaching
in a Bible college. Several colleges have arranged a series of
faculty meetings extending through one or several school
years in which the Biblical principles of education are ex-
plored and discussed. The North American Association of
Bible Institutes and Bible Colleges and Fort Wayne Bible
College have jointly sponsored annual summer seminars for
Bible institute-college teachers on the improvement of instruction through a better understanding of Biblical philosophy.

But the problem in its totality is far from solved. Bible colleges, like Christian liberal arts colleges, sometimes employ
teachers who have little understanding or intellectual affinity
with the Christian system. A more effective solution to the
problem is the establishment of evangelical graduate schools
or a university in which prospective teachers can secure graduate preparation in the non-Biblical fields under Christian

scholars of the first rank. That a university of this kind is envisioned by leading evangelicals in both the United States and Canada inspires hope for stronger Bible college faculties in the non-Biblical fields.

## Adequate Support

*The problem of adequate support for Bible institutes-colleges is intensified by current trends in education.* In general, Bible schools are dependent on voluntary support. Few have substantial endowments. One-third of them are independent and therefore do not enjoy denominational subsidies. Even some of the denominational schools receive no support from their denominations directly; what support they receive comes voluntarily from local churches and individuals. And among those that are supported by their denominations, the amount is usually a fraction of what a college needs above operational income. As a result, there are relatively few Bible colleges that are adequately supported by their constituent bodies. Most schools are handicapped by inadequate facilities and underpaid teachers.

This condition reflects the general lack of responsibility among evangelicals in supporting Christian education. Many groups have a commendable interest in missions and generously support missionaries, but they express little concern for the schools that prepare missionaries.

Added to the present state of affairs are three factors that make the situation critical. Christian colleges of all types are called upon to increase their facilities substantially to care for the great increase of college students during the next decade. Educational costs are rising appreciably. The state is taking over more and more responsibility for higher education, placing the Christian college increasingly at a disadvantage. Supported by taxes, the state and provincial universities provide education at comparatively low tuition costs. In some states, junior college education is provided without charge, and in a few states, the goal is free senior college education as well.

What is the future of voluntarily supported Christian colleges, particularly Bible colleges? T. L. Hungate of Columbia University takes a very dismal view of the future of private institutions. He thinks that increasing governmental control and support of higher education is inevitable. In *Financing the Future of Higher Education,* he says, "The proposed change in pattern of support would strike a heavy blow at private institutions. Some will close, some will consolidate, some will do better work with less money, some will restrict their fields of service. Some will become state institutions."[2] Hungate also expects that contributions to Protestant colleges will decline, while Catholics are likely to strengthen their institutions.[3]

Hungate, of course, does not reckon on the faith that released divine resources in the founding of many Christian colleges. Not only their founding, but the record of developing many a Bible college and preparing hundreds of young people for Christian service is replete with remarkable providences and answers to prayer. Furthermore, the generosity of evangelicals should not be discounted when they are aroused by a vital need.

What should be the policies of Bible colleges in relation to government subsidy of private education? There is no one answer, for each administrator will follow his judgment and conscience in the light of circumstances. Many educators oppose federal aid to education, fearing governmental control. Some oppose governmental aid on principle but accept the benefits so long as the conditions imposed do not encroach on private rights and freedoms. The danger here is that evangelicals who want to uphold the principle of separation of the church and state and who oppose the efforts of the Roman Catholic hierarchy to secure government support for their parochial schools will compromise their position and thereby weaken a cherished bulwark of freedom.

In Canada the Federal government has a system of provincial grants for operating expenses to private as well as public institutions of higher learning which in 1958 ranged from $157.70 per student in British Columbia to $268.39 in Alberta. Grants are also being made for new construction and capital equipment, but the conditions that are imposed make it practically impossible for Bible colleges generally to accept either kind of aid. For example, in one province it would be necessary for a Bible college to come very much under the jurisdiction of the provincial university, even to locating its facilities on the university campus, in order to qualify for aid.

As for grants from industry, so far, Bible colleges have not received substantial sums from this source even though they are making an invaluable contribution to public welfare by strengthening the moral and spiritual foundations of society. Many industries, as a matter of policy, do not aid religious institutions. Some larger corporations state publicly that grants are channeled only to those colleges, like engineering schools, whose services are helpful to them. Fortunately, not all are limited by policies of this kind, and some aid has come from industry.

So long as independent colleges want to remain essentially free, they will need to depend for the most part on *voluntary* support. This becomes a challenge to the leadership of Bible colleges to exercise faith and to arouse constituents to their privilege as well as their responsibility to support their colleges. It is unthinkable that Christians in affluent America do not have adequate resources. It is a matter of vision opening wealth that is withheld.

The latest statistics on financing Bible colleges give evidence that Christians are rising to the challenge of supporting these institutions. In the 1960-61 school year, the forty-eight member colleges of The Accrediting Association of Bible Colleges experienced an average increase of seven per cent in enrollment. In the same year, income for operating expenses increased by 20.6 per cent! In addition, the plant value of these schools increased by nine per cent through new buildings and facilities during the same year.

## SUMMARY

The story of the Bible institute-college movement is a demonstration of the power of the life-giving Word of God. Because God speaks to every generation through His Word communicated by Spirit-energized evangels, the need for "schools of the prophets" which give first place to the Bible is continuous. The world for whom Christ died needs to know the transforming message of the gospel. The church needs to hear prophetic voices from the pulpit to call it to obedience to its Lord. The man of God can only be shaped in heart and mind by an experiential knowledge of the will of God revealed in the Word. *The Bible is indispensable through the whole range of the Christian mission.*

Bible colleges have derived their inspiration, their ideals, their processes, and their goals from the Bible. Their continued usefulness will be determined by adherence to its principles; then grace and power will be released into human life by the Holy Spirit who quickens truth into living reality.

Bible colleges are confronted at once by a great peril and a great opportunity. The peril is to be conformists; the opportunity is to meet the world's perennial hunger for the bread of life. Only as they keep first values first and strive for the best in Christian education, will they be able to meet the challenge of our times.

# APPENDIX AND NOTES

*Appendix*

# BIBLE INSTITUTES AND BIBLE COLLEGES OF THE UNITED STATES AND CANADA

The following list of Bible schools is as complete and up-to-date as it was possible to compile as of January 1, 1962. With but one or two exceptions—in which regular theological programs are offered during evening hours—all are essentially day schools. No attempt was made to include the several hundred evening Bible schools offering adult education.

Some institutions are single-purpose units, while others are multi-purpose—embracing several educational units. For the definition of a Bible institute and a Bible college, see Chapter One.

No evaluation of a school's quality is implied by inclusion in this list (or inadvertent exclusion). It is known that it includes some strong and some relatively weak schools, and some of unknown quality. If any Bible institutes or Bible colleges have been omitted, it has been done inadvertently, and the author will appreciate receiving information about them.

AENON BIBLE SCHOOL OF THE PENTECOSTAL AS-
SEMBLIES OF THE WORLD, 251 N. 20th Street, Colum-
bus, Ohio. Founded 1941. Pentecostal Assemblies of the
World. Day, evening, and correspondence schools.

ALBERTA BIBLE COLLEGE, 2720 Centre Street, N., Calgary, Alberta. Founded 1932. Christian Church. Classical Ministerial Course (ThB), English Ministerial Course (BSL). Evening school. Day school enrollment, 18. Tuition fees for 32-week school year, $180. Good work opportunities. Write to Principal for information.

ALBERTA BIBLE INSTITUTE, 4704 55th Street, Camrose, Alberta. Founded 1933. Church of God (Anderson, Ind.). Two-, three-, and four-year programs.

THE AMERICAN BAPTIST THEOLOGICAL SEMINARY, COLLEGE OF THE BIBLE, 1800 White's Creek Pike, Nashville 7, Tenn. Founded 1924. National Baptist Convention, U.S.A., Inc. Programs: Bible (AB), Christian Education (AB). Seminary and extension divisions. Day school enrollment, 60. Tuition free. Registration, health, library and other fees, $90 for 36-week school year. Board and room, $42 per month. Some work opportunities. Write to Academic Dean for information.

APPALACHIAN BIBLE INSTITUTE, Inc., Bradley, W. Va. Founded 1950. Independent. Associate member of The Accrediting Association of Bible Colleges. Programs: General Bible (diploma). Enrollment, 70. Tuition free. Registration fee, $25 for each of three 12-week terms. Work-loan scholarships available, $10-$40 per month. Some work opportunities. Write to President for information.

ARIZONA BIBLE INSTITUTE, 3025 W. McDowell Road, Phoenix, Ariz. Founded 1946. Interdenominational. Programs: Ministerial (ThB, AB, 3-yr. diploma), Missions (AB, 3-yr. diploma), Christian Education (AB, 3-yr. diploma), Sacred Music (AB, 3-yr. diploma). Enrollment, 70. Tuition fees for 36-week school year, $193. Board and room, $595. Good work opportunities. Write to Registrar for information.

ASBURY BIBLE COLLEGE, 1200 Blackhawk Road, Moline, Ill. Founded 1960. Interdenominational. Ministerial (ThB, cert.), Music Evangelism (cert.), Christian Worker's Course (cert.). High school. Summer and correspondence schools. Tuition free. Room and board for 32-week school year, $450. Good work opportunities. Write to Registrar for information.

ATLANTA CHRISTIAN COLLEGE, 2531 Dodson Drive, East Point, Ga. Founded 1937. Christian Church. Associate member of The Accrediting Association of Bible Colleges. Programs: Ministerial (AB, BSL, ThB). Evening division. Day school enrollment, 91. Tuition fees, $215 for 36-week school year. Good work opportunities. Address President for information.

ATLANTIC BIBLE INSTITUTE, Hampton Station, New Brunswick. Established 1948. Non-denominational. Bible School, high school.

AZUSA COLLEGE, Highway 66 at Citrus, Azusa, Calif. Founded 1899. Interdenominational. Accredited by The Accrediting Association of Bible Colleges. Programs: Biblical Literature and Theology (AB), Ministerial (AB), Missions (AB), Psychology (AB), Education (AB), Music (AB). Enrollment, 197. Tuition fees for 36-week school year, $448. Good work opportunities. Scholarships available. Write to Registrar for information.

BALTIMORE BIBLE COLLEGE, 2200 Mt. Royal Terrace, Baltimore 17, Md. Founded 1957. American Evangelistic Association. Programs: Missionary (ThB), Ministerial (ThB), Christian Education (BRE). Enrollment, 55. Tuition fees for 36-week school year, $189. Room and board, $486. Good work opportunities. Admissions: acceptable high school record, Christian commitment, approved character, agreement with school's objectives. Write to Registrar for information.

BAPTIST BIBLE COLLEGE, 3255 Lowell Blvd., Denver 11, Colo. Founded 1952. Baptist. Programs: Biblical Education (AB), Elementary and Church Education (AB), Music (AB). Enrollment, 56. Tuition fees for 36-week school year, $320. Work opportunities fairly good. Fifty percent tuition grants for children of ministers and missionaries. For information write to Director of Admissions and Records.

BAPTIST BIBLE COLLEGE, 628 E. Kearney, Springfield, Mo. For information on curricula and admission, write to Principal.

BAPTIST BIBLE INSTITUTE, 1306 College Drive, Graceville, Fla. Founded 1943. Southern Baptist (Florida Baptist State Convention). Programs: 3-year diploma courses in Pastoral Training, Religious Education, and Music. Summer school. Enrollment, 202. Tuition fees, $195 for 36-week school year. Room and board, $475. Some work opportunities. Scholarships available to licensed or ordained ministers. Admissions: persons who have had one year of Christian experience, over 21 years of age, approved character, agreement with the objectives of the Institute. Direct inquiries to Office of Dean.

BAPTIST BIBLE INSTITUTE, North 15th and Dunbar Streets, Mayfield, Ky. Founded 1949. Southern Baptist. Member of Association of Southern Baptist Bible Institutes. Programs: Liberal Arts-Theological (AB), 3-year course (cert.). Evening, correspondence, and summer school divisions. Day school enrollment, 42. Registration fees, $30. Some work opportunities. For information address Office of President.

BAPTIST BIBLE INSTITUTE, 629 W. Main Street, Oklahoma City, Okla. For information on curricula and admissions, write to Principal.

BAPTIST BIBLE SEMINARY (Undergraduate), Johnson City, N. Y. Founded 1932. General Association of Regular Baptists. Accredited by Board of Regents of New York State. Programs: Theological (ThB), Religious Education

(BRE), diploma course (3 yrs.). Enrollment, 433. Tuition fees, $475 for 32-week school year. Good work opportunities. Write to Registrar for information.

THE BAPTIST SCHOOL OF THE BIBLE, 13407 Kinsman Road, Cleveland 20, Ohio. For information on curricula and admissions, write to Principal.

BARRINGTON COLLEGE, Barrington, R. I. Founded 1900. Interdenominational. Accredited by The Accrediting Association of Bible Colleges and the New England Association of Colleges and Secondary Schools. Programs: Theological (5-yr. ThB); Bible (3-yr. diploma); Church Vocation—Missions, Christian Education, Pastoral Studies (AB); Vocational—Education, Secretarial Studies, Social Service (AB); Music (BM); Liberal Arts majors (AB). Evening, summer, and correspondence schools. Day school enrollment, 428. Tuition fees for 36-week school year, approximately $650. Room and board, $600. Admission: upper two-thirds of high school, acceptable aptitude scores, sympathy with spiritual objectives of college, and willingness to abide by its social and moral regulations. Write to Registrar for information.

BEREA BIBLE INSTITUTE (Institut Biblique de Bérée), 1751 Henri-Bourassa Boulevard E., Montreal 12, Province of Quebec. Founded 1941. Pentecostal Assemblies of Canada. Serves French-speaking peoples. Working knowledge of French required for admission. Offers 3-year Bible School Course. Tuition fees, $225 for 28-week school year.

BEREAN BIBLE COLLEGE, 460 31st Avenue North West, Calgary, Alberta. Founded 1948. Undenominational. Three-year general Bible course (diploma). Evening and correspondence schools. Day school enrollment, 85. Free tuition. Modest living costs.

BEREAN BIBLE SCHOOL, 1020 S. Hall Street, Allentown, Pa. Founded 1950. Bible Fellowship Church. Associate member of The Accrediting Association of Bible Colleges. Three-year diploma courses in Theology, Bible Missions, Christian Education. Evening school. Day school enrollment 33. Total expenses for 36-week school year, $855. Good work opportunities. Admission: high school-college preparatory course preferred, willingness to submit to Christian education disciplines and school's objectives. Write to Registrar for information.

BERKSHIRE CHRISTIAN COLLEGE, 200 Stockbridge Road, Lenox, Mass. Founded 1897. Advent Christian. Accredited by The Accrediting Association of Bible Colleges. Programs: Pastoral (AB), Missions (AB), Christian Education (AB), Pre-Professional (AB). Junior college division. Enrollment, 96. Tuition fees, $450 for 36-week school year. Room and board, $483. Good work opportunities. Write to Director of Admissions.

BETHANY BIBLE COLLEGE, 800 Bethany Drive, Santa Cruz, Calif. Founded 1919. Assemblies of God. Accredited by The Accrediting Association of Bible Colleges. Programs leading to AB in Bible, Christian Education, Sacred Music, Missions, Pastoral Theology, and Pre-Seminary. Enrollment, 309. Tuition fees for 36-week school year, $420. Room and board, $576. Good work opportunities. Limited scholarships available. Admissions: high school record or equivalent, Christian commitment, approved character, agreement with school's objectives. Direct inquiries to the Registrar.

BETHANY BIBLE COLLEGE, 19 Beacon Street, Yarmouth, Nova Scotia. Founded 1945. Reformed Baptist Church. Programs: Ministerial (3-yr. diploma), Missionary (3-yr. diploma), Christian Worker (cert.), Music (cert.). Correspondence school. High School. Business department. Enrollment in Bible College, 13. Tuition fees for 36-week school year, $134. Board and room, $284. Some work opportunities. Write to Registrar for information.

BETHANY BIBLE INSTITUTE, Hepburn, Saskatchewan. Founded 1927. Mennonite Brethren. Three-year diploma courses in General Bible, Christian Education and Sacred Music. Enrollment, 146. Tuition free. Incidental fees, $24 for 24-week school year. Write to Principal for information.

BETHANY BIBLE TRAINING SCHOOL, 3435 Van Buren Street, Chicago, Ill. For information on curricula and admissions, write to Principal.

BETHANY FELLOWSHIP BIBLE AND MISSIONARY TRAINING INSTITUTE, 6820 Auto Club Road, Minneapolis 20, Minn. Founded 1948. Independent. Three-year Bible-Theology course for missionary preparation (diploma). Twenty-nine week school year and summer work program. Enrollment, 90.

BETHEL BIBLE INSTITUTE, R. R. 1, King Road, Abbotsford, British Columbia. Founded 1939. Mennonite (General Conference). Bible Diploma Course with minors in Youth Work and Sunday School. Evening school. Day school enrollment, 50. Tuition fees, $220 for 26-week school year. Some work opportunities. Write to Office of Principal for information.

BETHEL BIBLE INSTITUTE, 806 Avenue "A" North, Saskatoon, Saskatchewan. Founded 1935. Pentecostal Assemblies of Canada. Standard Theological course (three years), Christian education (two years). Modest fees.

BEULAH HEIGHTS BIBLE INSTITUTE, 892 Berne Street, S. E., Atlanta 16, Ga. Founded 1918. International Pentecostal Assemblies. Three-year diploma course.

BIBLE BAPTIST SEMINARY, 3001 W. Division, Arlington, Tex. Founded 1939. World Baptist Fellowship. Undergraduate and graduate theological programs.

BIBLE CHRISTIAN TRAINING INSTITUTE, 1001 E. 35th Street, Brooklyn 10, N. Y. Founded 1939. Non-denominational. For information on curricula and admissions, write to Principal.

THE BIBLE INSTITUTE OF LOS ANGELES, BIOLA COLLEGE, 13800 Biola Avenue, La Mirada, Calif. Founded 1908. Interdenominational. Accredited by The Accrediting Association of Bible Colleges and Western College Association. Programs: majors in Bible, Christian Education, Church Music, and liberal arts leading to AB; three-year Bible institute course (diploma); School of Missionary Medicine (one year); Talbot Theological Seminary. Evening and correspondence schools. College and Institute enrollment, 808. Tuition fees for regular school year, $626. Board and room, $640. Good work opportunities. Write to Office of Admissions for information.

BIBLE INSTITUTE OF MONTREAL, INC., (French Bible Institute), Box 850, Huntingdon, Province of Quebec. Founded 1950. Interdenominational. Diploma courses: 3-year and 4-year Bible Courses (taught in French). Certificate courses: High School Preparatory (for French-speaking students); concentrated French language courses and summer school (for English-speaking students). Tuition fees, $40 for 36-week school year plus 7 hours gratis work weekly (or $200 per year without work). Board and room, $432. A few work opportunities. Write Registrar for further information.

BIBLE INSTITUTE OF NEW ENGLAND, Hartford, Vt. Founded 1958. Independent (subsidiary of Northeastern Gospel Crusade). General Bible Courses with missionary emphasis (diploma). Evening school. Day school enrollment, 20. Tuition free. Registration fee for 34-week school year, $20. Board and room, $408. Some work opportunities. Write to Office of Registrar for information.

BIBLE MISSIONARY INSTITUTE, 3500 Blackhawk Road, Rock Island, Ill. Founded 1958. Bible Missionary Church.

Programs: Theological (diploma), Christian Worker's Course (diploma), Music-Evangelism (diploma). Enrollment, 77. Tuition fees, $250 for 36-week school year. Good work opportunities. Write to Registrar for information.

BIBLE SCHOOL OF THE ONTARIO CONFERENCE OF MENNONITE BRETHREN CHURCHES, 19 Ottawa Street, North Kitchener, Ontario. Founded 1944. General Bible Course with courses in Theology, Christian Education, Music, Missions, Languages (diploma, ETTA diploma and cert.). Enrollment, 22. Tuition fees for 30-week school year, $92. Limited work opportunities. Some scholarships. Write to Office of Principal for information.

BIBLE STANDARD COLLEGE, 1231 Olive Street, Eugene, Oreg. Founded 1925. Open Bible Standard Churches. Programs: Standard Bible (diploma), Sacred Music (diploma), Junior College (diploma). Enrollment, 115. Tuition fees, $270 for 36-week school year. Good work opportunities. Scholarships for outstanding proficiency in music. Write to Registrar for information.

BIBLE TRAINING INSTITUTE, 506 Gulley Street, Goldsboro, N. C. Founded 1944. United Holy Church of America. Programs: Christian Education (diploma), Missionary (ThB), Ministerial (ThB). Enrollment, 40. Tuition fees, $150 for 28-week school year. Write President for information.

BOISE BIBLE COLLEGE, 1723 Eastman Street, Boise, Idaho. First Church of Christ. Programs: Ministerial (AB and BSL). Enrollment, 29. Tuition fees, $75 for 36-week school year. Good work opportunities. Direct inquiries to Registrar.

BRIERCREST BIBLE INSTITUTE, Caronport, Saskatchewan. Founded 1935. Interdenominational. Member of ETTA. Programs: Pastoral (diploma), Christian Educa-

tion (diploma), Music (diploma), Missions (diploma).
High school division. Enrollment, 324. Tuition fees, $340
for 26-week school year. Write to Director of Admissions
for information.

BRITISH COLUMBIA BIBLE INSTITUTE, 3451 St. Marys
Avenue, North Vancouver, British Columbia. Founded
1941. Pentecostal. Three-year Ministerial, Christian Education, and Music programs. Enrollment, 87. Tuition fees,
$125 for 26-week school year. Board, $286. Work opportunities fair. Admission: Approved Christian character,
agreement with school rules and objectives, high school
graduation preferred. Direct inquiries to Registrar.

BROCKVILLE BIBLE COLLEGE, 243 Perth Street, Brockville, Ontario. Founded 1918. Standard Church of
America. For information on curricula and admissions,
write to Principal.

BUFFALO BIBLE INSTITUTE, 910 Union Road, Buffalo
24, N. Y. Founded 1938. Interdenominational. Programs:
General Bible (diploma), Pastoral Theology (cert.), Missionary (cert.), Christian Education (cert.), and ETTA
(cert.). Evening school and summer school. Day school enrollment, 67. Tuition fees, $235 for 37-week school year.
Good work opportunities. Address inquiries to President.

CALIFORNIA BIBLE INSTITUTE, 5570 Castro Road, El
Sobrante, Calif. Founded 1957. Free Will Baptist. Bible
major (diploma). Evening school. Day school enrollment,
31. Tuition fees for 36-week school year, $150. Good work
opportunities.

CALIFORNIA LUTHERAN BIBLE SCHOOL, 1345 South
Burlington, Los Angeles 6, Calif. Founded 1951. Independent, Lutheran. Two-year programs: General Bible, parish
workers, institutional workers.

CALVARY BIBLE COLLEGE, 402 Carroll Street, Sunnyvale, Calif. Founded 1949. Non-denominational. Day and evenings schools. Diploma and degree (BRE, ThB) programs.

CALVARY BIBLE COLLEGE, 75th and State Line Road, P. O. Box 8426, Kansas City 14, Mo. Independent. Accredited by The Accrediting Association of Bible Colleges. Courses: Pastors (AB, BS, ThB), Missions (AB, BS), Christian Education (AB, BRE, BS), Music (BSM, BS), Christian Workers (BS), Secretarial Science (BS). Evening schools in Kansas City and St. Louis. Day school enrollment, 250. Tuition fees for 36-week school year, $490. Address inquiries to Registrar.

CANADIAN BIBLE COLLEGE, 4400 Fourth Avenue, Regina, Saskatchewan. Founded 1941. The Christian and Missionary Alliance. Accredited by The Accrediting Association of Bible Colleges. Programs: Bible and Theology (BRE, diploma), Bible and Missions (BRE, diploma), Christian Education (BRE, diploma), Music and Christian Education (BRE, diploma), Bible and Missionary Nursing (BRE), Theological (ThB), and Missionary (ThB). Summer school. Enrollment, 114. Tuition fees for 33-week school year, $189. Board and room, $360. Some work opportunities. Limited scholarships available to upper classmen. Write to President for information.

CANADIAN LUTHERAN BIBLE INSTITUTE, Box 400, Camrose, Alberta. Founded 1932. Lutheran. Two-year courses.

CANADIAN MENNONITE BIBLE COLLEGE, 600 University Boulevard, Tuxedo, Winnipeg 9, Manitoba. Founded 1947. Conference of Mennonites in Canada. Programs: Bachelor of Christian Education, Bachelor of Theology, Sacred Music (diploma). Evening division. Day school enrollment, 100. Tuition fees, $207 for 36-week school year. Board and room, $450. Good work opportunities.

CANADIAN NAZARENE COLLEGE, 259 Church Avenue, Winnipeg 4, Manitoba. Founded 1921. Church of the Nazarene. Programs: Theology (ThB), English Bible (diploma), Music (BSM). Enrollment, 42. Tuition fees, $260 for 28-week school year. Board and room, $336. Good work opportunities. Some scholarships. Write to Registrar for information.

CANADIAN NORTHWEST BIBLE INSTITUTE, 10047 108th Street, Edmonton, Alberta. For information on curricula and admissions, write to Principal.

CARVER BIBLE INSTITUTE, 65 Haynes Street, S.W., Atlanta, Ga. For information on curricula and admissions, write to Principal.

CENTRAL BAPTIST COLLEGE, Box 791, Conway, Arkansas. Missionary Baptist. Bible major with minor in English or History (AB), Religious Education (BSRE). Junior college. Enrollment, 124. Tuition fees for 36-week school year, $150. Some work opportunities and scholarships. Write to Office of President.

CENTRAL BAPTIST SEMINARY, 225 St. George Street, Toronto 5, Ontario. Founded 1949. Evangelical Baptist. Programs: English Bible (2-yr. and 3-yr. diploma), full high school not required; undergraduate degrees in Theology: LTh, BRE—admission Grade XII; ThB—admission Ontario Grade XII general course or equivalent; graduate degrees: BD, MRE, MTh—Admission BA or equivalent college standing. Enrollment, 102. Tuition fees for 31½ weeks, $107.50. Board and room, $441. Good work opportunities.

CENTRAL BIBLE INSTITUTE, 3000 N. Grant Avenue, Springfield, Mo. Founded 1922. Assemblies of God. Accredited by The Accrediting Association of Bible Colleges. Programs: 3-year diploma and AB courses in Bible, Religious Education, Missions, and Music. Summer school.

Graduate school. Enrollment, 482. Tuition fees for 36-week school year, $502. Some work opportunities. Direct inquiries to Registrar.

CENTRAL CHRISTIAN COLLEGE OF THE BIBLE, 405 N. Ault Street, Moberly, Mo. Founded 1957. Non-denominational. Programs: Ministerial (ThB, AB, BSL), Christian Education (BCE). Evening school. Day school enrollment, 50. Tuition fees for 36-week school year, $212. Some work opportunities. Write to Dean for information.

CENTRAL PILGRIM COLLEGE, Bartlesville, Okla. Founded 1910. Pilgrim Holiness Church. Programs: Bachelor of Theology, Bachelor of Arts, Ministerial (3-yr. and 4-yr. diploma), Christian Workers (3-yr. diploma). Evening school, high school, junior college (AA). Enrollment, 145. Tuition fees for 36-week school year, $268. Excellent work opportunities. Some scholarships available. Write to Director of Admissions for information.

CENTRAL WASHINGTON SCHOOL OF THE BIBLE, P. O. Box 427, Selah, Washington. Founded 1948. Independent. Ministerial program (BMA, BSL), Church Workers' Certificate.

CENTRAL WESLEYAN COLLEGE, Division of Religion, Central, S. C. Founded 1906. Wesleyan Methodist. Accredited by The Accrediting Association of Bible Colleges. Programs: Bible and Theology majors (AB). Junior college, liberal arts college, and summer school. Enrollment, 26 (total 238). Total costs for 36-week school year, $896. Some work opportunities. Some scholarships available to upper 10 percent of graduating classes. Request information from Public Relations Office.

CHICAGO BIBLE COLLEGE, 6007 N. Sheridan Road, Chicago 40, Ill. Founded 1950. Non-denominational. Programs: Ministerial (3-yr. diploma), Theology (ThB), Missions (ThB), Christian Education (BRE). Enrollment,

35. Tuition fees 36-week school year, $217. Good work opportunities. Address Registrar for information.

CHRIST COLLEGE AND SEMINARY, "Wildwood", Vaudreuil, Province of Quebec. Founded 1959 in New York. Opening of day school in Quebec, 1962. Bible college program (diploma). Evening school. Tuition, $200. Good work opportunities. Write to Office of Dean for information.

THE CHRISTIAN TRAINING INSTITUTE, 10810 78th Avenue, Edmonton, Alberta. Founded 1940. North American Baptist. Bible College (ThB). Bible School (ETTA diploma). Offers Grade 12 and first year university. Enrollment, 80. Tuition fees vary from $66.50 to $179.50. Good work opportunities.

CHURCH OF CHRIST BIBLE INSTITUTE, 112 East 125th Street, New York 35, N.Y. Founded 1929. Non-denominational. Day Bible institute and evening divisions.

CHURCHES OF CHRIST SCHOOL OF EVANGELISTS, 550 N. E. 76th Avenue, Portland, Oreg. Founded 1952. Independent. Four- and five-year programs.

THE CINCINNATI BIBLE SEMINARY, Bible College Division, 2700 Glenway Avenue, Cincinnati 4, Ohio. Founded 1924. Church of Christ (Christian). Programs: Ministerial (AB, ThB, BSL), Music (5-yr. BSM), 3-year certificates in English Bible, Minister's Assistant, and Church Music. Evening school, summer school, graduate school. Day school enrollment, 382. Tuition fees for 35-week school year, $267. Good work opportunities. Write to Registrar for information.

CIRCLEVILLE BIBLE COLLEGE, 459 E. Ohio Street, Circleville, Ohio. Founded 1948. Churches of Christ in Christian Union. Programs: General Christian Workers (BSL), Ministerial (ThB), Bible Training Course (2-yr.

cert.). Correspondence school and summer school. Enrollment, 59. Tuition fees for 36-week school year, $270. Some work opportunities. Write to Registrar for information.

CLEAR CREEK BAPTIST SCHOOL, Pineville, Ky. Founded 1926. Bible institute program. For information, write to Principal.

COALDALE BIBLE SCHOOL, Box 331, Coaldale, Alberta. Founded 1929. Mennonite Brethren. Bible institute program. For information, write to Principal.

COLLEGE OF THE ROCKIES, 4700 Kendrick Street, Golden, Colo. Founded 1951. Interdenominational. Programs: Pre-Seminary (AB), Ministerial (AB, ThB), Christian Education (BRE), Nurses (BS), Christian Workers (3-yr. diploma), ETTA. Enrollment, 25. Tuition fees for 36-week school year, $210. Good work opportunities. Limited scholarships. Write to Department of Admissions.

COLLEGE OF THE SCRIPTURES, 4601 Shepherdsville Road, P. O. Box 217, Louisville, 18, Ky. Founded 1945. Christian. Five-year program. For information, write to Principal.

COLUMBIA BIBLE COLLEGE, Monticello Road, Columbia, S. C. Founded 1923. Interdenominational. Accredited by The Accrediting Association of Bible Colleges. Programs leading to BABE and BBE. Graduate School of Missions (MABE and BD). Enrollment, 469. Tuition fees, $110 for 34-week school year. Good work opportunities. Address inquiries to Director of Admissions.

COOK CHRISTIAN (INDIAN) TRAINING SCHOOL, P. O. Box 7158, Phoenix 11, Ariz. Founded 1940. Interdenominational. Programs: Church Worker (diploma), Junior College (diploma), Christian Education (1-yr. cert.). Evening school. Day school enrollment, 38. Total cost for 38-week school year, $650. Tuition and work scholarships available as needed. Write to Director of Admissions for information.

COVENANT BIBLE INSTITUTE, 245 21st Street East, Prince Albert, Saskatchewan. Founded 1941. Evangelical Covenant Church of Canada. Programs: General Bible (diploma), Christian Education (diploma). Enrollment, 25. Tuition fees for 28-week school year, $275. Limited work opportunities. Address inquiries to President.

DAKOTA BIBLE COLLEGE, P. O. Box 1381, Huron, S. Dak. Founded 1942. Church of Christ. Programs: Ministerial (AB, ThB), Christian Education (BSL). Enrollment, 10. Tuition fees for 36-week school year, $100. Limited work opportunities.

DALLAS BIBLE INSTITUTE AND BIBLE COLLEGE, 3608 Swiss Avenue, Dallas 4, Tex. Founded 1945. Non-denominational. AB in Biblical Education with minors in Greek, Music, Writing. Bible Institute diploma. Evening and correspondence schools. Day school enrollment, 94. Tuition fees for 36-week school year, $251. Good work opportunities. Write to Office of Registrar for information.

DALLAS CHRISTIAN COLLEGE, Carroll at San Jacinto, Dallas 6, Tex. Founded 1950. Christian Church. Programs: Ministerial (AB, ThB, BSL), Christian Education (BRE), Music (BSM). Evening school. Day school enrollment, 65. Tuition fees for 36-week school year, $188. Good work opportunities. One-half tuition scholarships available to children of ministers and missionaries, and wives of students. Write to Office of President for information.

DECATUR BIBLE INSTITUTE, P. O. Box 281, Decatur, Ill. For information on curricula and admissions, write to Principal.

DETROIT BIBLE COLLEGE, 17370 Meyers Road, Detroit 35, Mich. Founded 1945. Interdenominational. Accredited by The Accrediting Association of Bible Colleges. Programs: 3-year diploma courses in General Bible, Missions, Christian Education, and Music-Christian Education; Music-Christian Education (BRE), Bible-Theology (ThB). Enrollment, 225. Tuition fees for 36-week school year, $250. Good work opportunities. Address inquiries to Director of Admissions.

EASTERN BIBLE INSTITUTE, Maranatha Park, Green Lane, Pa. Founded 1938. Assemblies of God. Associate member of The Accrediting Association of Bible Colleges. Programs: Ministerial (diploma), Missionary (diploma), Christian Education (diploma). Evening school and summer school. Day school enrollment, 185. Tuition fees for 36-week school year, $215. Some work opportunities. Write to Director of Admissions for information.

EASTERN CHRISTIAN COLLEGE, P. O. Box 223, Bel Air, Md. Founded 1946. Churches of Christ. Ministerial programs. Modest fees. Write to the Office of President for information.

EASTERN PENTECOSTAL BIBLE COLLEGE, Argyle and Sunnyside Streets, Peterborough, Ontario. Founded 1939. Pentecostal. Ministerial Course (diploma). Enrollment, 125. Tuition, board and room for 34-week school year, $495. Good work opportunities. Write to Registrar for information.

EASTERN PILGRIM COLLEGE, 1412-20 E. Cedar Street, Allentown, Pa. Founded 1921. Pilgrim Holiness Church. Accredited by The Accrediting Association of Bible Colleges. Programs: Ministerial (diploma, BS), Christian Education (BS, BRE), Christian Workers (diploma). Correspondence school, summer school, high school, junior college. Total enrollment, 210. Tuition fees for 36-week school year, $560. Good work opportunities. Write to Office of President for information.

ELIM BIBLE INSTITUTE, Lima, N. Y. Founded 1924. Elim Missionary Assemblies. Programs: Ministerial (diploma), Missionary (diploma), Christian Education (diploma). Enrollment, 65. Tuition fees for 34-week school year, $210. Good work opportunities. Write to Registrar for information.

ELIM BIBLE SCHOOL, P. O. Box 387, Altona, Manitoba. Founded 1936. Mennonite. Three-year General Bible Course (diploma). Member of Evangelical Teacher Training Association.

EMMANUEL BIBLE COLLEGE, 20 Ahrens Street East, Kitchener, Ontario. Founded 1940. United Missionary Church. Programs: Ministerial (ThB, diploma), Missions (diploma), Christian Education (diploma). Evening school. Day school enrollment, 28. Tuition fees, $160 for 30-week school year. Board and room, $360. Good work opportunities. Some scholarships for returning students. Address inquiries to Registrar.

EMMAUS BIBLE SCHOOL, 156 N. Oak Park Avenue, Oak Park, Ill. Plymouth Brethren. Associate member of The Accrediting Association of Bible Colleges. Programs: Missionary (3-yr. diploma), Christian Education (3-yr. diploma), General Bible (3-yr. diploma), Bible Language (3-yr. diploma). One-year course (cert.). Evening school and correspondence school. Day school enrollment, 108. Tuition free. Incidental fees, $50 for 36-week school year. Write to Registrar for information.

FORT WAYNE BIBLE COLLEGE, 800 W. Rudisill Boulevard, Fort Wayne 6, Ind. Founded 1904. Missionary Church Association. Accredited by The Accrediting Association of Bible Colleges and Indiana Department of Public Instruction. Programs: Standard Bible (diploma), Bible and Theology (AB, ThB), Pastoral Training (AB, ThB), Missions (AB, BS), Missionary Nursing (BS), Christian Education (AB, BRE), Social Science (AB), Elementary Education (BS), Music Education (BS), Christian Education and Music (BS), Speech (BS), Music Education (BME), Sacred Music (BSM). Correspondence school. Day school enrollment, 379. Tuition fees for 36-week school year, $592. Room and board, $530. Good work opportunities. Write to Registrar for information.

FRANKFORT PILGRIM COLLEGE, Frankfort, Ind. Founded 1927. Pilgrim Holiness Church. Programs: Religion (AB), Theology (ThB), Ministerial (3-yr. diploma), Christian Workers (2-yr. diploma). Evening school, high school. Day school enrollment 178. Tuition fees for 36-week school year, $336. Write to Director of Admissions for information.

FREE WILL BAPTIST BIBLE COLLEGE, 3606 W. End Avenue, Nashville 5, Tenn. Founded 1942. Free Will Baptist. Accredited by The Accrediting Association of Bible Colleges. Programs: English Bible (AB), Missionary Nursing (BS), Business Education (cert.). Summer school. Enrollment, 259. Tuition fees for 35-week school year, $280. Good work opportunities. Address inquiries to Registrar.

FRIENDS BIBLE COLLEGE, Haviland, Kans. Founded 1917. Friends. Associate member of The Accrediting Association of Bible Colleges. Programs: Bible Training Course (diploma), Christian Workers (cert.). High school. Enrollment, 101. Tuition fees for 38-week school year, $350. Some work and scholarship opportunities. Address inquiries to Office of Admissions.

FRUITLAND BAPTIST BIBLE INSTITUTE, Box 1120, Hendersonville, N. C. Founded 1946. Baptist. Programs: Ministerial (diploma), Christian Education (diploma). Enrollment, 173. Tuition fees for 24-week school year, $50. Board and room, $284. Some work opportunities. Admissions: Christian character, church approval, Christian commitment, agreement with school's objectives. Write to Director for information and catalog.

FULL GOSPEL BIBLE INSTITUTE, Eston, Saskatchewan. Founded 1944. Apostolic Church of Pentecost. Three-year course. Write to Registrar for information.

FUNDAMENTAL BIBLE INSTITUTE, 205 N. Union Avenue, Los Angeles 26, Calif. Founded 1939. American Council of Christian Churches. General Bible (3-yr. diploma), Pastoral and Missionary (4-yr. diploma). Enrollment, 18. Tuition free. Registration fee, $10. Forty-week school year.

GLEN COVE BIBLE SCHOOL, Glen Cove, Maine. Founded 1959. Non-denominational. Division of Christian Schools, Inc., which also conducts a Christian high school and an elementary school.

GOD'S BIBLE SCHOOL AND COLLEGE, 1810 Young Street, Cincinnati 10, Ohio. Founded 1900. Interdenominational. Programs: Ministerial (ThB), Christian Workers (2-yr. diploma). Correspondence school, high school, liberal arts college. Enrollment in Bible college 103. Tuition fees for 36-week school year, $220. Good work opportunities. Address inquiries to Office of Admissions.

GRACE BIBLE COLLEGE, 1011 Aldon Street, S. W., Grand Rapids 9, Mich. Founded 1945. Grace Fellowship. Programs: Ministerial (ThB, BRE), Christian Education (BRE), Christian Education-Music (BRE), Two-year Layman's Course (diploma). Enrollment, 72. Tuition and fees for 36-week school year, approximately $300. Board and room, $670. Fair work opportunities. Admission: High school graduate, Christian character, willingness to conform to school standards. Write Registrar for information.

GRACE BIBLE INSTITUTE, 1515 South Tenth Street, Omaha 8, Nebr. Founded 1943. Inter-Mennonite. Accredited by The Accrediting Association of Bible Colleges.

Programs: General Bible (3-yr. diploma), Christian Education (BRE, AB), Pastoral Ministries (AB), Missions (AB), Psychology and Philosophy (AB), Music (BSM). Evening school. Day school enrollment, 377. Tuition fees for 36-week school year, $342. Room and board, $475. Good work opportunities. Write to Director of Admissions for information.

GRAHAM BIBLE COLLEGE, 214 Seventh Street, Bristol, Tenn. Founded 1951. Interdenominational. Programs: Christian Teachers Course (diploma), General Bible (cert., AB), Missions (AB). Evening school. Day school enrollment 10. Tuition fees for 36-week school year, $150. Board and room, $385. Direct inquiries to Office of the President.

GRAND RAPIDS BAPTIST THEOLOGICAL SEMINARY AND BIBLE INSTITUTE, 811 Wealthy Street, S. E., Grand Rapids 6, Mich. Founded 1941. General Association of Regular Baptists. Diploma programs: General or Pastor's Course, Missions, Christian Education, Music, Pre-Seminary. Evening school. Seminary. Day school enrollment in Bible Institute, 221. Tuition fees for 36-week school year, $270. Good work opportunities. Write to Office of the Registrar for information.

THE GRAND RAPIDS SCHOOL OF THE BIBLE AND MUSIC, 110 Crescent Street N.E., Grand Rapids, Mich. Founded 1946. Three-year programs leading to diploma in Missions, Music, Christian Education, Church Secretary, and General Bible; Pastor's Course (3- and 5-yr. diploma), Pastor-Music Course (4-yr. diploma). Evening division. Day school enrollment, 209. Tuition fees for 36-week school year, $125. Good work opportunities. Write to Registrar for information.

GREAT LAKES BIBLE COLLEGE, 106 E. North Street, Lansing 5, Mich. Founded 1949. Church of Christ (Christian). Programs: Christian Education (BRE), Ministerial

(ThB), Church Secretarial (cert.), Bible (cert.). Enrollment, 90. Tuition fees for 36-week school year, $250. Good
work opportunities.

GRUNDY BIBLE INSTITUTE, Grundy, Va.

GULF COAST BIBLE COLLEGE, 1001 W. 11th Street,
Houston 8, Tex. Founded 1953. Church of God (Anderson, Ind.). Curricula: Christian Education (cert.), Ministerial (3-yr. diploma, ThB). Junior college (AA) and
liberal arts (AB) divisions. Enrollment, 110. Tuition fees
for 36-week school year, $142. Good work opportunities.
Write to Registrar for information.

HILLCREST CHRISTIAN COLLEGE, Medicine Hat, Alberta. Founded 1939. Evangelical United Brethren. Bible
Course (diploma). High school (general diploma and
senior matriculation). Tuition fees for 24-week school year
in Bible school, $85. High school fees for 10-month school
year, $197. Some work opportunities. Write to Registrar
for information.

HOLINESS METHODIST SCHOOL OF THEOLOGY, 2111
29th Avenue N., Minneapolis 11, Minn. Founded 1914.
Holiness Methodist Church. Programs: Theological (ThB,
BSL), Missions (ThB, BSL), Bible Certificate (2 years).
Enrollment, 27. Modest fees for tuition, board and room.

IMMANUEL COLLEGE, 644 Memorial Drive, S.E., Atlanta
12, Ga. Founded 1953. Baptist. Programs: Institute (ThG),
Theology (AB, ThB), Religious Education (BRE). Evening, correspondence, high school, seminary divisions.
Summer school. Day school enrollment, 13. Tuition fees
for 36-week school year, $155. Good work opportunities,
limited scholarships. Write to Registrar for information.

INTERMOUNTAIN BIBLE COLLEGE, 1420 N. 12th,
Grand Junction, Colo. Founded 1946. Churches of Christ
(Independent). Programs: Ministerial (AB, BSL), Re-

ligious Education (BCE), Nursing (correlated with Mesa College) leading to RN. Enrollment, 15. Tuition fees for 34-week school year, $200. Good work opportunities. Some scholarships.

INTERNATIONAL BIBLE COLLEGE, Box 1480, Estevan, Saskatchewan. Founded 1936. Church of God (Cleveland, Tenn.). Three-year program. For information, write to Registrar.

INTERNATIONAL BIBLE COLLEGE, 2369 Benrus Boulevard, San Antonio 1, Tex. Founded 1945. Independent. Four-year program. For information, write to Principal.

JOHNSON BIBLE COLLEGE, Kimberlin Heights, Tenn. Founded 1893. Christian Church. Programs: Ministerial (AB, BSL), Sacred Music (BSM). Enrollment 189. Tuition fees for 36-week school year, $270. Board and room, $500. Good work opportunities. Tuition scholarships available to needy students. Address inquiries to Office of President.

JOHN WESLEY COLLEGE, 1906 Boulevard Street, Greensboro, N. C. Founded 1932. Programs leading to AB and ThB degrees.

KANSAS CITY COLLEGE AND BIBLE SCHOOL, 7401 Metcalf, Overland Park, Kans. Founded 1938. Church of God (Holiness). Five-year theological program. For information, write to Dean of Admissions.

KENTUCKY CHRISTIAN COLLEGE, Grayson, Ky. Founded 1919. Church of Christ (Christian). Associate member of The Accrediting Association of Bible Colleges. Ministerial Course (AB). Enrollment, 154. Total cost for 36-week school year, $640. Limited work opportunities. Write to Office of President for information.

KENTUCKY MOUNTAIN BIBLE INSTITUTE, Vancleve, Breathitt County, Ky. Founded 1931. Interdenominational. Three-year diploma. Curricula: Ministerial, Chris-

tian Education, Missionary. Enrollment, 110. Tuition fees
for 36-week school year, $170-$190. Board and room, $306.
Some work opportunities. Write to Office of Dean for
information.

KINGSTON BIBLE COLLEGE AND ACADEMY, Box 154,
Kingston, Nova Scotia. Founded 1930. International
Christian Mission, Inc. Programs: Two-, three-, and four-
year programs in the Sacred Scriptures; Christian Education. Correspondence school.

KING'S MISSIONARY TRAINING INSTITUTE, King's
Garden, Seattle 33, Wash. Founded 1955. Interdenominational. Bible School (3-yr. diploma), Missionary Orientation (1-yr. diploma). Evening school. Day school
enrollment, 8. Tuition fees for 36-week school year, $150-
$250. Some work opportunities. Write to Office of the
Registrar for information.

LANCASTER SCHOOL OF THE BIBLE, 835 Bluegrass
Road, Lancaster, Pa. Founded 1933. Interdenominational.
Associate member of The Accrediting Association of Bible
Colleges. Programs: Bible-Missions (4-yr. diploma) , Bible-
Christian Education (3-yr. diploma), Bible-Pastoral (3-yr.
diploma). Evening school. Day school enrollment, 103.
Tuition fees for 34-week school year, $350. Good work
opportunities. Write to Dean for information.

LEE COLLEGE, Bible College, Cleveland, Tenn. Founded
1918. Church of God. Accredited by The Accrediting Association of Bible Colleges. Biblical Education (AB),
Christian Education (AB). High school, junior college,
correspondence school. Day school enrollment in Bible
College, 207. Tuition fees for 36-week school year, $374.
Board and room, $410. Some work opportunities. Write
to Registrar for information.

LEXINGTON BAPTIST COLLEGE, 163 N. Ashland
Avenue, Lexington, Ky. Founded 1950. Baptist. General
Bible Course (3-yr. diploma), Bachelor of Arts.

L.I.F.E. BIBLE COLLEGE, INC., 1100 Glendale Boulevard, Los Angeles 26, Calif. Founded 1925. International Church of the Foursquare Gospel. Programs: Ministerial (ThB, diploma), Christian Education (BRE). Evening school, correspondence school. Day school enrollment, 250. Tuition fees for 36-week school year, $368. Good work opportunities. Write to Office of Admissions for information.

LINCOLN CHRISTIAN COLLEGE, Box 178, Lincoln, Ill. Founded 1944. Christian Church. Accredited by The Accrediting Association of Bible Colleges. Programs leading to AB in Ministerial Science, Missions, Sacred Music, Secretarial Science, Christian Education. Graduate school, evening school, summer school. Day school enrollment, 402. Tuition fees for 36-week school year, $222. Good work opportunities. Qualified applicants who are members of a recommended Christian Church (Church of Christ) are eligible to a $130 scholarship. Write to Registrar for information.

LINDA VISTA BAPTIST BIBLE COLLEGE AND SEMINARY, 6940 Linda Vista Road, San Diego 11, Calif. Founded 1946. Baptist. Programs: Majors in Bible, Christian Education, Education, and Library Science leading to AB. Seminary, summer school. Day school enrollment in Bible College, 45. Tuition fees for 36-week school year, $324. Good work opportunities. Inquiries about scholarships invited. Write to Registrar for information.

LIVING WORD BIBLE INSTITUTE, Box 278, Swan River, Manitoba. Founded 1952. Christians of Evangelical Faith of Canada. Bible institute program.

LONDON COLLEGE OF BIBLE AND MISSIONS, 518 Queen's Avenue, London, Ontario. Founded 1935. Interdenominational. Accredited by The Accrediting Association of Bible Colleges. Programs: Ministerial (ThB), Missionary (ThB), Christian Education (BRE), Christian

Education and Music (BRE), Christian Education and Missions (BRE, honours), Pre-Seminary (BRE), General Bible (3-yr. diploma). Enrollment, 91. Tuition fees for 32-week school year, $150. Good work opportunities. Write to Registrar for information.

THE LOUISVILLE BIBLE COLLEGE, 1707 S. Third Street, Louisville, Ky. Christian Church. Ministerial Training (AB, BSL, MA). Enrollment, 40. Tuition fees for 33-week school year, approximately $200. Good work opportunities.

THE LUTHERAN BIBLE INSTITUTE, 6125 Olson Highway, Minneapolis 22, Minn. Founded 1919. Independent, Lutheran. Courses: General Bible (diploma), Parish and Institutional Worker (diploma), Laymen (diploma), Christian World Service (diploma). Evening, correspondence, and summer schools. Day school enrollment, 243. Tuition fees for 31-week school year, $225. Board and room, $635.50. Excellent work opportunities. Write to Office of the President for information.

LUTHERAN BIBLE INSTITUTE IN SEATTLE, 13016 Greenwood Avenue N., Seattle 33, Wash. Founded 1944. Lutheran Church. General Bible Course (diploma), Parish Workers Course (diploma). Evening school, correspondence school, summer school. Day school enrollment, 103. Tuition fees for 30-week school year, $225. A few scholarships and grants available to needy and worthy students. Write to Office of President for information.

THE LUTHERAN BIBLE INSTITUTE OF AMERICA, Pomander Walk, Teaneck, N. J. Founded 1948. Lutheran. Programs: General Bible (diploma), Parish Workers' Training Program (diploma), Christian Day School Teacher Training (diploma). Evening School. Day school enrollment, 55. Tuition fees for 36-week school year, $270. Good work opportunities. Full scholarships available to qualified overseas applicants. Some on basis of need. Write to Office of Admissions for information.

LUTHERAN BRETHREN SCHOOLS, Bible Department, Fergus Falls, Minn. Founded 1903. Church of the Lutheran Brethren. General Bible Course. High school, seminary. Enrollment, 38. Tuition costs for 34-week school year, $130. Some work opportunities. Write to Office of President for information.

LUTHERAN COLLEGIATE BIBLE INSTITUTE, Outlook Saskatchewan. Evangelical Lutheran Church. Two-year Bible institute program. High school.

LUTHERAN LAY TRAINING INSTITUTE, 3126 W. Kilbourn Avenue, Milwaukee 8, Wis. Founded 1961. Lutheran Church-Missouri Synod. Two-year terminal course to train laymen for work of church. Enrollment (first year), 22. Educational fees for 36-week school year, $220. Board and room, $445. Admission: 20 years of age (minimum), acceptable high school record, membership in Lutheran Church-Missouri Synod, recommendation of pastor, entrance tests.

MANAHATH EDUCATIONAL CENTER, 410 Fifth Street, Altoona, Pa. Evangelical Methodist. Programs in Bible (AB), Christian Education (BS), Missions (BS).

MANHATTAN BIBLE COLLEGE, 1407 Anderson Avenue, Manhattan, Kansas. Founded 1927. Disciples of Christ. Accredited by The Accrediting Association of Bible Colleges. Programs: Ministerial (AB), Christian Education (AB, BS), Sacred Music (AB). Enrollment, 81. Tuition fees for 36-week school year, $276. Limited work opportunities. Write to Registrar for information.

MARITIME CHRISTIAN COLLEGE, Box 383, 223 Kent Street, Charlottetown, Prince Edward Island. Founded 1960. Churches of Christ. Programs: Ministerial (5-yr. ThB; 3-yr. cert.), Church Secretarial (2-yr. cert.). Evening school. Day school enrollment, 5. Tuition fees for 35-week school year, $150. Some work scholarships. Direct inquiries to Office of President.

MEMPHIS CHRISTIAN COLLEGE, 3101 Knight Road, Memphis 8, Tenn. Founded 1959. Christian Churches. Ministerial program (AB). Enrollment, 22. Tuition fees for 36-week school year (three quarters), $156. Half-tuition scholarship available to freshmen. Write to the Office of the President for information.

MENNO BIBLE INSTITUTE, R. R. #2, Didsbury, Alberta. Founded 1937. Mennonite Conference of Alberta. Three-year general Bible course; Christian Education (ETTA diploma).

MENNONITE BRETHREN BIBLE COLLEGE, 77 Kelvin Street, Winnipeg 5, Manitoba. Founded 1944. Mennonite Brethren Church. Accredited by The Accrediting Association of Bible Colleges. Arts Division affiliated with Waterloo Lutheran University. Programs: Theology (ThB), Religious Education (BRE), Sacred Music (diploma). Enrollment, 145. Tuition fees for 36-week school year, $186.50. Board and room, $372. Some work opportunities. Write to Office of Registrar for information.

MENNONITE BRETHREN BIBLE INSTITUTE, Box 460, Clearbrook, British Columbia. Founded 1943. Mennonite Brethren Church. Courses: Standard Bible (diploma), Bible and Christian Education (diploma), Bible and Sacred Music (diploma). Enrollment, 90. Tuition fees for 32-week school year, $150. Limited work opportunities. Address the Principal for information.

MIAMI BIBLE INSTITUTE, 900 N. W. 30th Street, Miami 37, Fla. Founded 1952. Non-denominational. Three-year Bible Course (diploma), one-year Bible Course (cert.). Evening school. Day school enrollment, 51. Tuition fees for 36-week school year, $170. Good work opportunities. Write to Registrar for information.

MICHIGAN BAPTIST INSTITUTE, 2211 N. Center Road, Flint, Mich. Founded 1959. Baptist State Convention. Three-year program. For information, write to Principal.

MID-SOUTH BIBLE COLLEGE, 1271 Poplar Avenue, Memphis, Tenn. Founded 1949. Non-denominational. Four-year Bible College Course (AB), Three-year Bible Institute Course (diploma), One-year Basic Bible Course (cert.). Evening school. Day school enrollment, 50. Tuition fees for 36-week school year, $180. Board and room, $60 per month. Good work opportunities. Write to Registrar for information.

MIDWEST BAPTIST COLLEGE, 1632 Georgetown Road, Danville, Ill. Founded 1961. Baptist (independent). Programs: Ministerial (diploma), Christian Education (diploma), Music (diploma). Evening school. Day school enrollment, 42. Tuition fees for 32-week school year, $66. Admission: Approved character, high school graduation for diplomas; non-high school for certificates. Limited work opportunities. Write to Registrar for information.

MIDWEST CHRISTIAN COLLEGE, P. O. Box 9665, Oklahoma City, Okla. Founded 1946. Christian Church. Ministerial (AB, BSL), Christian Education (BCE), Music (BSM), one- and two-year certificate courses in Bible. Enrollment, 76. Tuition fees for 36-week school year, $250. Good work opportunities. Write to Office of President for information.

MIDWESTERN BAPTIST SCHOOLS, 825 Golf Drive, Pontiac, Mich. Founded 1954. Independent Baptist. Programs: Bible (AB), Christian Education (BRE). Evening school, graduate division, summer school. Day school enrollment, 110. Tuition fees for 36-week school year, $125. Good work opportunities. Write to Dean of Administration for information.

MIDWESTERN SCHOOL OF EVANGELISM, 908 North Court Street, Ottumwa, Iowa. Founded 1946. Church of Christ. Programs: Ministerial (BSL), Christian Education (cert.). Enrollment, 57. Tuition fees for 36-week school year, $113. Board and room, $390. Good work opportunities. Admissions: Acceptable high school record, Christian commitment, approved character, agreement with school's objectives. Write to Registrar for information.

**MILLAR MEMORIAL BIBLE INSTITUTE,** Pambrun, Saskatchewan. Founded 1933. Independent. Three-year program. Enrollment, 90.

**MINNESOTA BIBLE COLLEGE,** 1507 University Avenue S.E., Minneapolis 14, Minn. Founded 1913. Churches of Christ (Christian). Accredited by The Accrediting Association of Bible Colleges. Programs: Ministerial (ThB), Christian Teachers (BCE), Christian Service (BSL), Evangelists' and Ministers' Assistant of Music (cert.), Secretarial Arts (cert.). Enrollment, 180. Tuition fees for 36-weeks, $255. Good work opportunities. Scholarships for high school valedictorians and children of ministers and missionaries. Write to Registrar for information.

**MOKAHUM INDIAN BIBLE SCHOOL,** Route 2, Cass Lake, Minn. Founded 1948. Interdenominational. Christian Workers Course (diploma), Ministerial (diploma). Enrollment, 16. Tuition fees for 28 weeks, $316. Some work opportunities. Work scholarships available. Write to Principal for information.

**MONTANA INSTITUTE OF THE BIBLE,** Route 1, Box 156, Billings, Montana. Founded 1953. Interdenominational. Programs: Bible (diploma), Theology (diploma), Christian Education (ETTA cert.), Missions (diploma). Evenings and correspondence schools. Day school enrollment, 20-34. No tuition. All expenses, $450 for 34-week school year. Some work opportunities. Admission: Qualified high school graduate or equivalent, Christian, approved character, agreement with school objectives.

**MOODY BIBLE INSTITUTE,** 820 N. LaSalle Street, Chicago 10, Ill. Founded 1886. Interdenominational. Accredited by The Accrediting Association of Bible Colleges. Courses leading to diploma: General Bible, Missionary, Pastors,

Christian Education, Christian-Education-Music, Jewish Missions, Sacred Music, Missionary Technical. Evening, correspondence, and summer schools. Day school enrollment, 972. Tuition free. Board and room, $654 for 36-week school year. Incidental fees additional. Good work opportunities. Write to Dean of Education for information.

MOOSE JAW BIBLE COLLEGE, Box 460, Moose Jaw, Saskatchewan. Founded 1940. Free Methodist. Programs: Christian Worker's (1-yr., ETTA cert.), Bible (2-yr. diploma), Bible Music (2-yr. diploma), Theology (ThB). Evening school. Write to Office of President for information.

MOUNTAIN VIEW BIBLE COLLEGE, Didsbury, Alberta. Founded 1926. United Missionary Church. Programs: Pastors (BSL), Missionary (BSL), three-year diploma courses in Bible, Christian Education, Bible-Music. Enrollment, 61. Tuition fees for 26-week school year, $324. Limited work opportunities. Some scholarships. Write to Office of Admissions for information.

MT. ECHO BIBLE INSTITUTE, Great Valley, N. Y. Founded 1953. Interdenominational. Courses: Basic Bible (3-yr. diploma), General Bible (3-yr. diploma), Theological (4-yr. diploma), Missionary (4-yr. diploma), Christian Education (4-yr. diploma). Evening school. Day school enrollment, 9. Tuition, free. Good work opportunities. Write to Dean of Education for information.

MT. VERNON BIBLE COLLEGE, Route 5, Mt. Vernon, Ohio. Founded 1957. International Church of the Foursquare Gospel. Standard Ministerial Course (diploma). Evening school. Day school enrollment, 31. Tuition fees for 36-week school year, $166. Board and room, $550. Good work opportunities. Write to Registrar for information.

MULTNOMAH SCHOOL OF THE BIBLE, 8435 N. E. Glisan Street, Portland 20, Oreg. Interdenominational.

Accredited by The Accrediting Association of Bible Colleges. Diploma Bible Course, Degree Bible Course (ThB), Certificate Bible Course. Evening school. Day school enrollment, 401. Tuition fees for 36-week school year, $265. Good work opportunities. Write to Registrar for information.

NAVAJO BIBLE SCHOOL, Window Rock, Ariz. For information on curricula and admissions, write to Director.

NEBRASKA CHRISTIAN COLLEGE, 910 Park Avenue, Norfolk, Nebr. Founded 1945. Christian Church (Church of Christ). Programs: Ministerial (AB, BSL, ThB), Christian Education (BCE), Sacred Music (BSM); certificates for two-year courses in Church Music, Church Secretarial, English Bible. Enrollment, 89. Good work opportunities.

NEW BRUNSWICK BIBLE INSTITUTE, Victoria, Carleton County, New Brunswick. Founded 1944. Interdenominational. Bible Course (diploma). Enrollment, 75. Fees for 31-week school year, $310. Write to Principal for information.

NEW TRIBES BIBLE INSTITUTE, 618 North 20th Street, Milwaukee 3, Wis. Founded 1955. Independent. Three-semester program of special preparation for missionaries.

NIPAWIN BIBLE INSTITUTE, Box 1330, Nipawin, Saskatchewan. Founded 1935. Interdenominational. Three-year Bible Course (diploma), Christian Education (ETTA cert.). Evening school. Day school enrollment, 15. Tuition fees for 26-week school year, $60. Write to Dean for information.

NOGALES BIBLE SCHOOL, 267 Western Avenue, Nogales, Ariz. Founded 1935. Free Methodist. Three-year Bible institute program. Correspondence school.

NORTH CENTRAL BIBLE COLLEGE, 910 Elliot Avenue South, Minneapolis 4, Minn. Founded 1930. Assemblies of

God. Associate member of The Accrediting Association of Bible Colleges. Programs: Bible and Theology (AB), Missions (AB), Religious Education (BRE), Music (diploma). Enrollment, 356. Tuition fees for 36-week school year, $337. Good work opportunities. Limited number of scholarships. Write to Admissions Office for information.

NORTHEASTERN BIBLE INSTITUTE, Oak Lane, Essex Fells, N. J. Founded 1950. Interdenominational. Accredited by The Accrediting Association of Bible Colleges. Bible major with minors in Ministerial Studies, Missions, Christian Education (diploma), Bible and Sacred Music (diploma). Summer school. Day school enrollment, 151. Tuition fees for 36-week school year, $282. Room and board, $630. Good work opportunities. Write to Registrar for information.

NORTHWEST BAPTIST BIBLE COLLEGE, 3358 S. E. Marine, Vancouver, British Columbia. For information on admissions and curricula, write to Principal.

NORTHWEST BIBLE COLLEGE, 1900 Valker Road, Minot, N. Dak. Founded 1934. Church of God. Courses: Religion (AB), Christian Education (3-yr. diploma). Junior College (AA). Enrollment, 47. Tuition fees for 36-week school year, $280. Good work opportunities. Admission: Christian character and acceptable high school grades. Write to Registrar for information.

NORTHWEST BIBLE COLLEGE, 11102 N. E. 53rd Street, Kirkland, Wash. Founded 1934. Assemblies of God. Accredited by The Accrediting Association of Bible Colleges. Bible majors leading to AB with minors in Theology, Missions, Christian Education; Sacred Music; Bachelor of Theology (5 yrs.). Junior College. Enrollment, 212. Tuition fees for 36-week school year, $455.50. Board and room, $525. Good work opportunities. Write to Registrar for information.

NORTHWEST CHRISTIAN COLLEGE, Eleventh and Alder, Eugene, Oreg. Founded 1895. Christian. Associate member, American Association of Schools of Religious Education. Programs: Ministerial (AB, ThB), Missionary (AB), Christian Education (AB, BS), Music (AB, BS), Church Secretary (BS).

NYACK MISSIONARY COLLEGE, Nyack, N. Y. Founded 1882. The Christian and Missionary Alliance. Accredited by The Accrediting Association of Bible Colleges and New York State Education Department. Programs: Theological (BS, ThB), Missionary (BS), Christian Education (BS), Sacred Music (BSM), Music Education (BS), Pre-Seminary (AB). Correspondence and summer schools. Day school enrollment, 519. Tuition fees for 36-week school year, $599. Good work opportunities. Limited scholarships. Write to Director of Admissions for information.

OAK HILLS BIBLE INSTITUTE, Route 3, Bemidji, Minn. Founded 1946. Interdenominational. Three-year diploma courses with Bible major and minors in Christian Education, Missions, Ministerial. Enrollment, 74. Tuition fees for 24-week school year, $155. Board and room, $240. Limited work opportunities. Write to Registrar for information.

OMAHA BAPTIST BIBLE COLLEGE, 1052 Park Avenue, Omaha 5, Nebr. Founded 1953. General Association of Regular Baptists. Programs: Ministerial (ThB), Bible (3-yr. diploma), Christian Education (AB, BS), Missions (AB, BS), Music (AB, BS), Pre-Seminary, (AB, BS). Enrollment, 175. Total fees for 36-week school year, $840. Good work opportunities. Write to Registrar for information.

OPEN BIBLE COLLEGE, 850 18th Street, Des Moines 14, Iowa. Founded 1930. Open Bible Standard Churches, Inc. Four-year diploma courses with Bible-Theology major and minors in Ministerial, Missions, Christian Education, Sacred Music, Social Studies. Evening and summer schools.

Day school enrollment, 47. Tuition fees for 36-week school year, $370. Scholarships available to applicants from top 20 percent of high school classes. Write to Registrar for information.

"OPEN DOOR" BIBLE INSTITUTE, Box 5393, St. Louis 15, Mo. Founded 1955. Independent. Three-year diploma course. Evening and correspondence schools.

OREGON BIBLE COLLEGE, Box 231, Oregon, Ill. Founded 1939. Church of God Conference. Ministerial and Christian Education (ThB). Enrollment, 22. Total expenses for 36-week school year, $815. Write to President for information.

ORTHODOX BAPTIST INSTITUTE, 320 N. Washington Street, Ardmore, Okla. Founded 1944. Independent Baptist. General Bible Courses (diploma, ThB). Junior college. Enrollment, 20. Tuition free. Limited work opportunities. Write to President for information.

OWOSSO COLLEGE, Bible College Division, 1020 S. Washington, Owosso, Mich. Founded 1909. Pilgrim Holiness Church. Accredited by The Accrediting Association of Bible Colleges. Courses: Bachelor of Theology, Bachelor of Arts in Bible, Ministerial Diploma. Evening school, high school, summer school, liberal arts college. Day school enrollment, 191. Tuition, board and room for 36-week school year, $950. Good work opportunities. Leadership qualities and high grade average to qualify for scholarships. Write to Office of President for information.

OZARK BIBLE COLLEGE, 516 N. Wall, Joplin, Mo. Founded 1942. Non-denominational. Ministerial (BSL). Five-year program with a choice of eight majors (ThB). Enrollment, 254. Tuition costs for 36-week school year, $250. Good work opportunities. Write to President for information.

OZARK BIBLE INSTITUTE, INC., Ozark, Ark. Founded 1946. Interdenominational. Christian Workers Course (2-yr. cert.), Bible and Missionary Course (3-yr. diploma), ETTA (cert.). Enrollment, 38. Total expenses for 36-week school year, $420. Some work opportunities.

PACIFIC BIBLE SEMINARY, 4835 E. Anaheim, Long Beach 4, Calif. Founded 1928. Churches of Christ (Christian Church). Bible Major (AB), Ministerial (ThB). Summer school. Day school enrollment, 160. Tuition costs for 36-week school year $362. Good work opportunities. Write to Academic Dean for information.

PACIFIC COLLEGE, 1717 S. Chestnut Avenue, Fresno 2, Calif. Founded 1944. Mennonite Brethren. Majors in Bible and Christian Education. Liberal arts (AA). Accredited by Western College Association. Enrollment, 102. Tuition fees for 36-week school year, $450. Board and room, $540. Good work opportunities. Scholarships available to top ten percent of high school class. Write to Registrar for information.

THE PEACE RIVER BIBLE INSTITUTE, Sexsmith, Alberta. Founded 1935. Interdenominational. Three- and four-year Bible Institute courses (diploma). Enrollment, 28.

PENTECOSTAL BIBLE COLLEGE AND HIGH SCHOOL, 2701 N Street, Sacramento 16, Calif. Founded 1945. Pentecostal Church of God of America, Inc. Programs: Theology (AB, GTh), Music (BSM), Religious Education (BRE), Missions (AB). Evening, correspondence, summer schools. High school. Bible college enrollment, 40. Total costs for 36-week school year, $700. Some scholarships available to qualified students.

PENTECOSTAL BIBLE INSTITUTE, 405 Clayton Avenue, Tupelo, Miss. Founded 1945. United Pentecostal Church. Ministerial Course (ThB), Christian Worker (BCE), Missionary (BCE). Correspondence school, high school. Day school enrollment, 75. Tuition fees for 32-week school year, $240. Good work opportunities. Write to the Registrar for information.

THE PEOPLES BIBLE COLLEGE, Box 6—West End Station, Colorado Springs, Colo. Founded 1942. Independent. Emmanuel Association. Five-year Ministerial and Missionary Course (ThB); three-year Christian Workers Diploma Course. Elementary and high schools.

PHILADELPHIA COLLEGE OF BIBLE, 1800 Arch Street, Philadelphia 3, Pa. Founded 1913. Denominationally unrelated. Accredited by The Accrediting Association of Bible Colleges. Three-year (diploma) and four-year (BS) programs offered in Bible-Missions, Bible-Music, Bible-Christian Education, Bible-Pre-Theology. Evening, correspondence, and summer schools. Day school enrollment, 425. Tuition fees for 35-week school year, $390. Board and room, $540. Good work opportunities. Write to Director of Admissions for information.

PIEDMONT BIBLE COLLEGE, INC., 716 Franklin Street, Winston-Salem, N. C. Founded 1945. Independent. Accredited by The Accrediting Association of Bible Colleges. Programs: Religious Education (BRE, diploma), Theology (ThB), Bible (3-yr. diploma). Evening school. Day school enrollment, 183. Tuition fees for 36-week school year, $292. Board and room, $500. Good work opportunities. Write to Office of Registrar for information.

PIEDMONT BIBLE INSTITUTE, Cramerton, N. C. Founded 1956. Free Will Baptist. For information on admissions and curricula, write to Principal.

PILLSBURY CONSERVATIVE BAPTIST BIBLE COLLEGE, Owatonna, Minn. Minnesota Baptist Convention. Bible college program leading to AB with major or minor in Christian Education, Pastorology, Evangelism, Missions, Biblical Languages, Sacred Music; two-year Practical Christian Work Course.

PINE CREST BIBLE INSTITUTE, Salisbury Center, N. Y. Founded 1958. Assemblies of God. Accredited by New York State Department of Education. Courses leading to diploma in Bible, Theology, Missions, Religious Education. Two 18-week semesters. Enrollment, 42. Good work opportunities. Write to Dean of Education for information.

PLATTE VALLEY BIBLE COLLEGE, Box 636, Scottsbluff, Nebr. Founded 1951. Christian Church-Church of Christ. Ministerial courses, (AB, BSL, ThB), Medical Missions (MMM). Enrollment, 44. Tuition fees for 36-week school year, $230. Scholarships available. Address inquiries to Office of the President.

POWELLHURST BAPTIST BIBLE COLLEGE, 2665 S.E. 122 Avenue, Portland 36, Oreg. Founded 1946. Conservative Baptist. Bachelor of Arts in Bible. Evening school. Day school enrollment, 26. Tuition fees for 34-week school year, $90. Board and room, $450. Good work opportunities.

PRACTICAL BIBLE TRAINING SCHOOL, Bible School Park, Broome County, N. Y. Founded 1900. Interdenominational. Bible school program. Enrollment, 142. Tuition fees for 29-week school year, $156. Board and room, $279. Good work opportunities. Write to the President for information.

PRAIRIE BIBLE INSTITUTE, Three Hills, Alberta. Founded 1922. Interdenominational, independent. Four-year and three-year General Bible-Missions Courses (diploma). Correspondence school, grade school, and high school. Day school enrollment in Bible School, 662. Board, room, and tuition for 26-week school year, $318.80. Limited work opportunities. Write to Registrar for information.

PUGET SOUND COLLEGE OF THE BIBLE, 101 N. W. 58 Street, Seattle 7, Wash. Founded 1950. Non-denominational. Ministerial (AB), Missions (AB), Religious Education (BRE), Theological-Pre-Seminary (ThB). Enrollment, 70. Tuition fees for 36-week school year, $300. Good work opportunities. Limited number of scholarships available on basis of academic excellence. Write to Registrar for information.

REED COLLEGE OF RELIGION, 9309 S. San Pedro Street, Los Angeles 3, Calif. Founded 1938. Not denominationally related. Theology (ThB), Christian Education (AB, BCE, MCSA). Evening school. Modest fees. Write to the President for information.

REFORMED BIBLE INSTITUTE, 1869 Robinson Road, S.E., Grand Rapids 6, Mich. Christian Reformed. Associate member of The Accrediting Association of Bible Colleges. Four Bible diploma courses: Missionary-Education, Parish Worker, Music, General Bible. Evening and correspondence schools. Tuition, free. Other fees for 38-week school year, $55. Room and board, $380 to $551. Write to Registrar for information.

RIO GRANDE BIBLE INSTITUTE, Box 840, Edinburg, Tex. Founded 1946. Independent. Three-year Bible institute program in Spanish. Missionary Language School offers one-year program in Spanish.

ROANOKE BIBLE COLLEGE, 707 Pennsylvania Ave., Elizabeth City, N. C. Founded 1948. Church of Christ. Four-year program.

ROCKMONT COLLEGE, Longmont, Colo. Founded 1914. Interdenominational. Associate member of The Accrediting Association of Bible Colleges. Courses leading to AB in Bible, Music, Elementary Education, Social Studies, Pre-Seminary, Electronic Communication. Enrollment, 52. Tuition fees for 36-week school year, $398. Good work opportunities. Write to Director of Admissions for information.

ST. LOUIS CHRISTIAN COLLEGE, Box 12, Florissant, Mo. Founded 1956. Independent Christian and Churches of Christ. Programs: Ministerial (AB), Music (AB), Christian Education (BCE, BSL). Evening classes and summer school. Day school enrollment, 80. Tuition fees for 36-week school year, $196. Write to Office of President for information.

ST. PAUL BIBLE COLLEGE, 1361 Englewood Avenue, St. Paul 4, Minn. Founded 1916. The Christian and Missionary Alliance. Accredited by The Accrediting Association of Bible Colleges and University of Minnesota. Programs: Pre-Seminary (AB), Bible and Theology (AB), Missionary Education (BS), Missionary Nursing (BS), Religious Education (BRE), Music (BM), Non-Professional (3-yr. diploma; 2-yr. cert.). Junior college. Summer school. Enrollment, 264. Tuition fees for 36-week school year, $470. Good work opportunities. Write to Admissions Office for information.

ST. PETERSBURG BIBLE INSTITUTE, P. O. Box 22, St. Petersburg, Fla. Founded 1947. Interdenominational. Ministerial (diploma), Missions (diploma), Pre-Seminary (AB in Bible), Chaplains' Seminary (BD). Tuition fees for 36-week school year, $120. Admission: Acceptable high school record, Christian commitment, approved character, good health, agreement with school's objectives. Write to Registrar for information.

SALEM BIBLE COLLEGE, Route 2, Woodsdale Road, Salem, Ohio. Founded 1956. Interdenominational. Major in Religion (AB). High school. Evening and summer schools. Day school enrollment, 65. Board, room, and tuition costs for 36-week school year, $600. Some work opportunities.

SAN JOSE BIBLE COLLEGE, 790 S. 12th Street, P. O. Box 1090, San Jose, Calif. Founded 1939. Christian Churches and Churches of Christ. Programs: Pre-Seminary (AB), Ministerial (AB, ThB), Christian Education (BRE), Music-Christian Education (BRE), Christian Education and Church Secretary (BRE), Christian Workers' (3-yr. diploma, 2-yr. cert.). Evening and summer schools. Day school enrollment, 118. Tuition, $8.50 per unit plus $20 incidental fees. Board and room for 36-week school year, $500. Good work opportunities. Write to Registrar for information.

SEATTLE BIBLE TRAINING SCHOOL, 7704 24th Avenue, N.W., Seattle 7, Wash. Founded 1955. Non-denominational. For information on admissions and curricula, write to Director of Admissions.

SHENANDOAH CHRISTIAN COLLEGE, 1232 Sylvan Road, S.E., Roanoke, Va. Founded 1955. Independent, non-denominational. Bible and Arts (diploma). Evening school. Day school enrollment, 12. Tuition fees for 34-week school year, $200. Board and room, $520. Some work opportunities. Write to Registrar for information.

SIMMONS UNIVERSITY, 1811 Dumesnil Street, Louisville 10, Ky. Founded 1879. Baptist. Ministerial (ThB), Missions (BM), Business Department (diploma). Evening and summer schools. Day school enrollment, 40. Tuition fees for 33-week school year, $65. Write to Registrar for information.

SIMPSON BIBLE COLLEGE, 801 Silver Avenue, San Francisco 24, Calif. Founded 1921. The Christian and Missionary Alliance. Accredited by The Accrediting Association of Bible Colleges. Programs leading to AB in Pastoral Theology, Missions, Vocational Missions, Christian Education, Pre-Seminary, Music-Christian Education; Church Secretarial (BRE). Evening and summer schools. Day school enrollment, 176. Tuition fees for 36-week school year, $415. Good work opportunities. Write to Office of the President for information.

SOUTH WESTERN BAPTIST SCHOOLS (Baptist Bible Institute and College), 4135 N. 19th Street, Phoenix, Ariz. Founded 1960. Conservative Baptist. Three-year Christian Worker's Course. Bachelor of Arts in Bible, Christian Education, Missions, Sacred Music.

SOUTHEASTERN BIBLE COLLEGE, 1401 South 29th Street, Birmingham, Ala. Founded 1935. Interdenominational. Programs: Pastor's Course (AB, ThB), Missions (AB), Christian Education (BRE), General Education (AB), Sacred Music-Christian Education (BSM), Pre-Seminary (AB), General Bible (3-yr. diploma). Evening and summer schools. Day school enrollment, 88. Tuition fees for 36-week school year, $200. Some work opportunities. Several scholarships available to qualified candidates. Admissions: Acceptable high school record, recommendations, Christian commitment, agreement with school's objectives. Write to Registrar for information.

SOUTH-EASTERN BIBLE COLLEGE, 1000 Longfellow Boulevard, Lakeland, Fla. Founded 1935. Assemblies of God. Accredited by The Accrediting Association of Bible Colleges. Diploma and AB programs in Christian Education, English Bible, Theology, Music, Missions; Business Education (diploma). Summer school. Enrollment, 284. Tuition fees for 36-week school year, $445. Good work opportunities. Write to Office of President for information.

SOUTHEASTERN CHRISTIAN COLLEGE, Winchester, Ky. Founded 1949. Church of Christ (undenominational). Divisions: Bible Institute, Evening School, Junior College, Seminary. Day school enrollment, 140. Some work opportunities. Some scholarships available to qualified candidates. Write to Registrar for information.

SOUTHERN BIBLE COLLEGE, 10950 Beaumont Highway, Houston 20, Texas. Founded 1927. Pentecostal Church of God of America (Joplin, Mo.). Programs: Ministerial (ThB, AB, BS), Missionary (AB, BS), Christian Education (AB, BS). Three-Year Diploma. Evening, correspondence, summer schools. Junior College. Day school enrollment in Bible College, 18. Tuition fees for 36-week school year, $379. Board and room, $360. Very good work opportunities. Scholarships available to valedictorians and salutatorians, and recommended, worthy foreign students. Write to President for information.

SOUTHERN BIBLE TRAINING SCHOOL, INC., 1415 Fleetwood Street, P. O. Box 26103, Dallas, Tex. Founded 1927. Independent. Bible Institute Program (diploma); Advanced Course, requiring two years of college as prerequisite, (ThB). Evening school. Day school enrollment, 40. Tuition fees for 34-week school year, $50. Good work opportunities. Write to Office of Registrar for information.

SOUTHERN CHRISTIAN COLLEGE, 314 S. Park Boulevard, San Antonio 4, Tex. Founded 1945. A co-educational, bi-lingual (English-Spanish) school of mission evangelism. Training offered in Ministry, Music, Secretarial, Nursing, Graphic Arts, Flying. Write to the President for information.

SOUTHERN PILGRIM COLLEGE, Kernersville, N. C. Founded 1946. Pilgrim Holiness Church. Associate member of The Accrediting Association of Bible Colleges. Programs: Bachelor of Theology (5 yr.), Bachelor of Religion (4 yr.), Ministerial Course (3-yr. diploma), Christian Worker's Course (2-yr. cert.). High school. Day college enrollment, 58. Tuition fees for 36-week school year, approximately $325. Room and board, $400. Write to Registrar for information.

SOUTHLAND BIBLE INSTITUTE, R.F.D. 2, Box 345, Pikeville, Ky. Founded 1945. Interdenominational. Christian Worker's Course (diploma). Evening and summer schools. Day school enrollment, 30. Free tuition. Incidental fees for 36-week school year, $35. Board and room, $460. Write to Registrar for information.

SOUTHWEST CHRISTIAN SEMINARY, 522 West Lynwood, Phoenix, Arix. For information on admissions and criteria, write to Principal.

SOUTHWESTERN ASSEMBLIES OF GOD COLLEGE, Waxahachie, Tex. Founded 1927. Assemblies of God. Bible College accredited by The Accrediting Association of Bible Colleges. Programs: Ministerial (AB, BS, diploma), Missions (AB, BS, diploma), Religious Education (AB, BS, diploma). Junior College, high school, summer school. Bible College enrollment, 185. Tuition fees for 36-week school year, $470. Some work opportunities. Write to Office of Registrar for information.

SOUTHWESTERN BIBLE COLLEGE, 5000 N. W. 10th, Oklahoma City, Okla. Pentecostal Holiness Church. School of Theology (ThB). High school and junior college. Enrollment, 158. Tuition fees for 36-week school year, $234. Good work opportunities. Write to Registrar for information.

STEINBACH BIBLE INSTITUTE, Box 1420, Steinbach, Manitoba. Founded 1936. Inter-Mennonite. Diploma courses in General Bible, Pastors, Missions, Christian Education, Sacred Music. Evening school, junior college, and high school. Day school enrollment, 204. Tuition fees for 24-week school year in Bible school, $65. Some scholarships available to qualified candidates. Admission: Approved character, agreement with school's objectives. Write to Registrar for information.

SWIFT CURRENT BIBLE INSTITUTE, 510 Cheadle Street East, Swift Current, Saskatchewan. Founded 1936. General Conference of Mennonites in Canada. Three-year program (diploma) .

TENNESSEE TEMPLE SCHOOLS (Bible School), 1815 Union Avenue, Chattanooga, Tenn. Baptist (independent). Programs: Bible (BB), Bible-Missionary (BB), Bible-Child Evangelism (BB), Bible-Christian Education (GTh). Evening school, elementary school, liberal arts college, and seminary. Day enrollment in Bible School, 257. Tuition fees for 34-week school year, $325. Good work opportunities. Work and missionary scholarships.

TOCCOA FALLS BIBLE COLLEGE, Toccoa Falls, Ga. Founded 1907. Independent. Accredited by The Accrediting Association of Bible Colleges. Programs: Bible-Theology (AB, BS), Bible-Missions (BS), Christian Education (BS), Church Music (BS). High school. Enrollment in Bible College, 181. Tuition fees for 36-week school year, $230. Some work opportunities. Write to Admissions Office for information.

TORONTO BIBLE COLLEGE, 16 Spadina Road, Toronto 4, Ontario. Founded 1894. Interdenominational. Courses: Christian Education (diploma), Missionary (diploma), Pastor's (diploma), Bachelor of Theology. Evening school. Day school enrollment, 170. Tuition fees for 33-week school year, $100 to $120. Good work opportunities. Write to the Registrar for information.

THE TORONTO CHRISTIAN SEMINARY, 272-278 High Park Avenue, Toronto 9, Ontario. Founded 1958. Church of Christ (Christian). Programs: Bible (AB), Bachelor of Sacred Literature, College Bible (one-year cert.), Christian Worker's (2-yr. cert.), Church Secretarial (2-yr. cert.), Minister's Assistant (3-yr. cert.). Presently operated as night school. Enrollment, 29. Tuition for 36-week school year, $120. Good work opportunities. Write to Office of Dean for information.

TRANSYLVANIA BIBLE SCHOOL, Freeport, Pa. Founded 1938. Independent. Four-year program. For information on admissions and curricula, write to Principal.

TRINITY COLLEGE, Clearwater, Fla. Founded 1932. Interdenominational. Three-year Christian Workers' Course;

"B.A." in Biblical Education. For information on admission and curricula, write to Principal.

TRINITY SCHOOLS OF THE SOUTH, 1985 LaVista Road, N.E., Atlanta 6, Ga. For information on admissions and curricula, write to principal.

UNION BIBLE SEMINARY, INC., P. O. Box 315, Westfield, Ind. Founded 1911. Friends background; interdenominational. Bible Diploma Course. Grade school and high school. Enrollment, 85. Tuition for 36-week school year, $146. Room and board, $370. Good work opportunities.

UNITED BAPTIST BIBLE TRAINING SCHOOL, Moncton, New Brunswick. Founded 1949. United Baptist Convention. Standard Bible Diploma Course with minors in Christian Education, Church Secretarial, and Missions.

VANCOUVER BIBLE INSTITUTE, 1601 W. 10th Avenue, Vancouver 9, British Columbia. Founded 1919. Baptist General Conference. Courses: Missionary Pastors' (4-yr. diploma), Bible-Christian Education (3-yr. diploma), Leadership Training (1-yr.). Evening school. Day school enrollment, 54. Tuition fees for 30-week school year, $226. Board and room, $440. Some work opportunities. Several scholarships available to candidates on basis of high scholarship and Christian character. Grants-in-aid available to children of ministers and missionaries. Write to the Registrar for information.

VENNARD COLLEGE, University Park, Iowa. Founded 1910. Interdenominational. Accredited by The Accrediting Association of Bible Colleges. AB with Bible major with Ministerial, Christian Education, Missions, Christian Social Service, Church Music minors. Bible Certificate Course. Correspondence school. Day school enrollment, 101. Tuition fees for 36-week school year, $399. Board and room, $495. Some work opportunities. Write to Academic Dean for information.

VIRGINIA BIBLE COLLEGE, 301 W. 32nd Street, Norfolk 8, Va. Founded 1960. Baptist, unaffiliated. Four-year Bible college program. For information on admissions, write to Principal.

WASHINGTON BIBLE COLLEGE, 1441 Rhode Island Avenue, N.W., Washington, D.C. Founded 1918. Associate member of The Accrediting Association of Bible Colleges. Biblical Education with majors in Pastoral Work, Missions, Christian Education, Music (AB). Evening, correspondence, and summer schools. Seminary. Day school enrollment, 144. Tuition fees for 36-week school year, $135.50. Good work opportunities. Write to Registrar for information.

WEST COAST BIBLE COLLEGE, 6901 N. Maple, Route 1, Clovis, Calif. Founded 1949. Church of God (Cleveland, Tenn.). Two-year Bible College program (AA), Junior College (AA). High school. Enrollment, 72. Tuition, board and room costs for 36-week school year, $762.50. Some work opportunities. Write to Office of Registrar for information.

WESTERN BAPTIST BIBLE COLLEGE, 1800 Elm Street, El Cerrito, Calif. Founded 1935. General Association of Regular Baptist Churches. Accredited by The Accrediting Association of Bible Colleges. Programs: Bible major (3-yr. diploma, AB with wide choice of minors); Bible-Nursing (BS); Bible-Business Administration (BS); five-year programs leading to ThB in Bible-Theology, Missions, Pastoral Education, Biblical Languages; Bible-Christian Education (5-yr. BRE). Evening and summer schools. Day school enrollment 202. Tuition fees for 36-week school year, $350. Board and room, $600. Good work opportunities. Admission: Acceptable high school record, approved character. Write to Registrar for information.

WESTERN BAPTIST BIBLE COLLEGE, 2119-25 Tracy Avenue, Kansas City 8, Mo. Founded 1890. Baptist. Programs: Bible-Theology (ThB, AB), Christian Education (AB), Missions (AB), Pastoral Studies (AB), Sacred Music (AB). Evening school. Day school enrollment, 40. Good work opportunities. Scholarships available to worthy, needy students with good scholastic record. Write to Office of the Registrar for information.

WESTERN BIBLE INSTITUTE, P. O. Box 4032, Denver, Colo. Founded 1948. Interdenominational. Courses leading to diploma in Bible, Music, and Missions. Evening school. Day school enrollment, 58. Tuition fees for 36-week school year, $165. Board and room, $540. Good work opportunities. Write to Director of Admissions for information.

WESTMINSTER COLLEGE AND BIBLE INSTITUTE, Box 989, Tehuacana, Tex. Founded 1953. Congregational Methodist. Bachelor of Religion. Junior college.

WILLIAM CARTER COLLEGE, INC., 2306-08 E. Ash Street, Goldsboro, N. C. Founded 1952. Interdenominational. Programs: Ministerial (ThB), Pre-Seminary (AB), Christian Education (BRE). Day school enrollment limited to 100. Tuition fees for 36-week school year, $240. Board and room, $468. Good work opportunities. Admissions: Acceptable high school record, Christian commitment, approved character, agreement with school's objectives. Write to Registrar for information.

WINKLER BIBLE SCHOOL, Winkler, Manitoba. Founded 1925. Mennonite Brethren. General Bible Course (diploma), Sunday School Course (ETTA diploma). Enrollment, 73. Tuition fees for 26-week school year, $325. Write to Principal for information.

WINNIPEG BIBLE INSTITUTE AND COLLEGE OF THEOLOGY, 2 Evergreen Place, Winnipeg 13, Manitoba.

Founded 1925. Interdenominational. Standard Bible Course (diploma), Christian Education (BRE), Theological (ThB). Evening school. Day school enrollment, 66. Tuition fees for 28-week school year, $70. Good work opportunities. Admission to College of Theology: Completion of Manitoba Grade XII (or equivalent), Christian dedication, recommended character, agreement with school's objectives. Write to Registrar for information.

WINSTON-SALEM BIBLE COLLEGE, 151 Wheeler Street, Winston-Salem, N. C. Founded 1950. Church of Christ. Ministerial courses (BSL, AB, ATh). Evening school. Enrollment, 7. Tuition fees for 36-week school year, $75. Limited work opportunities. Scholarships available to qualified candidates. Write to Main Office for information.

ZION BIBLE INSTITUTE, 846 Broadway, East Providence, R. I. Founded 1924. Non-denominational (Pentecostal). Bible institute program. For information on admissions and fees, write to Director of Admissions.

# NOTES

## CHAPTER ONE

1. Lenice F. Reed, "The Bible Institute Movement in America" (unpublished Master's thesis, Wheaton College, Illinois, 1947), pp. 1-2.

2. Among the first graduate studies were Hubert Reynhout, Jr.'s thesis prepared for the requirements of a Master's degree in the Department of Education at the University of Michigan in 1947 on "A Comparative Study on the Bible Institute Curriculum," and Harold W. Boon's doctoral dissertation on the development of Bible institutes and Bible colleges in relation to theological education in 1950 at New York University.

3. An extensive coverage of Bible college education was published by *Christian Life* in a special section of articles and reports entitled "The World of Bible Education," Vol. 21, No. 2 (June, 1959), pp. 29-44.

4. S. A. Witmer, "Bible College Education," *School and Society*, Vol. 80 (October 16, 1954), pp. 113-116; Frank E. Gaebelein, "The Bible College in American Education Today," *School and Society*, Vol. 80 (May 9, 1959), pp. 223-225.

5. Frank E. Gaebelein, *Christian Education in a Democracy*, The Report of the Committee of the National Association of Evangelicals, Chapter VII, "A New Form of American Education," by S. A. Witmer (New York: Oxford University Press, 1951), pp. 157-181.

6. *Ibid.*, p. 223.

7. *Ibid.*, pp. 223-224.

8. *Pensées* (London: Everyman Edition, 1931), p. 422.

9. Philip E. Jacob, "Patterns in Student Values," *Current Issues in Higher Education, 1957* (Washington: Association for Higher Education), p. 89.

10. Evening schools for the training of lay workers are generally called "Bible institutes."

11. *Manual,* Accrediting Association of Bible Colleges, 1960, p. 8.

CHAPTER TWO

1. Elwood P. Cubberley, *The History of Education* (New York: Houghton Mifflin Company, 1948), p. 703.

2. *Ibid.,* p. 703.

3. *Canadian Universities and Colleges, 1958* (Ottawa: The National Conference of Canadian Universities), pp. 13, 24, 39.

4. Matthew 25:18-20.

5. *Education Directory, 1960-61, Part 3* (Washington: U. S. Department of Health, Education, and Welfare, Office of Education, 1960), pp. 85-90.

6. Gaebelein, *op. cit.,* p. 167.

7. Kenneth Scott Latourette, *The Nineteenth Century in Europe* (Vol. II of Christianity in a Revolutionary Age. 2 vols.; New York: Harper & Bros., 1959), pp. 114-116.

8. *The Encyclopedia of Missions,* (Vol. I, ed. Edwin Murrsell Bliss. New York: Funk & Wagnells, 1891), p. 392.

9. *Ibid.,* p. 392.

10. *Ibid.,* p. 346.

11. A. B. Simpson, "Editorial," *The Gospel in All Lands* (May, 1880), p. 55.

12. Donald McKaig, "The Educational Philosophy of A. B. Simpson" (unpublished doctoral dissertation, New York University, 1947).

13. *Ibid.,* pp. 29-30.

14. Charles R. Erdman, *D. L. Moody, His Message for Today* (New York: Fleming H. Revell Company, 1928), pp. 130-131.

15. Richard Ellsworth Day, *Bush Aglow* (Philadelphia: The Judson Press, 1936), p. 264.

16. The President's Committee on Education Beyond the High School, *Second Report to the President* (Washington: U. S. Government Printing Office, 1957), pp. 1-2.

17. The Accrediting Association of Bible Colleges recognizes any Bible school as a "Bible college" provided that its program academically is of college grade, whether it offers three- or four-year programs and whether it is named "school," "institute," or "college."

18. Letter by Principal John McNicol of Toronto Bible College to Rev. S. H. Sutherland dated December 11, 1942.

19. The name was abbreviated in 1958 to The Accrediting Association of Bible Colleges.

20. About ten schools organized the Southern Accrediting Association of Bible Institutes, Bible Colleges, and Bible Seminaries with somewhat lower standards in 1952-53 largely for the purpose, according to its president, of securing governmental recognition for veterans' training. Since the effort was unsuccessful, the organization functions mainly for fellowship.

21. Enock C. Dyrness, "The Bible College and Accreditation," *Newsletter,* Vol. II, No. 2 (May, 1958), p. 1.

## CHAPTER FOUR

1. Oscar E. Feucht, "The Bible Institute Movement and the Church" (address given at Workshop on Lutheran Bible Institutes, River Forest, Illinois, July 27, 1953).

2. James E. Southerland, "The Role of Bible Schools in the Southern Baptist Convention" (inaugural address, February 13, 1959, quoted by permission).

3. Quoted by Thomas F. Zimmerman, "Where is the 'Third Force' Going?" *Christianity Today,* Vol. IV, No. 22 (August 1, 1960), p. 904.

4. I Corinthians 2:2, 4.

5. James DeForest Murch, in forthcoming book, *Christians Only: History of the Christian Churches and Churches of Christ* (Cincinnati: Standard Publishing Company).

6. *Yearbook of Christian Churches,* Edition of 1960 (New York: National Council of Churches, 1959), p. 22.

7. Murch, *op. cit.,* identifies the churches of this branch of the Disciples as Centrists.

8. *Ibid.*

9. *Yearbook of American Churches,* Edition of 1960. (New York: National Council of Churches of Christ, 1959), pp. 12-107.

CHAPTER FIVE

    1. A comprehensive list of Bible institutes and Bible colleges is found in the Appendix.

    2. Although named a seminary, its work is on the undergraduate level. Functionally and academically, therefore, it can be classified as a Bible college.

CHAPTER SIX

    1. Hebrews 4:12, R.S.V.

    2. Ephesians 1:10.

    3. The discussion which follows is based on excerpts from "How to Live in Two Environments" by S. A. Witmer published in *Christian Life,* Vol. 21, No. 2 (June, 1959), pp. 30, 31.

    4. S. Maxwell Coder, "The Philosophy of Education of Moody Bible Institute." Leaflet published by Moody Bible Institute Alumni Association.

    5. Edward D. Eddy, Jr., *The College Influence on Student Character* (Washington: American Council on Education, 1959), p. 16.

    6. Amos Alonzo Stagg, "Modern Youth and the Bible." Leaflet published by the American Bible Society, New York, N. Y.

    7. II Timothy 4:2, 3, 4.

    8. Abdel Ross Wentz, "A New Strategy for Theological Education" (Gettysburg: Lutheran Theological Seminary). Reprinted from *Christian Education,* April, 1937.

    9. *Ibid.,* pp. 6, 7.

    10. H. Richard Niebuhr, Daniel Day Williams, James M. Gustafson, *The Advancement of Theological Education* (New York: Harper & Brothers, 1957), p. 89.

    11. Edwin V. Hayden, "What Kind of Education for Your Preachers?" Pamphlet by the author, p. 9.

    12. *Manual, op. cit.,* pp. 20, 21.

    13. Matthew 7:23.

    14. *Manual, op. cit.,* p. 17.

CHAPTER SEVEN

    1. S. A. Witmer, *Preparation of Missionaries in Bible Institutes and Bible Colleges,* 1960. Pamphlet published by Accrediting Association of Bible Colleges, Fort Wayne, Indiana.

2. Bernard A. Helland, "The Commission to Communicate," *The Bible Banner*, Vol. XXXVII, No. 2, February, 1961, p. 8.

3. Esther 4:14.

## CHAPTER EIGHT

1. Letter from Herbert Klingbeil dated March 6, 1961.

2. Oscar E. Feucht, *Leadership Education Through Bible Institutes* (St. Louis: Board of Parish Education, The Lutheran Church—Missouri Synod, n.d.), p. 1.

3. The great majority of the 170 schools that are members of The Evangelical Teacher Training Association (Headquarters, Wheaton, Illinois) are regular Christian liberal arts colleges, seminaries, Bible colleges and Bible institutes; a small proportion are evening schools only.

4. Feucht, *op. cit.*, p. 2.

5. *Ibid.*, p. 3.

## CHAPTER NINE

1. See II Corinthians 3:1-6.

2. Elwood P. Cubberley, *The History of Education* (New York: Houghton Mifflin Company, 1948), p. 211.

3. William R. Moody, *The Life of Dwight L. Moody* (New York: Fleming H. Revell Company, 1900), p. 343.

4. Quoted by John H. Cable, *A History of the Missionary Training Institute* (Nyack: Nyack Missionary College, 1933), p. 33.

5. Matthew 10:40.

6. A. B. Bruce, *The Training of the Twelve* (New York: George H. Doran, n.d.), p. 99.

7. H. Richard Niebuhr, *The Purpose of the Church and Its Ministry* (New York: Harper & Brothers, 1956), pp. 131, 132.

8. *Report of the Fourth Biennial Meeting of the Association of Seminary Professors in Practical Skills*, 1956 (San Anselmo, California: San Francisco Theological Seminary), p. 84.

9. II Peter 1:3.

10. *Ibid.* 1:5-8.

11. *Manual, op. cit.*, pp. 15, 16.

12. Evaluations made in 1958 survey of Christian service conducted by The Accrediting Association of Bible Colleges.

CHAPTER TEN

1. John 7:17.
2. II Peter 3:18.
3. Lois E. LeBar, *Education That Is Christian* (New York: Fleming H. Revell, 1958), p. 30.
4. John 15:4.
5. John 6:63b.
6. Lois E. LeBar, "A Functional Philosophy of Christian Education" (address given to Commission on Research in Christian Education of the National Sunday School Association, Providence, Rhode Island, October 24, 1955).
7. II Peter 1:3, 4.
8. Luke 11:52.
9. John 16:13.
10. LeBar, *loc. cit.*
11. Oscar E. Feucht, *Leadership Through Bible Institutes* (St. Louis: Board of Parish Education, The Lutheran Church—Missouri Synod, n.d.), p. 45.
12. Andrew Murray, *The Spirit of Christ* (London: Nisbet and Company, 1888), p. 228.
13. Robert A. Traina, *Methodical Bible Study* (published by the author, 1952), p. 169.
14. Merrill C. Tenney, *Galatians: A Charter of Christian Liberty* (Grand Rapids: Wm. B. Eerdmans Publishing Company, 1950), p. 12 ff.
15. II Timothy 3:16, 17.
16. Catalog, 1958-59, Prairie Bible Institute, p. 3.
17. *Catalogue, 1958-1959,* The Biblical Seminary in New York, p. 12.
18. The inductive method, like any other method, can be misused or over-used. An example of excessive reliance on the method is to restrict students from using any texts, commentaries or helps outside the Bible. It is possible, too, to give so much place to method that the means becomes the end. More attention is given to the tool than the treasure it is designed to exploit.
19. Samuel M. Zwemer, *Thinking Missions With Christ* (Grand Rapids: Zondervan Publishing House, 1934), pp. 13, 14, 17.

CHAPTER ELEVEN

   1. II Corinthians 5:17a.

   2. Romans 8:16, 17.

   3. I John 3:1a.

   4. Romans 8:29.

   5. Ephesians 4:13.

   6. Herman Harrell Horne, *Jesus the Master Teacher* (New York: Association Press, 1942), pp. 189-190.

   7. I John 2:16.

   8. John 17:15.

   9. Galatians 5:22, 23.

   10. *Manual, op. cit.,* pp. 17, 18.

   11. Letter to Dr. William T. Watson, President, Trinity College. Quoted by permission.

CHAPTER TWELVE

   1. Guy E. Snavely, *The Church and the Four-Year College* (New York: Harper & Brothers, 1955).

   2. Thad Lewis Hungate, *Financing the Future of Higher Education* (New York: Teachers College, Columbia University, 1946), p. 253.

   3. *Ibid.,* p. 144.

# THE AUTHOR

S. A. Witmer lives a rich, full life. His many hobbies include flying (he has held a license since 1945), photography, astronomy, world travel and writing.

Dr. Witmer and his wife, Edith McLean Witmer, make their home in Fort Wayne. Their daughter Ruth and her husband, Dr. Ian Cook, are engaged in medical missionary work among the Mosquito Indians of Honduras. Family travels have taken the Witmers on flying trips to Central America and Mexico, and as far north as the Eskimo territory of northwest Canada.

Dr. Witmer is a frequent contributor to scholarly, lay and religious journals—among them *Moody Monthly, Christian Life, Christianity Today, School and Society, Eternity, King's Business, United Evangelical Action,* and *Alliance Witness.*

During World War II he served as a chaplain in the U. S. Air Force, and is now a member of the Education Commission, National Association of Evangelicals, and of the Committee on Pre-Seminary Education, National Education Association.